Untouchable!

Voices of the Dalit
Liberation Movement

Untouchable!

Voices of the Dalit Liberation Movement

Edited by Barbara R. Joshi

The Minority Rights Group Ltd.

Zed Books Ltd.

Untouchable! Voices of the Dalit Liberation Movement was
first published by Zed Books Ltd., 57 Caledonian Road,
London N1 9BU, UK, and 171 First Avenue,
Atlantic Highlands, New Jersey 07716, USA; and
The Minority Rights Group, 29 Craven Street,
London WC2N 5NT, UK, in 1986.

Edition for India published by Selectbook Service Syndicate,
Shiel Sadan, E-10, Kailash Colony, New Delhi-110 048,
India, in 1986.

Cover designed by Jacque Solomons.
Printed in the United Kingdom at The Bath Press, Avon.

British Library Cataloguing in Publication Data

Untouchable!: voices of the Dalit liberation
movement.
1. Untouchables — Political activity —
History — 20th century
I. Joshi, Barbara
322.4'4'0954   DS422.C3

ISBN 0-86232-459-9
ISBN 0-86232-460-2 Pbk

Hostal Navarro Ramos is shinier and better-assembled than Landazuri, but with less warmth and character (S-1,500 ptas, D-2,300 ptas, Db-3,500 ptas, Tb-4,300 ptas, Cuesta de Gomerez 21, tel. 958/25-05-55, NSE).

The tidy and simple **Hostal Viena,** run by English-speaking Austrian Irene (pronounced "ee-RAY-nay"), is on a quieter side street (S-1,500 ptas, Sb-2,500 ptas, D-3,000 ptas, Db-3,500 ptas, T-4,000 ptas, Tb-4,500 ptas, Q-4,500 ptas, Qb-5,500 ptas, CC:VM, Hospital de Santa Ana 2, just off Cuesta de Gomerez, tel. & fax 958/22-18-59). Irene can help with lodgings at the nearby **Hotel Austria,** which has comfortable, recently-remodeled rooms (Db-3,500–5,000 ptas, Cuesta Gomerez 4, tel. 958/22-70-75).

Hostal Gomerez is run by English-speaking Sigfrido Sanchez de León de Torres (who will explain to you how Spanish surnames work if you've got the time). Clean and basic, and listed in nearly every country's student-travel guidebook, this is your best cheapie (S-1,400 ptas, D-2,500 ptas, T-3,400 ptas, Q-4,300 ptas, breakfast in room-250 ptas, Cuesta de Gomerez 10, one floor up, tel. & fax 958/22-44-37).

Sleeping near Plaza Carmen
Just a few blocks from the TI lies the pleasant Plaza Carmen and the beginning of the Calle Navas, a pedestrian street offering several good values. The friendly **Hotel Lisboa is** right on Plaza Carmen (D-4,000 ptas, Db-5,200 ptas, CC:VM, Plaza de Carmen 27, tel. 958/22-14-13, fax 958/22-14-87), offering well-maintained, spacious rooms with firm beds, and helpful owners. A few blocks down the Calle Navas is the modern, sharp, and professional **Hotel Navas** with stately rooms (Db-11,000 ptas, breakfast buffet-1,400 ptas, CC:VMA, Calle Navas 24, tel. 958/22-59-59, fax 958/22-75-23). A few more blocks down Calle Navas is the youthful, easygoing **Hotel Nizza** (Sb-4,000 ptas, Db-5,700 ptas, they have a few fine two-room quads, and a cheery breakfast room, Calle Navas 16, tel. 958/22-54-30, fax 958/22-54-27).

Hotel Los Tilos is on a lively but traffic-free square behind the cathedral, a five-minute walk from Plaza Carmen. The place feels a bit like an old elementary school, but some rooms have balconies over the square, and it's in a great café, shopping, and people-watching neighborhood (Sb-4,500 ptas, Db-6,500 ptas, Tb-8,500 ptas, some rooms with air-con, breakfast buffet-650 ptas, elevator, CC:VM; Plaza Bib-Rambla 4, tel. 958/26-67-12, fax 958/26-68-01, friendly manager Jose-Maria SE).

Sleeping near the Alhambra
(zip code: 18009)

I don't know why people want to stay near the Alhambra, but here are three popular options. The stately old **Hotel Washington Irving** is pleasant, spacious, and slightly run-down, offering the best reasonable beds in this prestigious neighborhood (Sb-8,500 ptas, Db-11,000 ptas, Tb-13,000 ptas, Qb-15,000 ptas, breakfast-750 ptas, elevator, CC:VMA, Paseo del Generalife 2, tel. 958/22-75-50, fax 958/22-88-40, SE). There are two famous, overpriced, and difficult-to-get-a-room-in hotels actually within the Alhambra grounds.

The **Parador Nacional San Francisco** is a converted 15th-century convent, usually called Spain's premier *parador* (Sb-25,000 ptas, Db-35,000 ptas, breakfast-1,300 ptas, free parking, CC:VMA, Real de la Alhambra s/n, tel. 958/22-14-40, fax 958/22-22-64, SE). You must book ahead to spend the night in this lavishly located, stodgy, classy, and historic place. Do drop in for coffee or a drink.

Next to the *parador* is **Hotel America**, which is small (just 13 rooms), cozy, elegant, snooty, and very popular (Sb-8,500 ptas, Db-11,000 ptas, Tb-16,000 ptas, breakfast-950 ptas, CC:VMA, tel. 958/22-74-71, fax 958/22-74-70, SE). Book three to four months in advance.

Eating in Granada

The most interesting, reasonable meals are a steep walk up in the Albaicín quarter. (For directions to restaurants, see "More Sights—Granada: Albaicín," above.) From the San Nicolás viewpoint, head a few blocks north (away from the Alhambra) to Calle Pages. For a memorable orgy of seafood specialties, reasonably priced, at great outdoor tables in a colorful square atmosphere, eat at **El Ladrillo** (on Placeta de Fatima just off Calle Pages in the Albaicín). Their *media barca* (half boat) is a fishy feast that can stuff two to the gills. The nearby **Ladrillo II** offers indoor dining (both open daily, lunch from 13:00, dinner from 20:00, Calle Panaderos 35, off Plaza Larga, tel. 958/29-26-51). Try the quiet patio in the otherwise unquiet **Café-Bar Higuera**, just off Placeta de Fatima.

Contents

Tables

Photographs appear on pages 8, 27, 68, 78, 93, 94, 95, 109, 110, 114, 115, 123.

Line drawings appear on pages 58, 82, 154.

The Minority
Rights Group

The Minority Rights Group is an international human rights organization investigating a whole range of minority – and majority – situations in the world arising from discrimination and prejudice. Its reports cover refugees, the oppression of women and children, migrant workers, threatened indigenous peoples and destructive religious and ethnic conflicts, among others. MRG also works through the UN and other international bodies to increase awareness of human rights issues and to give oppressed groups a voice in the international arena. For further information write to: MRG, 29 Craven Street, London WC2N 5NT.

The Minority Rights Group Working Group On Untouchables consists of Untouchable activists and interested academics in India, Britain and North America who aim to inform and influence public opinion and to provide an international forum for all issues involving Untouchables. It aims for the total abolition of Untouchability.

For Ram Pyari, who wanted justice for her children.

Acknowledgements

Any book owes much to many, and this is doubly true in the case of an edited collection. I will not attempt to duplicate here the many introductions and expressions of appreciation for specific contributors that will appear in the following pages. However, there are several individuals and organizations who have played a far larger role than will appear on the surface of this book.

Friends in the Dalit community in North America have been a sustaining source of commitment as well as information; my special thanks to both the Ambedkar Mission (Canada) and VISION (USA).

In many ways this particular book has evolved from work with the Minority Rights Group, which has provided a common meeting ground for the scholars and activists who compose my often divergent worlds. Kaye Stearman, MRG's deputy director and fellow South Asianist, has been critically important as both inspiration and source of professional expertise. Several of the articles and illustrations in this book were originally developed as part of a 1983 conference on 'Minority Strategies: Comparative Perspectives on Racism and Untouchability' that owed much to the technical advice of Susanne Roff, executive director of MRG (New York). The conference was hosted by Columbia University's Southern Asian Institute and the City University of New York. Major funding was provided by the New York Council for the Humanities, the Ford Foundation, the Smithsonian Institution and the National Science Foundation; in a very real sense, these institutions also provided the funding for this book.

Several participants in this project were responsible for important contributions to which their own names are not directly attached. Dr Eleanor Zelliot was one of the first scholars to explore the intellectual richness of Dalit India; this book and the conference that preceded it are only a few of the many projects that are deeply indebted to her research and generosity. Mr Vasant Moon has been an important source of documentation, photographic as well as bibliographic. Achyut Yagnik and Anil Bhatt are responsible for introducing the Gujarati Dalit poetry that appears in this book, as well as the study of Dalit conditions that has appeared elsewhere. Gail Omvedt and Bharat Patankar will appear in the following pages as secondary sources and as translators; they are also companions on a journey. Bhuvan will not appear in the following pages at all, but has been a factor in all of them.

Introduction

DHARAM SUTRA
(An ancient Indian religious text)

> If a Shudra [low caste person] listens to a recitation of the Vedas [Hindu religious texts] his ears shall be filled with molten tin or lac. If he recites Vedic texts his tongue shall be cut out . . . He who tells [religious] law to a Shudra and he who teaches him religious observances, he indeed together with that Shudra sinks into the darkness of the hell called Asamvritta.

REJECTION
V. L. Kalekar (*Asmita Darsha*, 1979)

> No! No! No!
> A triple rejection
> To your economic, social, political, mental, religious, moral
>   and cultural pollution.
> You ever-living, ever-luminous suns!
> Your very touch brings a contagious disease.
> But I am a new sun
> Independent, self-luminating,
>   Possessed of a new spirit.
> I reject your culture.
> I reject your Parmeshwar-centred tradition.
> I reject your religion-based literature.
> My brothers!
> I have proclaimed my hatred
> My hate is unyielding
> It is without end.
> I have taken into account the unceasing battles
> I may bend but I won't break.

[Protest poetry from the 'Dalit' (Oppressed) literary movement developed by intellectuals from 'Untouchable' castes. Translation courtesy of Dr Jayashree Gokhale-Turner.]

Untouchable. Most of the world assumes that some force — Mahatma Gandhi, modernization or progressive legislation — has obliterated this ancient Indian nightmare, or at least reduced it to marginal significance.

Reality is at bitter odds with assumptions. For the past several years, official Indian figures on violent attacks against Untouchables have routinely exceeded 10,000 cases per year. Indian human rights workers report a far larger number go unrecorded, buried by collusion between police and local privilege (for example, Randeria and Yagnik, 1983; see the bibliography for details of this and all subsequent references). Justice is rare, even when charges are filed. In one grimly typical case, a state high court recently acquitted all those accused of the mass murder in daylight of fourteen Untouchables in the central Indian village of Kestara in 1982. The Indian Constitution outlaws the practice of untouchability, but a recent sample survey by the semi-official Harijan Sevak Sangh found 53 per cent of the sample villages still barred anyone from hereditary Untouchable castes from using common village wells, and 71 per cent of the villages barred them from the local Hindu temple (*Report of the Commissioner for Scheduled Castes and Scheduled Tribes*, 1978-9; subsequent references to this annual report will be abbreviated — *RCSCST* and year of report). The semi-slavery of debt-bonded labour is also illegal, but a 1976 national survey by the Gandhi Peace Foundation estimated 2,600,000 cases in agriculture alone, of which 62 per cent were Untouchables (Marla, 1981). Conditions of 'free' Untouchable labourers are often little better. The 1971 census found that 52 per cent of the Untouchable workforce had become landless agricultural labourers, up from 34 per cent in 1961. (By 1984, only parts of the 1981 census were in print.) The latest Rural Labour Enquiry (for 1974–5) found 71 per cent of all Untouchable agricultural labourers were in debt, mostly to money-lenders, shopkeepers and landlords.

The myth that Untouchables are mute, passive figures is quite as well entrenched as the notion that their problems have been solved by the generosity of others. In fact, the rising tide of violence has been triggered by increasing numbers of Untouchables who no longer tolerate the linked oppression of caste and class (*Seminar*, Delhi: November, 1979; Joshi, 1982). Details vary. In one village it is Untouchable women who will no longer drag themselves through the heat to a distant, inferior, 'Untouchable' water supply. In another it is agricultural labourers who demand better wages and better access to land. In some regions there have also been waves of conversion — to a Buddhism shaped by Untouchable reformers; to Christianity; to Islam. This too triggers violence, and also bureaucratic harassment as officials of a theoretically secular state struggle to stem desertions from the dominant religion.

Meanwhile, an Untouchable lawyer from southern India writes to an Untouchable engineer who has settled in the United States, reporting the latest outrage — police firing has killed ten Untouchable fishermen. He is representing the fishing community in a judicial enquiry, but he also seeks financial support for a new local unit of the Dalit Panthers, a movement inspired by the Black Panthers who so disturbed a complacent White America. 'Our people should be ready to attack their oppressors.' In central India, the president of a welfare society established by Untouchable converts to Buddhism concludes a convention by calling for nationalization of land: 'unless there was total nationalization of land, the judicious and equitable distribution of the land among the needy masses could not be ensured. A handful of the rich people were appropriating the major portion of the cultivatable land, while the majority were deprived of it' (*Hitavada*, Bhopal: 15 January 1984). In Geneva, Switzerland, an Untouchable doctor has already taken his people's case to the United Nations in 1982, to be followed by an Untouchable lawyer in 1983. Back in India, young Untouchables develop their own touring drama troops and recycle the case for assertive self-respect back out to Untouchables in the villages and slums.

It is time for a larger audience to hear some of these very articulate voices. Most of the articles, editorials, poetry and letters that make up the following chapters come from Untouchable writers, who have kindly allowed me to republish their work here. However, since the writers and their world are still unfamiliar to most Western readers, an introduction is in order.

By the early 1980s there were more than 105 million Untouchables distributed throughout peninsular India. The exact number is difficult to determine, because government statistics do not account for those who are converts to non-Hindu religions, even when they are demonstrably treated as Untouchables by their neighbours. At the lowest estimate, the Untouchables account for more than one out of every seven Indians — more than the combined populations of the United Kingdom and France.

Nearly 90 per cent live in India's rural villages, compared to approximately 80 per cent of the higher-caste population. Although Untouchables are commonly clustered together in segregated hamlets at the edge of a village, they are a small and vulnerable minority in any given region, making resistance to exploitation and violence very difficult. The latest available statistics, from the 1971 census, show that 52 per cent of the Untouchable workforce were landless agricultural labourers, compared to 26 per cent of the non-Untouchable workforce. The Untouchable literacy rate was only 14.7 per cent compared to 29.5 per cent for the total population. There are new channels for mobility — several of the Untouchable writers and organizers whose work appears in the following chapters are the children of agricultural or urban labourers — but the channels are narrow and hazardous, and the survivors few.

Most of the Untouchable writers we will meet in subsequent chapters would introduce themselves as 'Dalit', a term popularized by Untouchable protest movements since the early 1970s. A literal translation of the word 'dalit' is 'the oppressed', but the term 'Dalit' has become a positive, assertive expression of pride in Untouchable heritage and a rejection of oppression. Because 'Dalit' deliberately refers to all forms of social and economic oppression it can be, and often is, extended by Untouchable writers and activists to other suppressed peoples — tribals, religious minorities, women, the economically oppressed of all castes. In other cases the term 'Dalit' is used to specify Untouchables and the writer or speaker then makes separate but linked reference to other oppressed groups. I will deliberately use the term 'Untouchable' because it still has greater clarity and impact for English-speaking audiences, but the very concept of 'Dalit' may prove a powerful Untouchable contribution to a broad spectrum of social and economic liberation movements.

Other descriptive terms often appear in writing by or about Untouchables. 'Harijan' ('Children of God'), the term introduced by Mohandas (Mahatma) Gandhi, is most familiar to higher-caste Indians and foreigners, but is seldom used by today's Untouchable activists, who dislike its patronizing tone and reject the strategy of reliance on higher-caste *noblesse oblige* with which it is associated. 'Scheduled Caste' has a specific legal connotation and covers most, but by no means all, those who are socially treated as Untouchables.

Accuracy often requires reference to separately named Untouchable castes (or *jatis*) — Mahar, Madiga, Bhangi and so on — for 'Untouchable' is by no means an homogeneous category. There are many different hereditary Untouchable castes and subcastes. Language has been one dividing line. India has fifteen official languages and many more distinctive dialects. Only recently has there been a substantial pool of Untouchables with a command of several languages, including English, who could serve as human links between Untouchable movements in different linguistic regions.

Each Untouchable caste has also been defined by the same social rules of endogamy (in the Indian context, marriage exclusively within the caste community) that shape the entire Indian caste system. The result has been the development of a variety of distinctive Untouchable cultures, with significant differences in the direction and pace of mobilization for change. Frequently it also means social conflicts that make co-operative efforts difficult. The problem is all the more acute because the invidious hierarchic ranking of hereditary castes that permeates the dominant society does not stop at the social border of Untouchability. Some Untouchable castes long regarded themselves as superior to others, and even imposed their own internal touch-me-not-ism. One of the hallmarks of the contemporary Dalit movement has been its explicit rejection of older divisive strategies by which a given Untouchable caste would seek its own liberation by trying — usually unsuccessfully — to distance itself from other Untouchable castes. By now the goal is liberation of all Dalits — and this means dismantling the burden of centuries.

The origin of the caste system is a subject of much debate and little hard evidence. The most popular theory traces the system to invasions of Aryan-speaking peoples, roughly in the period 1400 B.C., and the ability of the Aryans to subordinate the indigenous non-Aryan population. The higher the caste, the more Aryan it was. For higher-caste Indians this often provided an opportunity to assert common Aryan identity with colonial Englishmen, English racism notwithstanding. Low-caste Indians, including some Untouchables, inverted Aryanism, proclaimed themselves the original and rightful owners of India, and wrote of a pre-Aryan 'golden age'. The Aryan theory poses a number of problems, however. As the late Untouchable leader, Dr Ambedkar, pointed out, Untouchables from the Tamil-speaking region of south India look like high caste Tamils, not like Untouchable Punjabis in the north-west, who are indistinguishable from higher-caste Punjabis. His own theory was that the caste system represented the triumph of an ideology that served the interests of the Brahman priesthood, not the triumph of one specific ethnic group (Ambedkar, 'Castes in India', 1916; and *Untouchables – Who Are They and How They Became Untouchable*, 1948). Other scholars, for example D. D. Kosambi and Morton Klass, have asked how an inherently sparse herding and gathering people like the Aryans could have generated so massive a migration or invasion (Kosambi, 1965; Klass, 1980).

Recently the focus has shifted to the relationship between caste and control of economic surplus. Klass has hypothesized a caste system dating back to the earliest development of settled agriculture on the Indian subcontinent, with some clans of previously egalitarian food-gathering tribes asserting dominance over others in order to claim a greater proportion of the new surplus generated by the new technology. This hypothesis lends a new dimension to both Ambedkar's theory and to Kosambi's notes on the food-distributing role of a priestly class in the earliest pre-Aryan city states. Two Marxist scholars, Gail Omvedt and Bharat Patankar, have pointed out the significance of such an interpretation for strategic debate on the Indian Left, where caste has routinely been pushed to the side. They have added their own analysis to new arguments for greater realism about the staying power of caste, its intimate relationship with Indian class structure, and the need for simultaneous caste-class struggle (Omvedt, 1982).

Untouchability itself has been rationalized in Hindu religious thought as the ultimate logical extension of the concepts of *karma* and rebirth that are supposed to determine all caste identity. One was born into an Untouchable caste because of the accumulation of especially heinous sins in previous births. This burden of sin made the Untouchable a hazard to higher-caste persons, who would be 'polluted' by contact. The ancient Indian legal text, the *Manusmriti* (the laws of the mythic legal codifier, Manu) prescribed Draconic punishment for Untouchables who so defiled others. The Untouchable was assigned economically and socially critical tasks that were, however, considered 'polluting' in themselves – sweeping, tanning leather, handling a plough which would destroy insect life. Specific tasks came to be associated with specific castes, for example Chamars with leather work, but it was not an occupation itself that made an individual an Untouchable. The Untouchable was forbidden to hear sacred texts (Manu prescribed pouring molten lead in the ears of offenders) even though Untouchables played menial roles considered essential to many religious rituals. By 400 A.D., the Chinese traveller Fa-Hsieu described a world in which 'the Chandalas [Untouchables] are named "evil men", and dwell apart from others. If they enter a town or market they sound a piece of wood in order to separate themselves; then, men knowing who they are, avoid coming in contact with them.'

Contemporary reality for Untouchables is a world in which the basic substance of the past is sustained, even when the environment appears to change dramatically. Belief in the inherent inferiority of an hereditary population has dangerous economic and psychological advantages for all individuals in the dominant society: a vast pool of cheap, legitimately degraded labour; limits on competition for the goods and positions that shape modern prestige and power — land, white-collar professions, political leadership; limits on competition for scarce loans to marginal farmers and scarce jobs for industrial labour; an automatic boost to the self-esteem of all in the dominant society. An analysis of recent patterns of conflict makes it easier to see how this operates in different sectors of Indian life.

The overt social oppression of Fa-Hsieu's India is still most common in the vast rural sector — home to nearly 90 per cent of the Untouchable population — where Untouchables are a socially conspicuous, economically vulnerable part of the village community. One typical clash in 1980, in the north Indian village of Kafalta, left one higher-caste Hindu and fourteen Untouchables dead. The Untouchables had been guilty of trying to adopt the standard higher-caste style in a marriage procession (*RCSCST*, 1979–81).

This does not mean that village life has been static. Far from it. Democracy has shifted political power from small urban elites to a variety of numerically large farming castes, including some that were once snubbed as 'Shudra' — castes that rank higher than Untouchables but far below the 'Twice Born' Hindu castes. Post-Independence land reforms supported by this new power bloc have stripped away a narrow strata of super-landed who once controlled vast populations, creating a new middle peasant elite but also blocking truly equal access to land. The 'Green Revolution' of modern technology has further reinforced the status of the new peasant elite, who have had the capital to invest in hybrid seeds, fertilizer, irrigation pumps, tractors. In a number of areas, commercial and technological change has increased the demand for a large pool of labour that can be used intensively at peak periods, then shunted aside in slack seasons. Regional patterns and details vary, but the subsistence agriculture and feudal relationships that once shaped the Indian village have increasingly given way to a world defined by capital, contract, cash crop — and economic conflict (Frankel, 1971; Mencher, 1974; Shivkumar, 1979; Omvedt, 1982).

What has not changed is the linkage between land and power, the importance of caste-defined social ties in access to both, or the importance of Untouchability in defining 'where the bottom is'. The pattern comes through with sickening clarity in a case that might be classified as 'minor' — only one dead, an eight-year-old Untouchable child. In late 1980, several Untouchable huts in the village of Shankarpur in Bihar were set on fire. The homes were destroyed and a little girl burnt to death. A local district magistrate and a superintendent of police reported that the Untouchables themselves had set the fires and had then tried to implicate higher-caste landlords. Journalists were less than impressed by this improbable tale, especially when they found that the landlords were trying to regain control of small sections of land that had been awarded to the Untouchables by the government during a short burst of populist fervour a few years previously. A senior official was nudged into further enquiry but without result (*RCSCST*, 1979-81).

Untouchables are not the only victims of the increased frequency and intensity of rural economic conflict. It has become popular to describe this as 'class warfare', with the writer's tone varying from horror to hope. It is certainly warfare over economic exploitation, but 'class' suggests a degree of common identity and co-operative purpose among rural workers that is difficult to develop and harder to sustain. Frequently the non-Untouchable labourer clings to some shred of dignity by co-operating in excluding the Untouchable from the well shared by all other villagers. Increasingly, the Untouchable is heartily tired of routine denigration, and needs no scientific knowledge to notice that being relegated to the least desirable water supply is not unconnected with the relative frequency of disease and death. Landed elites are often shrewd enough to divide and rule by isolating the Untouchables.

Consider Dharampura, another village in Bihar. This village had been the scene of a long-simmering dispute between landowners (including the hereditary Brahman priest of the local temple) and sharecroppers (including Untouchables and also non-Untouchable Ahirs). In late 1977, a mob of about sixty persons, led by the priest, attacked the huts of Untouchable sharecroppers, killing four and wounding four others. The Ahir sharecroppers were spared but very effectively warned, and the Untouchables were isolated. The pattern is not unvarying, but it is bitterly common (*RCSCST*, 1977-8; Sharma, 1979).

Urban India is hardly a utopian escape — in the past few years, major cities from the south-east to the north-west have exploded in anti-Untouchable riots. Even occasions for simple social invisibility prove less frequent and less useful than we have usually assumed. In any given job or neighbourhood in India, co-workers and neighbours are normally well informed about one another's social antecedents; amateur social anthropology is an Indian national pastime. Even highly educated and geographically mobile Untouchables find to their cost that it is seldom possible to hide themselves and their extended kin networks from the curiosity of the potential employer or neighbour and his own kin network. This can lead to very overt touch-me-not-ism: refusal of jobs or apartment leases, the daily indignity of being excluded from a water tap. Invisibility is easiest in the least critical areas of life. It is indeed impossible physically to segregate inconspicuous Untouchables in the bedlam of urban public transportation, and the patrons of cinema houses are inured to the presence of unidentifiable strangers. For Untouchables who have lived with the constant strictures of village life this is a much prized relief, but it is important to avoid exaggerating its significance.

The more important element of urban life is that cities offer both facilities

Mass rally of Dalit activists in front of Parliament House, New Delhi, 1983. Like most Dalit meetings and demonstrations, the rally went unrecorded by the national press. *(Oppressed Indian)*

and organizational options that are not available in the villages. There are no village universities. Urban jobs may be in desperately short supply, but the city is where most of those few jobs in India that are not dependent upon access to land exist, and even the urban day-labourer is more likely to be able to escape a master's constant surveillance than is his village counterpart. The economics of concentrated numbers has made possible independent literary magazines, small businesses, large-scale protest organizing. Only 10 per cent of the Untouchable population is urban, but this means substantial absolute numbers (about 10 million) who have begun to develop much-needed institutions.

   Unfortunately, in the city also there is no escape from the basic facts of

Indian life: acute scarcity; the pervasive importance of social networking in access to scarce goods and services; and the persistent importance of hereditary status in these networks. The networks are simply a normal part of life for those whose status makes them the most frequent beneficiaries. The uninitiated may wish to consult R. S. Khare's case study, complete with a bemused but accurate flow chart, of one high-caste family's use of caste-kin networks in obtaining a job for their son (Khare, 1970). It is an excellent indirect commentary on the continuation of *de facto* 'protective discrimination' for upper-caste groups that is still far more effective than any legislated 'protective discrimination' for low-caste Indians.

Networks are critically important even at the level of the factory floor. Although there have been serious efforts to develop official employment exchanges, most job information and recruiting practices are still *ad hoc* and personalized. A study of the labour market in the large industrial city of Ahmedabad showed 70 per cent of all employees had only informal sources of job information, and 61 per cent had actually obtained jobs through the intercession of friends or relatives already in a given factory shop or department (Papola and Subrahmanian, 1973). Below the level of prestige positions, this routinized nepotism benefits a variety of castes, but earlier patterns of industrial access sharply limit the areas in which Untouchables stand to benefit.

The Untouchables' basic urban problem is that they cannot simultaneously hide their identity and actively manipulate the only social networks to which they have access. In the words of the Dalit poet, Daya Pawar

> You say you want to flee
> this ghost-ridden town!
> Oh yes, but how can you run far enough?
> You may go anywhere, but wherever you step
> you will stumble over the ochre-coloured gods.

Increasing numbers will neither hide nor apologize for Dalit ancestry. This can be dangerous. It certainly has been in Agra, the city of the Taj Mahal as well as an important regional commercial centre. Here Untouchables have some limited economic independence because their 'polluting' leather craft is the basis for a cottage industry and small-scale businesses. Many have also proclaimed cultural independence through conversion to their own autonomous form of Buddhism. An annual parade in honour of the late Untouchable leader, Dr Ambedkar, symbolizes all that Untouchables should *not* be in the eyes of many high-caste Hindus — proud, assertive, independent. The parade is deeply resented by the higher-caste population, and in 1978 conflict triggered a riot in which local police went on a rampage in Untouchable residential areas. They killed nine Untouchables, seriously injured more than 100 others, burned homes and left the walls of an Untouchable Buddhist shrine riddled with bullet holes (*RCSCST*, 1977–8). As yet, no police have been brought to trial.

Three months of anti-Untouchable riots in the state of Gujarat in 1981 brought the linkage between the cultural and economic underpinnings of Untouchability into much sharper focus (Yagnik and Bhatt, 1984; Joshi, 1982). The riots began in the industrial city of Ahmedabad, then spread to most other cities and many villages in the state. The initial incident was a protest by high-caste medical students about seven seats in Ahmedabad medical schools that had gone to Untouchables and to other minority students under a special affirmative action programme. Anti-Untouchable violence quickly spread to private sector factories, where there are neither affirmative action programmes nor simple anti-discrimination policies, and on out into the villages. Subsequent research showed a close correlation between levels and targets of violence and the relative degree of upward mobility among Untouchables in different regions and among particular Untouchable castes (Bose, 1981). The least mobile Untouchable caste had generally been left in peace, as had all the non-Untouchable minorities who were covered by the affirmative action programmes. On the other side, conflict was encouraged by high-caste dominated newspapers and professional associations, while mobs were recruited from industrial slum and university campus alike. The events in Gujarat are widely described as a caste war. It was — but it was a caste war over economic competition from people Indian society defines as beneath competition.

Although the professional middle class attracted most of the attention, the riot also underlined chronically destructive rifts in the Indian working class. The only significant labour union at the site of the fiercest fighting, Ahmedabad, is a textile union founded by Mahatma Gandhi in 1918 that still reflects his vision of co-operation between labour and paternalistic capital. Throughout the riots, the union refused to speak out on Untouchable rights, and when one internationally-known woman organizer insisted on speaking out for both peace and affirmative action she was dismissed from the union. It is easy to see the union's role in the riots as a reflection of its leaders' ties to the economic establishment — better to let workers vent their frustration on a long-despised minority than on millowners. Unfortunately it is also true that the union's rank and file needed no coaching in its hostility to Untouchables.

The Left has been a weak presence in Gujarat, but this has not always made a difference. There has been discouragingly little active leadership from the Left in developing a vision of working-class unity explicitly including Untouchables as equal partners. Organizers of the Left, like those of the Centre and Right, find it easier to avoid confronting the bigotry of those who make up the largest pool of potential supporters. Organizational expediency is reinforced by the short-term pressures of electoral politics. Indian politics is open to the Left; a variety of socialist and communist parties have formed state governments and are routinely represented in Parliament. Their presence as active electoral competitors has kept alive critical issues and options, but the immediate search for votes has also discouraged attention to thorny minority issues. The one segment of the Left that is least interested in electoral strategies, the so-called 'Naxalite' factions of the CPI-ML, is also the segment most committed to addressing Untouchable and tribal issues directly.

Added to tactical problems are leadership attitudes that spread from Right to Left, and from medical professionals in western Gujarat to academics in eastern Bengal. Most of India's modern intelligentsia reject traditional theories of Untouchable inferiority, just as their Western counterparts reject traditional theories of racial inferiority. It has also been just as adept at finding new rationalizations for maintaining old dominance. One discouragingly typical example is a leading social scientist and socialist. Early in his career he was employed as a teacher by the late Untouchable leader, Dr Ambedkar, in a school that Ambedkar had started. He does not deny his association with the school; indeed, he points to it as proof of his own lack of prejudice about Untouchables. However, he has reconstructed the past and now describes the relationship in terms of his own charity, not contract and paid employment – he, a high-caste Hindu, was a volunteer donating his knowledge to Untouchables. This modification of fact conveniently reinstates the traditional caste order of dominant and subordinate, giver and receiver; the situation is no longer a radical reversal of roles in which an Untouchable gave a high-caste Indian a badly-needed job. Charity, yes; equality, no.

Under these conditions it is inevitable that Untouchable equality means Untouchable pressure. The problem is that efficient pressure means resources: autonomous communication channels, the money and the skilled personnel to keep these channels alive, the audacity to challenge a society that demands daring and then rewards it with a combination of indifference and repression.

Most of the resources that Untouchables now use as building blocks for change are the product of political manoeuvre before Indian Independence, when unique political conditions gave Untouchables unusual leverage. The man most often associated with Untouchable mobility, Mohandas (Mahatma) Gandhi, actually played an ambiguous role, opposing touch-me-not-ism, but also opposing changes in Untouchable roles and job status that would undermine his vision of hereditary moral 'duty' (for example, quotations from 1927 in Gandhi, *An Autobiography*, 1959; or from 1937 in Gandhi, *The Removal of Untouchability*, 1954). For a number of years, even limited change remained a matter of personal practice, not public policy. As early as 1915 he had admitted an Untouchable family to his ashram, but the resulting storm of orthodox outrage convinced him that the issue of untouchability would have to be kept out of the Indian National Congress and the Indian Independence movement (Gandhi, *An Autobiography*, 1957). British education policy, however, had already produced small pockets of Untouchable literacy and a few leaders whose skill in the English language made possible an independent international role. It was this that dramatically restructured the debate.

By far the most influential of the Untouchable leaders was Dr Bhimrao Ambedkar. Ambedkar regarded the British and high-caste Indian nationalists as competing forms of colonialism; neither could be trusted, but the competition itself could be used as a means to institutionalize access to resources Untouchables would need for liberation (Ambedkar, *The Evolution of Provincial Finance in British India*, 1925; and *What Congress and Gandhi Have Done to the Untouchables*, 1945). He eventually manoeuvred a floundering British empire into far more significant protective and developmental policies for Untouchables than any the colonial empire had produced in its heyday. Gandhi and the Congress reversed course; an issue that had been politically untouchable had become politically imperative. Ambedkar lost a number of battles he considered critical, but by the time the British departed, the Congress as governing heir-apparent had committed itself to some policies that were subsequently written into the Indian Constitution, with Ambedkar serving as a member of the drafting committee.

The most visible feature of these policies is actually the single greatest source of frustration for the Untouchables. Ambedkar sought, and the British finally awarded, separate Untouchable electorates. Gandhi defeated the policy in a dramatic death fast. The compromise that emerged was a policy whereby a number of constituencies are 'reserved'; only Untouchables (or tribals in a separate set of constituencies) can stand for office, but non-Untouchables make up the vast majority of the electorate within the constituencies. The result is still guaranteed proportional representation, in spite of a combination of geographic dispersion, social hostility and economic dependency that would normally block any significant access to the political system at a level above the occasional city council seat. Access, but not the autonomy that was sought. Dominant society voters and power brokers determine the winning party in 'reserved' constituencies as fully as they do elsewhere — rarely do Untouchables compose as much as a third of the electorate — and dominant society elites determine distribution of party tickets and direction of party policy. Many Untouchable legislators themselves, as well as Untouchable activists, say the Untouchable representatives are expected to be docile field hands.

In practice, the balance of power has become more subtle, and sometimes more useful. Some of the representatives certainly earn the bitter Untouchable label of 'chamcha', puppet. There are others who use the multiparty divisions of Indian politics and the chronic internal tensions of the larger parties to more effective public purpose, and certainly many prove far more articulate in the legislative arena than a determinedly inattentive press would lead us to believe (Dushkin, 1972; Joshi, 1982). This is not a legislative minority in a position to force through grand new departures in Indian public policy, but it does contribute to the populist tilt of Indian policy. For example, Ambedkar himself lost a bid to write co-operative farming and nationalization of agricultural land into the Indian Constitution; for all but a few individuals, this vision of a radical redistribution of wealth and power was an idea before its time. Subsequent Untouchable politics has not loosened the grip of landed rural elites who rose in the wake of a more popular strategy, but it has added to ameliorative policies in the rural sector (Joshi, 1982).

Influence has been greater in policy areas where resistance is less overwhelming, including several that have been critical to Untouchable development. Education is one of these areas. Untouchables had already used British support to move their children into common village schools, determined village resistance notwithstanding, and there has been no retreat to segregation. Government-supported education has broad support throughout Indian society, and has expanded rapidly since Independence. Special affirmative action programmes for Untouchable and tribal students, pushed through by Ambedkar in the waning years of British rule, are profoundly unpopular — witness the Gujarat riots — and yet these too have been expanded. The provincial level programmes vary greatly in extent and quality but cover such items as free textbooks and supplies for low-income minority students in primary and secondary schools, and special admissions policies (lowered entrance requirements and a quota of seats) for a variety of minority students in technical schools and colleges. Because of restrictions in the Constitution, central government schemes focus on the narrower field of college ('post matric') scholarships for Untouchable and other minority students whose families fall below an income cut-off line (Joshi, 1980; MRG, 1983).

The results are unquestionably blunted by the incidence of parental poverty in the Untouchable population. As of 1977-8, only 75 per cent of Untouchable children in the 6–11 age group were in school, compared to 88 per cent of non-Untouchable children. For 11–14-year-olds the comparable figures were 25 per cent and 42 per cent. High-caste resistance adds to the effects of poverty. In the midst of Gujarat's anti-Untouchable riots, one of India's leading sociologists wrote an angry denunciation of fellow high-caste educators bent on dismantling affirmative action policies, accusing them of repeating British colonial harassment of Indian students in British schools and citing cases of Untouchable college students being told to their faces they had no business being anything but street-sweepers (Desai, 1981).

Nevertheless, the policies have pulled large blocks of students over the walls of poverty and caste and into school. In a recent national survey 60 per cent of all Untouchable students at both the secondary and college levels proved to be the children of village servants and labourers (Shah, 1982). Survival is precarious for an impoverished pool of first-generation educated, but in the following chapters we will meet specialists on economics and law whose parents were rural or urban labourers; college-educated sons of street-sweepers who are organizing a slum revolt; poets and dramatists from India's industrial slums who use their art to arouse their own people and challenge the dominant society.

The financial base for such action is still narrow. What there is has been built on the slow expansion of public sector affirmative action policies for Untouchables that Ambedkar first pushed through in the years before Independence. Resistance from private employers and high-caste dominated labour unions has been intense. Not until the 1970s did these policies include most public sector industries. There are still no effective anti-discrimination policies in the private sector, including industries dependent on government contracts, or even an effective reporting system to monitor Untouchable access to private sector jobs. Bureaucratic resistance continues to take a toll even when policies are in place; the reports of the independent Commissioner for Scheduled Castes and Tribes and those of a parliamentary watchdog committee formed at the insistence of Untouchable representatives, routinely document harassment and overt job discrimination. Still, the numbers edge up. In 1947, Untouchables accounted for 0.7 per cent of the most senior central government administrative posts; in 1979 it was 4.7 per cent, and at the level of skilled technical jobs in public sector industries the figure was 16.3 per cent (MRG, 1983).

This bridgehead in the public sector is not the equal of private wealth, either in land or urban capital, but it has improved the Untouchable resource base. I was abruptly reminded of this by one recent convention of public sector activists that drew 5,000 delegates from across the country to the capital in Delhi. Not all were Untouchables — there were a number of tribals and other minority groups — but most of the leadership and membership were Untouchable employees: railroad mechanics, lawyers, film technicians, doctors, printers. Public sector education plus public sector jobs have produced a swelling pool of skills, information and disposable income. Their own organization was already producing protest journalism in several different languages, running a small chain of medical and legal intervention centres in city slums, sending entertainer 'Awakening Squads' to villages and provincial towns. Individual members provided funding for everything from literary magazines to young people organizing rural labourers.

The importance of these autonomous channels was underlined by the capital's press, which reported a small 'national integration' display by children at an elite school but ignored the far better stories to be had at a massive open-air conference to which it had been invited. No one was surprised by the news blackout. It was merely symptomatic of a far broader indifference and resistance that had already alienated Untouchables and other minorities from the national elite and impelled the establishment of their own organizations. They would have to find their own ways of financing and amplifying independent voices. They had found some. They would find others. This book is an attempt to bring some of those independent and courageous Untouchable voices to a wider audience.

1. Roots of Revolt

There is no single time or place marked 'Start' for the modern Dalit movement. By the end of the 19th Century change was in the air, and a few Untouchables found access to new ideas and new resources. In local communities scattered across India they shaped a variety of ideologies and organizations as they sought to challenge an exploitative tradition. Standard histories have told us little about these diverse efforts; we have been told far more about occasional reforms from above than about struggle from below. Fortunately a growing number of Dalit intellectuals have sought directions for the future through a better understanding of the Dalit past. The result is renewed efforts at collecting, preserving, publishing, often by people who commit time from unrelated careers. It will be some time before we see all of a complex mosaic, but some of the pieces are already taking shape. The following article describes some of the early Dalit ferment in west-central India (the area now known as Maharashtra), the region that became the base of operations for the most influential figure in the Dalit movement, Dr B. R. Ambedkar. The author has formed his own collection of Dalit historical materials into a small public research centre and has served as one of the editors of Dr Babasaheb Ambedkar: Writings and Speeches, *an ongoing publication project of the government of Maharashtra. The article itself was originally presented to an international conference on racism and untouchability in New York City in 1983.*

From Dependence to Protest: The Early Growth of Education and Consciousness among 'Untouchables' of Western India

Vasant W. Moon (1983)

Education, Attitudes and Resources under Peshwa Rule in Western India

It has become one of the truisms of the historical profession that the peasants of traditional societies are the 'Silent Actors' of history. If this is true, the same applies to an even greater degree to the Untouchable communities of India. In attempting to trace the rise of an independent educational movement among Untouchables, we face an acute shortage of direct evidence about the realities of village social life for Untouchable castes even for most of the

19th Century. In this first section, therefore, I will restrict myself to some general observations about the conditions of these communities in the 19th and early 20th Centuries, as the background to the educational movements with which this paper is concerned.

We are all familiar, I think, with the social deprivations and humiliations which the religious writings of the Hindus demanded should be inflicted on the Untouchables. Their touch, shadow, and even the sound of their voices were deemed to be polluting. They were restricted to the most crude clothing and ornaments. Public wells were forbidden to them. They were not to learn to read or write, and were prohibited from listening to any of the traditional sacred texts. The punishments to be inflicted on transgressors were set out in gruesome detail. Any act of disrespect, especially to the priestly caste of Brahmans, was to be punished with the utmost rigour. To a certain extent, the same disabilities were laid down for the 'Shudra' lower castes of Hindus. Yet the peculiar social stigma suffered by Untouchables was something unique to them. As we shall see, the abhorrence of Untouchables was not something limited to the higher castes, but extended even to the lower 'clean' Hindu castes.

It is very difficult to say how far these religious texts were applied in practice to the Untouchables. But there does seem to be evidence that in western India the severity with which caste boundaries and disabilities were applied had increased since the middle of the 18th Century, when political power passed into the hands of the Chitpavan Peshwas, themselves drawn from one of the highest Brahman castes. In his description of western Indian social structure, written at the end of the 19th Century, R. V. Russell set out some of the disabilities that Untouchables suffered. Under native rule, the Mahar, the largest local Untouchable caste, was subject to painful degradations. He might not spit on the ground lest a Hindu should be polluted by touching it with his foot, but had to hang an earthen pot around his neck to hold his spittle. He was made to drag a thorny branch behind him to brush out his footsteps, and when a Brahman came by had to lie at a distance on his face lest his shadow might fall upon the Brahman. In Gujarat, they were not allowed to tuck up the loin cloth, but had to trail it along the ground. Even quite recently in Bombay, a Mahar was not allowed to talk loudly in the street while a well-to-do Brahman or his wife was dining in one of the houses. In the city of Poona, seat of the ruling Chitpavan Brahmans, conditions were even worse: 'The Mahars and Mangs were not allowed within the City of Poona between 3 p.m. and 9 a.m., because before 9 a.m. and after 3 p.m. their bodies cast too long a shadow, and whenever their shadow fell upon a Brahman it polluted him, so that he dare not take food or water until he had bathed and washed the impurity away.'

In view of conditions such as these, we are safe in assuming that under Peshwa rule at least, Untouchable communities had no access to education, even of the most rudimentary kind. What is much less certain, however, is the question of Untouchables' own attitudes to their status. It is hard to find any clear evidence of widespread or mass-based resistance. Dissent of a kind was, of course, expressed in the devotional *bhakti* movement in Maharashtra, with its emphasis upon the devotion of the individual believer, rather than the rigid hierarchies of caste. Protest was also expressed through the myth, widespread amongst Untouchable groups, of an earlier high-caste status that was lost by the community through error or misfortune, such as the consumption of meat in desperation during periods of famine, or some accidental annoyance caused to one of the deities. These examples apart, we have little evidence of consistent self-conscious movements of protest. It may have been that Untouchables themselves had internalized the religious values of Hinduism, and so perceived the ordering of society to be legitimate, or more likely because they realized that the chances were heavily stacked against a successful protest.

The Beginnings of Untouchable Education Under British Rule

Three factors were to assume importance for the growth of Untouchable movements as the 19th Century progressed. The first was the attitude and influence of British officials. The second was the effect of missionary activities on local Untouchable communities. The third was a growing realization among all Indians, including Untouchables, that in education lay the key to future political power, as the British government prepared to extend limited representative institutions to Indians themselves.

The issue of Untouchable education came increasingly frequently to the surface in the second half of the 19th Century, and, as we shall see, commonly took the following form. Christian missionaries in a particular area would concentrate their efforts of education and proselytization upon the Untouchables, as the most likely candidates for conversion. In doing so, they would encourage bright Untouchable students to apply for places in the government secondary schools. Upon their gaining admission, there would follow a large-scale desertion and vocal protest by the families of the 'clean' (*savarna*) Hindu students. This in turn would set off worried consultations amongst the British officials responsible for the area. While these were usually sympathetic to the cause of Untouchable uplift, not all of them were prepared to see empty classes in the secondary schools, and most of them attempted to arrive at a compromise, such as sitting the Untouchable students on an outside verandah, and hoping for a relaxation in the attitudes of the local higher-caste Hindus as they became accustomed to seeing the Untouchable students in the schools.

While practices such as these were not calculated to bring about any major change in the educational levels of Untouchables, other aspects of British policy did serve to heighten their sense of the importance of education. As it became clear that the British government was prepared to devolve at least local political power upon Indians themselves, castes at all levels of Indian society quickly realized that the largest share of this power would go to those with an English education, professional qualifications and administrative experience. By the 1880s, Untouchable leaders were becoming increasingly aware of the urgency of their need for education, if the Untouchable communities were to have any sort of influence upon Indian political life in the future.

Conflict Over Education: Some Case Studies of Untouchables in Government-aided Schools

The Recalcitrant Patel of Ranjangaon Ganpati: The Reverend R. Winson referred a complaint from Mahars to Mr W. A. East, Collector of Poona, under his letter of 14 January 1887. In his letter Rev. Winson pointed out that in September 1880, about seven years before, the Patel and the Kulkarni (village officers) of Ranjangaon Ganpati had compelled the Mahars of the village to close their school under violent threats, intimidation and persecution. On this complaint Mr Stewart, the Collector at that time, had come to Sirur, a *taluq* town, summoned the Patel and the Kulkarni, made enquiries and then suspended their services. After six months, they were reinstated on the understanding that they would never again resort to such treatment of Mahars, and that if they did they would be dismissed. A written promise had been obtained from them.

In spite of this, by a similar course of threat and persecution, the Patel had again forced the Mahars to close their school. Rev. Winson further stated that the Mahars appealed to the government for their protection and for the opening of their school. He therefore requested the Collector to do the needful, to relieve them of unjustifiable oppression and hindrance in their lawful pursuit.

Enquiry was held by Mr Snow, the Assistant Collector, on 1 February 1887. He found the charge against the Patel proved, that the Patel 'acted in a most violent, headstrong and foolish manner in threatening the Mahars'. In spite of the report of Mr Snow, Mr East proposed that the Patel should be continued and suggested that the missionaries should be warned against interfering in any way between the Patel and the Mahars.

The matter then came up before Mr Snow's superior, Mr W. Lee Warner. In his judgement on 10 July 1887, Mr Warner observed that neither Mr Snow nor Mr East had mentioned any incident proving exaggerated and false allegations or improper disobedience on the part of the Mahars, nor had he found any himself. Referring to the earlier decision about misconduct of the Patel, Mr Warner said that the Patel had been expressly told that he would surely be dismissed if any obstruction occurred in future. He was therefore at a loss to understand how a mild caution could suitably meet the case. Mr Warner further elaborated on official British policy, quoting the Secretary of State's despatch No. 5, dated 9 March 1866, para. 7, which observed

> There is every reason to believe in the beneficial effect upon the Hindu Population in Bengal of the Education imparted to them under English Gentlemen of Character and acquirements such as the Missionaries. There is ample scope for the labour of all — the benefits resulting from the efforts in this direction of missionaries have repeatedly been acknowledged,

and Her Majesty's Government would greatly regret that these efforts should be discouraged or that any ground should be afforded for supposing that Govt. or its officers are less disposed than before to afford encouragement to such valuable and disinterested exertions.

Mr Warner's personal observations on the effect of education on the Mahars in Satara and Ahmednagar districts are quite interesting. He noted that a social revolution was going on, in the movement of Mahars and other low castes from status to contract. The Mahars now could sell their labour and were not required to work the customary village service in exchange for a livelihood based on customary perquisites received from other villages as *baluta*. Mr Warner states

> The system of compelling the Mahars to stay at home is a device suggested by the specious pretence of precaution against crime, but really proposed by the village officers to suppress the movement towards their emancipation. In Ahmednagar where the Mahars have been most educated, they have risen from a condition of serfdom to free labour with the very best results.

[The case eventually worked its way to the Governor's office, where it encountered a final hurdle.]

The battle was still not fully won. When the matter of Ranjangaon schools went to the government, the Acting Chief Secretary noted (31 August 1887) his opinion, 'that it is desirable to wait and see the effects of education and time and the Railways to remove prejudices, rather than to threaten, and to warn the Patel of the penalties'. According to him, if orders were issued that Mahars, Dheds, Bhangis and other low castes must be admitted into the same room to sit by the side of the higher castes and the orders were obeyed, government schools would speedily be emptied. 'It is a concession and a large concession, by the people generally, that they allow Mahars etc. to be under the same roof though not within the same walls as themselves. Give education time, and the work will do itself.' To hurry it unnecessarily would see what work had been done at great risk of being undone, was the conclusion of the Acting Chief Secretary.

However the Governor opined that the government could undertake the opening of special schools for Mahars. He hoped that the higher castes would take a leading part in the education of the depressed classes in order to prevent the social subversion which would follow their entire emancipation from tutelage.

The case of the Patel of Ranjangaon had set the stone rolling. The initiative of Rev. R. Winson, the missionary from Sirur, and the personal interest shown by Mr L. Warner, Commissioner of the Division, shook the whole machinery of administration of the state government. The Patel, who had been appointed by the Governor, was ordered to be dismissed under Revenue Department letter dated 12 September 1887. It was also directed that instructions should be given to the new Patel that he not interfere in any way with the school or with the teachers. Thus ended the long-drawn-out battle of a missionary with the administration on the cause of education of low castes. The earlier apprehension of the officers that Rev. Winson was taking up the cause of Mahar boys and teachers only because these boys may be Christian converts was also proved wrong. Enquiry revealed that there was only one converted Christian from the Mahar community. The boys enrolled in the school were of low caste, but most were not converts.

Dapoli: Untouchable Soldiers vs. Orthodoxy: There is an interesting case of a similar battle, though with one important difference. In this event, the persons who carried through the war were Mahars themselves. They were retired British Army personnel. Ratnagiri District was the chief recruiting ground of the British Bombay Army, and a large portion of men enlisting there for service in infantry regiments were from the Untouchable Mahar and Chambar castes. After completion of their service, or retirement, they settled in some central or favourite village or town with some piece of land, cultivating their crops and bringing up their children, leading a peaceful quiet life. Of such men, a few commissioned and non-commissioned officers settled at Dapoli. This is the place where Dr Ambedkar, the emancipator of the Untouchables, spent his early childhood and received his primary education.

Subhedar Major Gagnak and nine other military pensioners, including Ambedkar's father, sent a petition on 1 July 1892 to the president of Dapoli Municipality asking that their sons be admitted into the Municipal school and taught along with other boys. They stated that this arrangement would induce their boys to study hard and to emulate the example of the boys of other castes in the hope of attaining a high rank in their class. Opening a separate school for Mahar and other low caste boys would entail additional expenditure to the government exchequer. (One of the signatories of this petition is 'Ramnak Malnak'. Mahars used to suffix 'nak' to their names until recently, later substituting 'ji'. Thus 'Ramnak Malnak' becomes 'Ramji Maleji', Dr Ambedkar's father. He was also one of 1,588 pensioners who petitioned the government in 1904 for readmission of Mahars into the Bombay Army after it was closed to them in 1892 by a change in British recruiting policy.)

This petition was forwarded by the Collector to the Chairman of the Municipality for report, who stated in reply on 5 August 1892 that if the Mahar boys were admitted into the school, the boys of other castes would leave it, and consequently the school would have to be closed. It would be better to open a separate school for Mahar boys and to engage a separate teacher.

The papers were placed before the quarterly meeting of the Municipality held on 6 August 1892, when it was resolved to inform the applicants that the request could not be granted as it would result in closing of the school. If, however, they could bring twenty-five boys of their caste, a separate school and separate teacher would be provided.

To this communication Subhedar Gagnak replied on 8 September 1892 that the petitioners could not undertake to secure an attendance of twenty-five low-caste boys to secure a new school for the reasons already mentioned. They asked for admission into the existing school and to have their boys taught with other boys. This reply was considered at a meeting of the Municipality on 9 September 1892 in which it was resolved that it was impossible to admit the Mahar boys into the existing school on account of the religious scruples of the parents of high-caste boys.

On 3 December 1892, the local Collector asked the Municipality whether something could not be done in this matter. In reply, the Municipality forwarded an extract of the resolution adopted on 9 September 1892 and stated that it was contemplated to extend the school and appoint an additional teacher for the benefit of Mahar boys, but this could not be effected for want of funds. Consequently these boys could not be admitted and allowed to sit in the verandah as proposed by the Collector. The Municipality then informed the petitioners that if they would consent to contribute Rs. 50/- to the cost of extension of the school, the Municipality would take up the work. The petitioners consented to this proposal. But nothing was done. The petitioners waited for about eleven months and sent the petition again in November 1893, hoping against hope, to the Additional Collector. After having exhausted their patience, they approached the Commissioner, Mr T. Nugent, on 8 February 1894.

The Commissioner observed that the government orders were disregarded not only in the case of Dapoli but elsewhere. In his letter to the Collector on 21 May 1894, he observed:

For over 18 months nothing seems to have been done to enable their [Pensioners'] sons to be educated at the Principle school, which is maintained for the benefit of boys of all castes and creeds and is paid for from the taxes and rates collected from persons of all castes and creeds. The Municipality make proposals which were unreasonable and inadequate. I found that through bigotry and obstructiveness of the Municipal members and inertness displayed by the Dist. Officers, the low caste boys were debarred from obtaining any education and were positively refused admission.

[The Mahars persisted, and the Collector eventually asked the government to block all grants to the Municipality. At this point the Municipal Council retreated, and Mahar children were seated in the classrooms, though at a distance from other boys.]

Policy and Public Conflict: It is easier to see the implications of these and other cases of conflict if we remember the British government had laid down a policy of imparting education to low castes, one sharply at variance with earlier Peshwa rule. Section 591 of the Education Commissioner's Report said 'that the principle has been laid down by the Court of Directors in their letter of 5th May, 1854, and in a subsequent reply to Government's letter dated 20/5/57'. According to these letters, 'nobody should be refused admission to a Government college or school merely on the ground of caste'. This principle was reaffirmed in 1863. It was applicable to all institutions which were maintained at the cost of public funds, provincial or local. The

Commission referred to the opposition to this principle which existed in Bombay itself, and rejected the opposition on the ground that education would advance them (low castes) in life and induce them to seek emancipation from this servile condition. The Commission therefore opined that this class of society requires special help, and they indicate the institution of schools as the best method.

The government of India officially commented on this principle further. 'His Excellency the Governor in Council attached great importance to the provision of adequate educational facilities for children of low caste parents.' In order to clarify any misapprehension the government of India wrote in letter no. 15/16, dated 19 June 1885 'that rule of admission irrespective of caste must be maintained'.

The principle of equality was also emphasized in Her Majesty's message of 21 April 1856 in the passage in which she personally altered Lord Malmsbury's draft. The final declaration read: 'We declare it to be our Royal will and pleasure that none be in any way favoured, none molested by reason of their faith, and that all alike enjoy the equal and impartial protection of law.'

In contrast, the Indian intelligentsia, composed mainly of the higher castes, routinely opposed every reform on the grounds of its interfering with religion, thus causing injustice and persecution not only to the Untouchables but to women and non-Brahmans as well.

Despite government orders and frequently sincere efforts on the part of officers of government, there existed widespread opposition to the admission of Mahars to educational institutions. Mr Waddington, Education Inspector from Negar, found during his inspection of government schools that the attendance of Mahars was limited, and even where they were admitted, a separate shed or room outside the school was provided for them . . . He observed that village officers were parties to inciting ill-will against the low castes. The Christian missions were hindered in opening schools owing to village officers threatening to stop Mahar *haqs* or rights of *watan*. [Both terms refer to hereditary perquisites provided in exchange for village services demanded of Mahars, and were essential to Mahar economic survival.] It was not only mission schools; even in government schools, caste feeling was strong to work to stop the spread of education among the lower castes . . .

Strategies of the protagonists varied. If the government did not yield to the protests of the caste Hindus they sometimes withdrew their pupils and opened new schools. When petitions for equal treatment from Untouchables were turned down by the authorities, the Untouchables sometimes opened separate schools and sometimes continued to fight for access to existing schools. Sometimes they were supported by the missionaries and sometimes government officers came to their rescue.

For example, the Director of Public Instruction in Central Provinces and Berar, in his Quinquennial Review in 1905, reported that 'At Nagpur, boys from the Depressed Class were required to sit in the verandah of the primary school apart from their fellow pupils. The community bitterly resented this and claimed equality of treatment. On meeting no response, they opened a

For *tapas*, prowl through the bars around the Plaza del Campo del Príncipe or Carrera del Darro (near Plaza Nueva). Several lively *tapas* bars line Calle Elvira at the west end of Plaza Nueva, such as the cheap, popular **Bodega Castoneda** where you can get a mouth-watering chef-like salad (*salad de casa*) or baked potatoes with a variety of toppings. For an inexpensive and decent menu on Cuesta de Gomerez, try **Restaurante Morillo** (at #20). **Naturi Albaicín** is a great vegetarian place (Calle Caldereria Nueva 10, tel. 958/22-06-27). The **Lisboa Cafeteria** (on Plaza Nueva at Calle Reyes Católicos) and **Croissanteria La Blanca Paloma,** nearly across the street (at #48), are good pastry shops.

Some interesting bars lie in the area between Plaza Nueva and the cathedral. **Bodega La Mancha,** on Calle Joaquin, has an impressive array of tasty sandwiches you can wash down with a *caña* (beer) or *calicassa* (mixed drink with secret ingredients). The atmospheric **Casteñada,** on Calle Almireceros, offers it own version of *calicassa*.

Teterias are *muy* popular. These small tea shops, open all day, are good places to sit and talk. Some are conservative and unmemorable, others are filled with incense, beaded cushions, and young hippies. All sell a wide range of teas (from all over the world) for about 250 ptas per person. Light meals are available, too.

Little hole-in-the-wall groceries are sprinkled throughout the city. For supermarkets, try **Mariscal** or **El Corte Inglés** (10:00–20:00, closed Sunday, supermarket in basement, both stores on Carrera del Genil, a few blocks off Puerta Real).

Transportation Connections—Granada

By train to: Barcelona (2/day, 12 hrs, handy night-train), **Madrid** (3/day, 1 handy night-train, 6–9 hrs, or go via Córdoba and catch the AVE train), **Toledo** (2/day, 9 hrs, transfer in Alcázar and Castillejo, 1 handy night-train, or go via Madrid), **Algeciras** (2/day, 5 hrs, transfer in Bobadilla), **Ronda** (3/day, 3 hrs), **Sevilla** (3/day, 4 hrs, transfer in Bobadilla; also 10 buses/day, 3 hrs), **Córdoba** (4/day, 4 hrs, transfer in Bobadilla; also 6 buses/day, 3 hrs).

By bus to: Nerja (3/day, 2 hrs, more frequent with transfer in Motril), **Málaga** (hrly, 2 hrs; also 3 trains/day, 3.5 hrs with transfer in Bobadilla), **Algeciras** (10/day, 5 hrs), **La Línea/Gibraltar** (2/day, 5 hrs).

SEVILLA

This is the flamboyant city of Carmen and Don Juan, where bullfighting is still politically correct and where little girls still dream of growing up to become flamenco dancers. While Granada has the great Alhambra, and Córdoba the remarkable Mezquita, Sevilla has a soul. It's a great-to-be-alive-in kind of place.

Sevilla, the gateway to the New World, boomed when Spain did. Explorers like Amerigo Vespucci and Magellan sailed from its great river harbor, and great local artists (Velázquez, Murillo, Zurbarán) made it a cultural center. Sevilla's Golden Age, with its New World riches, ended when the harbor silted up and the Spanish Empire crumbled.

Today Sevilla (pop. 700,000, Spain's fourth-largest city) is Andalucía's leading city, buzzing with festivals, life, color, and castanets. James Michener wrote, "Sevilla doesn't *have* ambience, it *is* ambience." Sevilla has its share of impressive sights, but the real magic is in this ambience: its quietly tangled Jewish Quarter, riveting flamenco shows, thriving bars, and teeming evening *paseo*.

Planning Your Time

If ever there was a big Spanish city to linger in, it's Sevilla. The sights are few and simple for a city of this size: the cathedral and the Alcázar (about three hours) and a wander through the Santa Cruz district (an hour). If you tried you could spend half a day touring its other sights (described below). An evening is essential for the *paseo* and a chance to see a flamenco show. With three weeks in Iberia, spend two nights and a day in Sevilla. On a shorter trip, at least zip down here via the slick AVE train for a day trip from Madrid. Córdoba (described at the end of this chapter) is worth a short stopover if you're taking the AVE. Sevilla's Alcázar is closed on Monday. Bullfights are on Sunday, April–September.

Orientation (tel. code: 95)

For the tourist, this big city is small. The major sights, including the lively Santa Cruz district and the Alcázar, surround the cathedral. Parallel to the river, the central boulevard, Avenida de la Constitución (with the central tourist information office, banks, post office, and so on) zips right past the cathedral to the Plaza Nueva (shopping district). Nearly everything is within easy walking distance. Taxis are reasonable (400 ptas minimum), friendly, and easy. The horse-and-buggy rides cost about 4,000 ptas per hour.

Tourist Information: There are several handy offices in Sevilla. The central TI is near the cathedral toward the river (Monday–Saturday 9:00–19:00, Sunday 10:00–14:00, Avenida de la Constitución 21, tel. 95/422-1404). Get the city map/guide (100 ptas); a current listing of sights, hours, and prices; a schedule of bullfights; and ideas for evening fun. The free monthly events guide, *El Giraldillo*, is in nearly readable Spanish and covers surrounding cities as well. If heading south, ask for the *Route of the White Towns* brochure and a Jerez map (100 ptas apiece). If you're arriving by bus from Portugal or by train, you'll find helpful TIs in or near your station (see below).

Arrival in Sevilla

By Train: Trains arrive at the sublime Santa Justa station (banks, ATMs, English-speaking TI, luggage storage). Bus #27 gets you into the city center to Plaza de la Encarnación. Bus #C2 takes you a block from Puerta Jerez, close to the TI (and most recommended hotels). Pay the driver 125 ptas as you board. The town center (marked by the ornate Giralda cathedral bell tower, visible from the front of the station) is a 30-minute walk or 500-pta taxi ride away.

By Bus: Sevilla's two major bus stations have information offices, cafés, and luggage storage. The decaying station at Prado de San Sebastian covers Andalucía. To get downtown

Sevilla

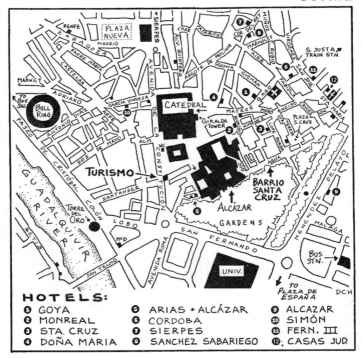

HOTELS:

❶ GOYA	❺ ARIAS • ALCÁZAR	❾ ALCAZAR
❷ MONREAL	❻ CORDOBA	❿ SIMÓN
❸ STA. CRUZ	❼ SIERPES	⓫ FERN. III
❹ DOÑA MARIA	❽ SANCHEZ SABARIEGO	⓬ CASAS JUD.

from the station, turn right on the major street Carlos V, then right again on Avenida de la Constitución to get to the central TI (ten-minute walk; city buses aren't worth the trouble).

The modern and well-equipped bus station at Plaza de Armas (across the river from the EXPO '92 site), serves southwest Spain and Portugal. To get downtown from this station, head toward the angled brick (apartment) building and cross the busy boulevard Expiración. Go a half-block up Calle Arjona to the stop for bus #C4, which goes into town (125 ptas, payable on bus; get off at Puerta de Jerez, near TI). But first, to get to Sevilla's best TI (just 2 blocks from this bus stop), continue up Calle Arjona to CIS at #28 (near Isabel II Bridge), where you'll get very helpful information, a free Sevilla map, and a magazine of current events called *Welcome & Hola* (TI open: daily 8:00–20:30, tel. 95/450-5600). From here you can catch bus #C4 or walk 15 minutes into the center (have the TI show you the way on your map).

Helpful Hints

The post office is on Avenida de la Constitución 32, kitty-corner between the Turismo and the cathedral (Monday–Friday 8:30–20:30, Saturday 9:30–14:00). The Locutorio Público has metered phone booths—the cost is slightly more expensive than calls made with Spanish phone cards, but you get a quiet setting with a seat (Monday–Friday 10:00–14:00 and 17:00–21:00, Saturday 10:00–14:30, Sierpes 11, near intersection with Calle de Rafael Padura). The downtown RENFE office gives out train schedules and sells train tickets (Monday–Friday 9:00–13:15 and 16:00–19:00, CC:VMA, Calle Zaragoza 29, tel. 95/421-7998, NSE). Many travel agencies sell train tickets at the same price as the train station; check the window for a posted sticker that shows a picture of a train.

Sights—Sevilla

▲▲**Cathedral**—This is the third-largest church in Europe (after the Vatican's St. Peter's and London's St. Paul's) and the largest Gothic church anywhere. When they ripped down a mosque on the site in 1401, the Reconquista Christians bragged, "We'll build a cathedral so huge that anyone who sees it will take us for madmen." Even today, the descendants of those madmen proudly display several enlarged photocopies of their *Guinness Book of Records* letter certifying, "The cathedral with the largest area is: Santa Maria de la Sede in Sevilla, 126 meters long, 82 meters wide, and 30 meters high." (Guinness doesn't have an "ugliest cathedral" category.)

Take a hike through the sanctuary and don't miss Columbus' tomb (with the four pallbearers, near the exit). The incredible main altarpiece has 4,000 pounds of gold (imported in Spain's post-1492 "free trade" era). Its 1,500 figures were carved by one man over 40 years. In the treasury (*tesoro*) you'll see the most valuable crown in Spain (Corona de la Virgen de los Reyes, 11,000 precious stones and the world's largest pearl made into the body of an angel), lots of relics (thorns, chunks of the cross, splinters from the Last Supper table), and some of the lavish Corpus Christi festival parade regalia. The *tesoro* consists of two rooms with separate entrances, both just before the exit. Cost for the whole works with the Giralda Tower thrown in: 600 ptas

(Monday–Saturday 10:30–17:00, Sunday 14:00–16:00). The free English pamphlet helps you navigate through a church bigger than many of Andalucía's white towns.

▲**Giralda Tower**—Formerly a Moorish minaret from which Muslims were called to prayer, it became the cathedral's bell tower after the Reconquista. Notice the beautiful Moorish simplicity as you climb to its top, 100 yards up, for a grand city view. The spiraling ramp is designed to accommodate riders on horseback, so gallop up the 34 ramps and orient yourself from this bird's-eye perspective (included in cathedral admission, same hours plus Sunday morning 10:30–13:30).

▲▲▲**Alcázar**—What you'll see today is basically a palace built by Moorish workmen (*mudejar*) for the Christian King Pedro I, who was called either "the Cruel" or "the Just," depending on which end of his sword you were on. The Alcázar is a thought-provoking glimpse of a graceful Al-Andalus (Moorish) world that might have survived its Castilian conquerors—but didn't. The Alcázar is intentionally confusing (part of the style designed to make experiencing the place more exciting and surprising), with an impressive collection of royal courts, halls, patios, and apartments. In many ways it's as splendid as Granada's Alhambra. The garden is full of tropical flowers, wild cats, cool fountains, and hot tourists. Sit in an interesting part of the palace and freeload off passing tours (600 ptas, Tuesday–Saturday 9:30–16:00, Sunday 10:00–13:00, closed Monday; off-season Tuesday–Saturday 10:30–17:00, Sunday 10:00–13:00, closed Monday, tel. 95/422-7163).

The disappointing **Archivo de Indias** (archive of the documents of the discovery and conquest of the New World) is in the Lonja Palace, across the street from the Alcázar (free, Monday–Friday 10:00–13:00, closed weekends).

▲▲**Barrio de Santa Cruz** (old Jewish Quarter)—Even if it is a little over-restored, this classy maze of lanes too narrow for cars, whitewashed houses with wrought-iron latticework, and *azulejo* tile–covered patios is a great refuge from the summer heat and bustle of Sevilla. Get lost among tourist shops, small hotels, flamenco bars, and peaceful squares. Even with the TI's helpful Barrio de Santa Cruz map (an inset on the 100 ptas city map), you'll get lost—which is the idea anyway. Locals are unfailingly kind in giving directions.

Hospital de la Caridad—Between the river and the cathedral is the charity hospital founded by the original Don Juan.

One of history's great hedonists, his party was crashed by a vision that tuned him in to his own mortality. He paid for the construction of this hospital for the poor and joined the Brotherhood of Charity. Peek into the fine courtyard. On the left the chapel has some gruesome art (above the door) illustrating how death is the great equalizer, and an altar sweet as only a Spaniard could enjoy (500 ptas, Monday–Saturday 10:00–14:00 and 15:30–18:30, closed Sunday, tel. 95/422-3232).

Torre del Oro/Naval Museum—This historic riverside "gold tower" once received the booty of the New World. Today it houses a mediocre little naval museum with lots of charts showing various knots, models of ships, dried fish, and an interesting mural of Sevilla in 1740 (100 ptas, Tuesday–Friday 10:00–14:00, weekends 11:00–14:00, closed Monday).

University—Today's university was yesterday's *fabrica de tabacos* (cigar factory), which employed 10,000 young female *cigareras*—including Bizet's Carmen. When built, it was the second-largest building in Spain, after El Escorial. Wander through its halls as you walk to the Plaza de España. The university's bustling café is a good place for cheap *tapas*, beer, wine, and conversation (Monday–Friday 8:00–21:00, Saturday 9:00–13:00, closed Sunday).

▲**Plaza de España**—The square, the surrounding buildings, and the nearby María Luisa Park are the remains of a 1929 fair that crashed with the U.S. stock market. This delightful area, the epitome of World's Fair–style building, is great for people-watching (especially at early-evening *paseo* time). Stroll through the park and along the canal. Check out the *azulejo* tiles (a trademark of Sevilla) that show historic scenes and maps from every corner of Spain. Walk up to one of the balconies for a fine overview.

▲**Museo de Bellas Artes**—Sevilla's top collection of art has 50 Murillos and works by Zurbarán, El Greco, and Velázquez (250 ptas, Tuesday–Sunday 9:00–15:00, closed Monday, Plaza Museo 9, tel. 95/422-0790).

▲**Basilica Macarena**—This altarpiece statue of the Weeping Virgin (Virgen de la Macarena), complete with crystal teardrops, is the darling of Sevilla's Holy Week processions. She's beautiful (and her weeping can be contagious). Tour the exhibits behind the altar and go upstairs for a closer peek at Mary. The church is free, the museum costs 300 ptas (daily

9:00–13:00 and 17:00–20:00, long walk or taxi to Puerta Macarena or take bus #C3 from Puerta Jerez).

▲**Bullfights**—Spain's most artistic and traditional bullfighting is done in Sevilla's Plaza de Toros, with fights on most Sundays, April through October (seats from 2,500 ptas, information at TI, your hotel, or tel. 95/422-3152). You can now follow a guide for 15 minutes through the strangely quiet and empty arena, its museum, and the chapel where the matador prays before the fight (250 ptas, Monday–Saturday 10:00–13:30, closed Sunday, skip the 100-pta info sheet). See the Appendix for more on the dubious "art" of bullfighting.

▲▲**Evening *Paseo***—Sevilla is meant for strolling. The areas along the river (see Eating, Triana District, below), around the Plaza Nueva, at Plaza de España, and throughout Barrio de Santa Cruz thrive every non-winter evening. Spend some time rafting through this sea of humanity and don't miss the view of Sevilla by night from the far side of the river.

▲▲**Flamenco**—This music and dance art form has its roots in the Gypsy and Moorish cultures. Even at a packaged "Flamenco Evening," sparks fly. The men do most of the flamboyant machine-gun footwork. The women concentrate on graceful turns and a smooth shuffling step. Watch the musicians. Flamenco guitarists, with their lightning finger-roll strums, are among the best in the world. The intricate rhythms are set by castanets or the hand-clapping (called *palmas*) of those who aren't dancing at the moment. In the raspy-voiced wails of the singers, you'll hear echoes of the Muslim call to prayer.

Like jazz, flamenco thrives on improvisation. Also like jazz, good flamenco is more than just technical proficiency. A singer or dancer with "soul" is said to have *duende*. Flamenco is a happening, with bystanders clapping along and egging on the dancers with whoops and shouts. Get into it.

For a tourist-oriented flamenco show, your hotel can get you nightclub show tickets for about 3,500 ptas (includes a drink). The Turismo has a current listing. **Los Gallos** gives nightly shows at 21:00 and 23:30 (Plaza de Santa Cruz 11, tel. 95/421-6981). Or you might try **El Patio Sevillano** (Paseo de Colón II, show times 19:30, 22:30, 23:45, tel. 95/421-4120) or **El Arenal** (Calle Rodo 7, shows at 21:30 and 23:30, tel. 95/421-6492). These prepackaged shows can be a bit sterile, but I find Los Gallos professional and riveting.

The best flamenco erupts spontaneously in bars through-out the old town (well past my bedtime). Just follow your ears in the Barrio de Santa Cruz or wander down Calle Salados, near Plaza de Cuba across the bridge. Flamenco rarely rolls before midnight.

Shopping

The popular pedestrian street Calle Sierpes and the smaller lanes around it near the Plaza Nueva are packed with people and shops. The street ends up at Sevilla's top department store, El Corte Inglés. While small shops close between 13:00 and 16:00 or 17:00, El Corte Inglés stays open (and air-conditioned) right through the siesta. It has a supermarket downstairs and a good but expensive restaurant (Monday–Saturday 10:00–21:30, closed Sunday). Flea markets hop on Thursday on Calle La Feria and Sunday along Alameda de Hércules.

Sleeping in Sevilla

(140 ptas = about $1, tel. code: 95, zip code: 41004)
Sleep Code: **S**=Single, **D**=Double/Twin, **T**=Triple, **Q**=Quad, **b**=bathroom, **t**=toilet only, **s**=shower only, **CC**=Credit Card (Visa, MasterCard, Amex), **SE**=Speaks English, **NSE**=No English.

Sevilla has plenty of $30 to $50 double rooms. All of my listings are centrally located in or near the atmospheric Santa Cruz neighborhood and within a few minutes' walk of the cathedral.

Room rates jump way up during the two Sevilla fiestas (roughly April 23–May 7 and December 20–January 4). Outside of fiesta times, the busiest and most expensive months are April, May, September, and October. June, July, and August are cheaper, and empty rooms are plentiful. Prices rarely include the 7 percent IVA tax. A price range indicates low-to-high season prices. Though English isn't rampant, hoteliers know the basic words (like the prices). The small, family *pensiónes* may or may not hold a phone reservation (get it in writing or stick with the larger hotels if you want certainty). Skip ground-floor rooms (because of noise), and ask for upper floors (*piso alto*).

Sleeping Deep in the Santa Cruz Neighborhood

Hostal Goya is two minutes down the street from the cathedral, with 20 fan-equipped rooms and a pleasant atrium

(Sb-4,500 ptas, Db-6,800 ptas, Tb-9,500 ptas, Qb-12,000 ptas, Mateos Gago 31, tel. 95/421-1170, fax 95/456-2988, NSE). The upper floors have tiny windows.

Hostal Monreal disguises its very basic rooms with a relaxing, cheery courtyard and tiled hallways that give you the sensation of climbing through a tile treehouse (S-2,750 ptas, D-4,000 ptas, Db-6,300 ptas, T-6,300 ptas, Tb-9,300 ptas, breakfast with o.j.-500 ptas, CC:VM, Rodrigo Caro 8, tel. 95/421-4166, NSE). Coming from the cathedral, take the first right off Mateos Gago. Pass on the ground-floor rooms.

Pension Santa Cruz is a nice little *pensión*, if you get past the gruff owner, with five rooms around a tiled courtyard (reach inside the gate to ring the bell, S-3,300–6,500 ptas, D-6,000–7,500 ptas, shower-400 ptas, Santa Cruz 12, at the end of Lope de Rueda, tel. 95/421-7695, NSE).

The next three hotels are just off the Plaza Maria.

Hostal Córdoba has tidy, quiet rooms and a showpiece plant-filled courtyard (S-3,000–4,500 ptas, Sb-4,000–6,500 ptas, D-4,000–6,500 ptas, Db-5,000–7,500 ptas, Farnesio 12, tel. 95/422-7498, NSE). From Plaza Santa Maria follow the smallest street (Ximenez de Enciso) as it curves right, then take the first right.

Hotel Fernando III is cavernous, central, comfortable, modern, and popular with tour groups (Sb-9,400 ptas, Db-11,800 ptas, breakfast-990 ptas, air-con, pool, garage, elevator, CC:VMA, San Jose 21, just off Plaza Santa Maria, tel. 95/421-7307, fax 95/422-0246, SE).

Hotel Las Casas de la Juderia, also off Plaza Santa Maria, has quiet, elegant rooms and suites, tastefully decorated with a Spanish flair, surrounding a peaceful courtyard (Sb-10,500 ptas, Db-14,000 ptas, Db/suite-16,000 ptas, Qb/suite-21,000 ptas, breakfast-1,100 ptas, lower prices off-season, air-con, elevator, CC:VMA, Calle Callejon de Dos Hermanas 7, tel. 95/441-5150, fax 95/442-2170, SE).

Sleeping near the Santa Cruz Neighborhood

Walking from the cathedral square straight up Argote de Molina (for 200 yards) you come to two fine options. **Hostal Sierpes** is a sprawling, 40-room place with wonderful lounges and a big, cool, airy courtyard. It's a user-friendly, youthful-feeling place, drenched in tradition, though unreliable with phoned reservations. When you arrive, show this book to the hardworking manager, Quintin or his equally serious son, Melquiades, for a 15 percent discount (Sb-3,500–6,000 ptas, Db-6,000–8,000 ptas, rooms with a bath rather than a shower cost 1,000 ptas extra, quieter rooms upstairs, garage 1,200 ptas; CC:VMA, Corral del Rey 22, tel. 95/422-4948, fax 95/421-2107, SE). Across the street, **Hostal Sanchez Sabariego** is a cozier, ten-room place. Its folksy garden courtyard is a joy. The higher floors are most peaceful (S-3,500 ptas, Db-5,500 ptas; agree on the price in writing; Corral del Rey 23, tel. 95/421-4470, NSE).

Hotel Alcázar, on the big and busy Menendez y Pelayo boulevard, is air-conditioned, with lavish, shiny public areas and everything you'd find in a modern, big-city American hotel (Sb-8,500 ptas, Db-13,500 ptas, includes breakfast, parking-1,000 ptas, air-con, CC:VMA, Menendez y Pelayo 10, tel. 95/441-2011, fax 95/442-1659, SE). Ask for a quiet room off the street.

Sleeping near the Cathedral

Hotel Residencia Doña María, facing the cathedral on Plaza Vírgen de los Reyes, brags that it's "very modern but furnished in an ancient style," with four-poster beds, armoires, and a rooftop swimming pool with a view of Giralda Tower (Sb-8,500–11,500 ptas, Db-16,000–32,000 ptas, skip the 1,300-pta continental breakfast, elevator, CC:VMA, Don Remondo 19, tel. 95/422-4990, fax 95/421-9546, SE).

Hotel Simón is a typical 18th-century mansion with a faded-elegant courtyard. The air-conditioned rooms vary in quality, and many are decorated with period furniture under high ceilings. Avoid rooms on the noisy street (Sb-6,000–7,500 ptas, Db-7,500–11,000 ptas, add 3,000 ptas for salon, breakfast-450 ptas, CC:VMA, 1 block west of Avenida de la Constitución and the cathedral at Calle García de Vinuesa 19, tel. 95/422-6660, fax 95/456-2241, SE). It's around the corner from Calle Arfe, my favorite *tapas* street.

Hotel El Rabida seems too good to be true: 100 peaceful rooms surrounding a spacious atrium lobby and a delightful garden courtyard, with a classy breakfast room and elevators (Sb-6,000 ptas, Db-8,500 ptas, add 500 ptas for a larger room—worth it, breakfast-400 ptas, Castelar 24, tel. 95/422-0960, fax 95/422-4375). From Avenida de la Constitución, go down Calle García de Vinuesa, and turn right on Calle Castelar.

Sleeping between the Alcázar and Avenida de la Constitución

In a quiet eddy of lanes behind the tourist office, **Hostal Arias** is cool, clean, quiet, and no-nonsense, with firm beds. All 15 rooms are air-conditioned, with telephones and full bathrooms. The manager, Manuel Reina, speaks American, as do some of his staff (Sb-4,800–6,800 ptas, Db-5,800–8,500 ptas, Tb 7,000–9,500 ptas, CC:VMA, Calle Mariana de Pineda 9, tel. 95/422-6840, fax 95/421-8389, e-mail: reina@arrkis.es). Around the corner, most of **Pension Alcázar**'s eight pleasant rooms have air-conditioning; top-floor rooms have only ceiling fans but a fine large terrace (Db-5,500 ptas, extra bed-1,000 ptas, Dean Miranda 12, tel. 95/422-8457, NSE).

Eating in Sevilla

Eating in the Cathedral/Santa Cruz Area

You'll find plenty of atmospheric-but-touristy restaurants. Many places line Alvarez Quintero, a street running north from the cathedral.

Do the *tapa* tango through several great neighborhoods. The Barrio de Santa Cruz is trendy, touristic, and more expensive but *muy romantico*. Walk from the cathedral up Mateos Gago a few blocks and melt into the narrow lanes on your right. You're very likely to enjoy some live music. The **Cervecería Giralda** (Mateos Gago 1), **Bodega Santa Cruz** (get a spot at the bar and see how they keep your tab, Rodrigo Caro 1), **Navascues** (Mateos Gago 13A), and the smart wine-bar, **Bodega Belmonte** (Mateos Gaga 24), all within a block of each other, are good places to start (all open daily).

Across from the cathedral, west of Avenida de la Constitución, is my favorite *tapas* area—follow Almirantazgo, Calle Arfe, and Calle García de Vinuesa. Calle Arfe and the nearby streets are lined with colorful bars and no tourists. Drop into the **Meson Sevilla** for chic *tapas* (open daily, Arfe 1).

Horno San Buenaventura is a popular, handy place for coffee, *tapas*, and dessert (next to cathedral, at intersection of Avenida de la Constitución and García de Vinuesa, restaurant upstairs).

There is an entertaining, covered, fish-and-produce **market** (with a small café/bar for breakfast inside) just beyond the bullring (on Calle Pastor y Landero at Calle Arenal, 9:00–13:00, closed Sunday).

Eating Across the River

In the Triana District, you'll find classy bars, cafés and restaurants lining Calle Betis along the river. Remember that lunch starts at 13:00 and dinner at 20:00. You'll get a good look at some of the EXPO '92 buildings from the Puente Isabel II. To reach the Triana District, cross the river at Puente San Telmo and walk to Puente Isabel II.

For dinner, you can splurge at the **Río Grande** restaurant (turn right after crossing Puente San Telmo) with its shady deck over the river—good view, good food, and good service (CC:VMA, Calle Betis s/n). Or eat the same thing—with the same view but fewer tablecloths—next door at **El Puerto** (closed Monday) for one-half the price.

If you're looking for a fight, pop into the workingmen's places 1 block away from the river and say something derogatory about a local matador. **La Taberna** is cheap, youthful, and lively after 23:00 (opens at 22:00, Duarte 3A, between the two bridges, near the police station).

On the south end of Puente Isabel II, the bar in the yellow bridge tower, **Restaurante Maria Angeles**, is a fine option with roof garden tables and a classy *tapas* bar downstairs, all with great views of the river and Old Town (tel. 95/433-7498). Many other good bars are nearby, such as **Kiosco de las Flores** (next door) or better, **Cafe de la Prensa**, at Betis 8.

Transportation Connections—Sevilla

To: Madrid (15 trains/day, 8 hrs; 2.5 hrs by AVE, 1,200 ptas reservation fee with railpass), **Córdoba** (15 trains/day, 2 hrs or 50 min by AVE; 10 buses/day, 2 hrs), **Málaga** (2 trains/day, 3 hrs; 10 buses/day, 4 hrs), **Ronda** (3 trains per day, 3 hrs, change at Bobadilla; 6 buses/day, 3 hrs), **Tarifa** (4 buses/day, 3 hrs), **La Línea/Gibraltar** (4 buses/day, 4 hrs), **Granada** (3 trains/day, 4 hrs; 8 buses/day, 4 hrs), **Arcos** (2 buses/day, 2 hrs), **Jerez** (7 buses/day, 2 hrs), **Barcelona** (4 trains/day, 10–12 hrs), **Algeciras** (3 trains/day, 5 hrs, change at Bobadilla; 10 buses/day, 4 hrs), **Lisbon** (3 buses/day, 6 hrs). Train information: tel. 95/454-0202.

From Sevilla to Portugal's Algarve (Tavira and Lagos/Salema)

To Tavira by bus: 2 buses/day, 3.5 hrs (from Sevilla's Plaza de Armas station), easy transfer in Huelva; 1 direct bus runs Thursday, Friday, Saturday, and Sunday, 3 hrs, no transfer.

To Lagos by bus/train: The direct bus between Lagos and Sevilla is a godsend (5 hrs, 1/day except Monday from June–October, 1/day Thursday–Sunday, April–May, about 2,600 ptas). The bus departs from Sevilla's Plaza de Armas bus station and arrives at the Lagos bus station, with stops at Algarve towns such as Tavira. Regrettably, there are no official bathroom stops. No one drinks freely on this bus. The bold and desperate ask the driver for a minute's wait at a stop. From Lagos catch a one-hour bus to Salema.

Other than the direct bus, it's a long day of bus, ferry, and train rides. Catch the Sevilla–Ayamonte bus (4/day from Plaza de Armas station, 2.5 hrs) to Ayamonte at the border (banks sell *escudos* in Ayamonte), take the ferry to Vila Real in Portugal (17/day, 15 min), then the train to Lagos (3/day, more frequent with transfer in Tunes, 4 hrs). Get an early start.

If you insist on taking the train from Sevilla, you'll need to transfer to a bus at Huelva (Sevilla–Huelva: 4 trains/day, 1.5 hrs; Huelva–Ayamonte: 6 buses/day, 1 hr). The Sevilla–Ayamonte bus is preferable, cheap, direct, and less hassle. In Vila Real the train station, the buses, and ferry dock are clustered together. Saturdays and Sundays are dead in Vila Real. Ayamonte is much livelier and tourist-friendly by comparison.

Drivers' note: Sevilla is Spain's capital of splintered windshields. Pay to park in a garage. Paseo de Cristobal Colón (Christopher Columbus) has free street parking but is particularly dangerous in the summer. Get advice from your hotel. For driving ideas south into Andalucía and west into Portugal's Algarve, see those chapters.

CÓRDOBA

Córdoba is one of Spain's three big Moorish cities. Even though it was the center of Moorish civilization in Spain for 300 years (and an important Roman city), Sevilla and Granada are far more interesting. Córdoba has a famous mosque surrounded by the colorful Jewish quarter, and that's it. The city's touristic merit just doesn't quite live up to its historical importance.

The **Mezquita** (may-SKEET-ah) was the largest mosque in Islam in its day. Today you can wander past its ramshackle "patio of oranges" and into the cavernous 1,200-year-old building. The interior is a moody world of 800 rose- and blue-marble columns and as many Moorish arches. If a guide told me I was in the basement of something important, I'd believe him. The center was gutted to make room for an also-huge Renaissance cathedral (750 ptas, Monday–Saturday 10:00–19:00, Sunday 13:00–19:00). The mosque is near the TI (tel. 957/47-12-35).

From the train station it's a 300-pta taxi ride or a pleasant 15-minute walk (left on Avenida de America, right on Avenida del Gran Capitan, which becomes a pedestrian zone; when it ends ask someone "*¿Dónde está Mezquita?*" and you'll be directed downhill through the whitewashed old Jewish Quarter).

Transportation Connections—Córdoba
Now that Córdoba is on the slick AVE train line, it's an easy stopover between **Madrid** and **Sevilla** (5 trains/day, about an hour from each city, reservations required on all AVE trains).

By bus to: Granada (7/day, 3 hrs), **Málaga** (4/day, 3 hrs), and **Algeciras** (2/day, 6 hrs).

ANDALUCÍA'S WHITE HILL TOWNS

Just as the American image of Germany is Bavaria, the Yankee dream of Spain is Andalucía. This is the home of bullfights, flamenco, *gazpacho*, pristine-if-dusty whitewashed hill towns, and glamorous Mediterranean resorts. The big cities of Andalucía (Granada, Sevilla, and Córdoba) and the Costa del Sol are covered in separate chapters. This chapter explores its hill-town highlights.

The Route of the White Towns, Andalucía's charm bracelet of towns, gives you wonderfully untouched Spanish culture. Spend a night in the romantic queen of the white towns, Arcos de la Frontera. Towns with "de la Frontera" in their names were established on the front line of the centuries-long fight to recapture Spain from the Muslims, who were slowly pushed back into Africa. The hill towns, no longer strategic, no longer on any frontier, are now just passing time peacefully. Join them. Nearby, the city of Jerez is worth a peek for its famous horses in action and a sherry *bodega* tour.

Planning Your Time

While the towns can be (and often are) accessed from the Costa del Sol resorts via Ronda, Arcos makes the best home base. Arcos, near Jerez and close to interesting smaller towns, is conveniently situated halfway between Sevilla and Tarifa.

On a three-week Iberian vacation, the region is worth two nights and two days sandwiched between Sevilla and Tarifa. Spend both those nights in Arcos. See Jerez (horses and sherry) school of their own.'

There was a different result in Chandrapur. Sir Frank Sly, Governor of the Central Provinces and Berar, records that the caste Hindus refused entry to Untouchable students in the government English school of Chandrapur in the year 1870. Mr Browning, the Director of Public Instruction, suggested opening a separate class for these boys, but Major Smith, Deputy Commissioner of Chandrapur, told the caste Hindus that they would have to abide by the principle of equal treatment. At this the caste Hindus withdrew their boys *en masse*. The Deputy Commissioner was firm, however, and reported to the government that he would prefer the school closed rather than allow the caste Hindus to practise discrimination in a public school. At last, caste Hindus surrendered and Untouchable children were admitted along with other boys. The local Collector was so excited over this victory that he intended to have a procession of these Untouchable children on an elephant to be taken through the city with a band of musicians playing before them, but the higher authorities advised him to desist from such action. Nevertheless the Indian papers condemned the action of Major Smith and his officers in admitting the boys to the school; *Indu Prakash, Native Opinion, Mitrodays* and all other newspapers wrote critical comments asking the government to mend the 'mischief done by the imprudence of Major Smith'. The *Indu Prakash*, in its issue of 16 May 1870, regretted that Lord Mayo, while in the city, concurred with the views of Major Smith (*Reports on Native Papers*).

It is interesting to find that all of the Hindu press, excepting only a few non-Brahman newspapers, was critical of the government's action permitting low-caste boys into the public schools. The only papers supporting Untouchable entry were the non-Brahman papers and Christian papers. This was true in spite of the fact that the low-caste Untouchables came from the caste Hindus' own religion. The caste Hindus did not object even to the admission of Muslim boys into schools with caste Hindus. But the same caste Hindu papers did not like the idea of separate education for European and Eurasian children who were Christians. *Indu Prakash* wrote in the issue of 12 October 1874, 'Separate schools for Europeans are condemned as unreasonable. They are not prohibited from taking advantage of existing institutions.'

Early Untouchable Organizing in the Cause of Education

It was foretold by Mr Cradock, the settlement Commissioner of Nagpur District, as early as the year 1900, that

> Mahars will not remain for years downtrodden and are already pushing themselves from the state of degradation . . . They have established a school of their own community . . . He at present lacks education and self-respect, but these will come, and the day may not be far distant when a Mahar will be found among the ranks of the native magistry (*Report of the Land Revenue Settlement of Nagpur District, 1900*).

The change was to come through education. In the beginning, as told earlier, Mahars tried to push their children into the public schools run by the government or by the missions. When they realized that this was not enough, they started establishing their own schools. One such early school was established in Nagpur in the last quarter of the 19th Century through the efforts of the Mahars. At the same time the Untouchables developed more sophisticated institutions to influence the general direction of Untouchable access to education.

By the end of the 19th Century, Mahars had started establishing their own institutions. In 1884, Janoji Khandare, a forest contractor, had started a free boys' hostel in Akola, a district town in Vidharba (statistics hereafter are from the report of the Janoji Khandare Free Boarding House, 1927-8). Mr Khandare used to approach other Mahar families, bringing these boys from various places for education, feeding them and teaching them under rigorous discipline. So long as he was alive, he himself bore the expenses of the hostel. A District Collector, after seeing the social concern of Janoji, allotted land of about 40 acres for maintenance of the hostel. This hostel is still being run by his descendants. The hostel produced several social and political workers of the 20th Century Mahar Movement. Besides education, students were forced to follow a daily programme which included prayers, gymnastics and games.

[After describing several similar examples, including the opening of the first Dalit-sponsored school for girls in this region, the author goes on to introduce the development of Dalit lobbying and legislative action on behalf of educational development.]

Efforts were made in other parts of Bombay Presidency too. One R.C. Rangrao had established schools and hostels on the Malabar coast in western India as early as 1896. In 1922, Mr Paranjpe, the Education Minister of Bombay Presidency, issued orders for compulsory primary education. The Untouchables held meetings in support of government action and demanded strict enforcement of this social reform (*Dhana Prakash*, 27 January 1923). The low-caste leaders used to organize conferences and meetings throughout the length and breadth of western India. The resolutions passed in those meetings invariably included some call for establishment of hostels and schools, and for people to send their children to the schools and help the cause of education by contribution to the institutions.

In order to get an idea of this type of organizing being carried out in the first two decades amongst the low castes it would be proper to cite some illustrations.

On the eve of a discussion in Nagpur on educational improvement of low castes, an invitation was distributed (on 18 December 1912) in which it was emphasized that the opportunity offered during the rule of King Edward V should not be missed. A 1913 conference of Mahars at Nagpur passed several resolutions, one of which was in honour of Mr K. C. Nandagoli, for establishing the first girls' school in 1911 at his own expense of Rs. 3000/-. On 29 May 1921, a Mahar conference in Berar, at Badnera in Amravati

District, passed the following resolutions, among thirteen others, which indicate the general trend of efforts to influence policy:

1. That Government should impart free and compulsory primary education.
2. That the numbers of scholarships in schools and colleges should be increased.
3. That the age limit for Depressed Classes boys appearing for the matriculation examination should be withdrawn.
4. That Depressed Classes students should be admitted to Normal schools without consideration of merit.
5. That since low-caste students were still barred from Government hostels, they incurred greater expenses than other students and so the amount of their scholarship should be increased.
6. That Free Boarding Houses for Depressed Classes students be established.
7. That Depressed Classes teachers who had qualified should be appointed as Inspectors of schools.

In the Legislative Council of the Central Provinces and Berar, Mr K. C. Nandagoli, a representative of the Depressed Classes, carried the effort to influence general public policy further. He moved a resolution on 16 March 1921, for the appointment of a committee to enquire into the problem of the Depressed Classes. The committee inquired into two aspects of the problem: first, the employment of Depressed Classes in the public services; secondly, the action which should be taken to facilitate their education. Lack of space here prevents me from going fully into the details of the report. However, it is worth noting that the final resolution adopted by the government conceded a number of the demands made by Mr Nandagoli. These included a specific assurance that no properly qualified Depressed Classes candidate for government employment would be discriminated against on account of his social position, nor would there be any such discrimination in the case of candidates applying for admission to the government schools. Government also accepted the point that Depressed Classes scholars incurred greater expenses for their living than other students and that their scholarships should be increased accordingly.

Conclusion

I have attempted here to sketch the emergence of conscious and vociferous Untouchable opposition to the social values and religious hierarchies of Hindu society. This movement later expanded under the leadership of Dr Ambedkar, but it was perhaps first of all in the field of education that the Untouchable communities gained some idea of the resistance which their efforts at uplift would encounter from other Hindus. From this experience came in part the remarkable transformation in consciousness which was evident by the 1920s. From the same experience grew also the conviction that if the Untouchable communities were to achieve any substantial change in their condition, it would not be as a result of any growing liberalization of attitudes amongst the Hindus, but rather in spite of their fiercest opposition. This bitter awareness of isolation and separation was to grow in strength to become the hallmark of the movement under Dr Ambedkar, and to culminate on that day in 1956 when he led hundreds of thousands into conversion to Buddhism in outright rejection of the Hindu social order.

Author's References

1. Report of the Committee Appointed by the Central Provinces and Berar Government to Enquire into the Problems of the Depressed Classes, under Government Resolution dated 29/6/21.

2. Interim Report: Review of the Growth of Education in British India by the Auxiliary Committee of the Indian Statutory Committee, 1928.

3. Report of the Varhad Mahar Reform Society, Yavatmal, 1929.

4. Report of the Janoji Khandare Free Boarding House, Akola, for the year 1927–8.

5. Report of the Native Papers for 1880 to 1895.

6. Education Department, vol. 58, of 1893 (file 383); and vol. 45 of 1895.

* * * *

Dr B. R. Ambedkar: The Man and His Teachings

It is indeed impossible to understand the contemporary Dalit revolt without understanding the late Dr Ambedkar, but it is also impossible to compress this angry, complex advocate of social and economic liberation into a few pages. Ambedkar was born in 1891 in Mhow, a village in central India. For a growing number of young Dalits across India, many born after his death in 1956, he has become a symbol of a world that can be achieved, free from social and economic injustice. At a time when few Untouchables ever got into a classroom – and few Indians of any caste acquired advanced degrees – Ambedkar earned a PhD from New York's Columbia University (1917), then went on to become a DSc from the London School of Economics and a Barrister-at-Law from Gray's Inn (both in 1923). In a world that denied Untouchables access to minor village councils, Ambedkar successfully crashed the elaborate political poker game played out by the British Empire and India's nationalist elites in the years before Independence: testimony to the Southborough Commission in 1919; representation on the Simon Commission of 1928–9 and the London Round Table Conferences of 1930–3; representation on the Bombay Legislative Council, then Labour minister, then member of the Constituent Assembly and constitutional drafting committee.

At different times in a crowded life Ambedkar was a leader of mass agitations, an experimenter in electoral politics, a religious iconoclast, a founder of night schools and colleges. Much that is central to Ambedkar's legacy lies in short sayings and expressions that have become part of a new folklore:

Be a lion; the Hindus sacrifice goats.

'Atta dipa bhav' – Be your own light.

Dr Ambedkar with other Dalit organizers of the 1930 Nasik Satyagraha, one of his few efforts to gain Untouchable access to a Hindu temple. By 1935 Ambedkar had renounced Hindu reform as a solution to Untouchable problems. *(Oppressed Indian)*

However, there is also a wealth of books, speeches, editorials that form a point of departure for contemporary debate within the Dalit movement. The following portions of this chapter explore the two central themes of his attack on the established Indian order: destruction of culturally defined inequality and destruction of economic inequality.

Ambedkar's revolt against established Indian culture was both an extension and a significant modification of a very old counter-culture tradition in India. Many societies have developed systems of cultural myths that legitimize hereditary inequality. In India it is the writings and practices of orthodox Hinduism that have served as the transmission belt for belief in the hereditary inequality of caste. Thus challenges to inequality of all types have commonly taken the form of challenges to Hinduism, a pattern that dates at least as far back as the inception of Buddhism, c. 400 B.C. Untouchables have long been a significant part of these counter-culture revolts. In the early 20th Century, some Untouchables continued to filter into the Christian and Muslim communities, while a number of others developed independent forms of socio-religious protest such as the Namashudra movement in Bengal and the Ad-Dharm movement in the Punjab.

Ambedkar's own writings and speeches repeatedly explore the relationship between culture and the psychology and political economy of power. On one level he comments on the views of philosophers as diverse as Plato and Bertrand Russell, as in his critique of Indian society in Annihilation of Caste, *written in 1936. At other times he explains his ideas in language and stories familiar to the common man, as he does in the following excerpt and in the much later* The Buddha and His Dhamma *(1956). Throughout there is*

27

one common thread: socio-economic transformation in India requires a
cultural revolution, one that will not only destroy the culture of the past
but also build something of value in its place. Rebuilding was quite as important
as tearing down, and it presented Ambedkar with a problem. Although he
defended individual development and creativity, he rejected the aggressively
self-serving individualism of Western capitalism as something guaranteed to
perpetuate Dalit subordination. He devoted most of his life to the search for
radical social democracy, but he also remained convinced that the arid and
inherently impermanent world of legislation and law courts would never be
enough to create a necessary sense of community. His own answer was an
attempt both to harness and to tame the psychological power of religion by
developing a modern, activist, atheist Buddhism, stripped of all belief in
supernatural forces and committed to the struggle for social and economic
equality. In 1956, Ambedkar joined 500,000 of his followers in a Buddhist
conversion ceremony, but the journey had begun long before and continues
to be influential, even among Dalits who seek solutions other than Buddhism.

*The following excerpt is from Ambedkar's speech to a mass meeting of
the Mahar community that was held in Bombay in May 1936. In it he expresses
his conviction that religions are purely man-made institutions. They can
provide cultural reinforcement for a rational and egalitarian society or they
can reinforce superstition and social tyranny. Since religion is a social
convention, Dalits can choose what conventions will help build a livable world.
The English translation of the speech used here appeared in* The Oppressed
Indian, *a contemporary journal published in New Delhi by a Dalit-led
organization that has branches throughout India and encompasses both
Buddhist and non-Buddhist Untouchables, as well as members of other
minority communities.*

What Path Freedom?

Dr B. R. Ambedkar (trans. Vasant W. Moon)

. . . There are two aspects of conversion. Social as well as religious; material as
well as spiritual. Whatever may be the aspect, or line of thinking, it is necessary
to understand the beginning, the nature of untouchability and how it is
practised. Without this understanding, you will not be able to realize the
real meaning underlying my declaration of conversion.

In order to have a clear understanding of untouchability and its practice
in real life, I want you to recall the stories of the atrocities perpetrated
against you. The instances of beating by caste Hindus for the simple reason
that you have claimed the right to enrol your children in government schools,
or the right to draw water from a public well, or the right to take a marriage
procession with the groom on horseback, are very common. You all know
such instances, as they happen before your eyes. But there are several other
causes for which atrocities are committed on the Untouchables by the caste

Hindus which, if revealed, surprise foreigners. The Untouchables are beaten for putting on clothes of good quality. They have been whipped because they used utensils made of metal like copper, etc. Their houses are burnt because they have brought land under cultivation. They are beaten for putting on the sacred thread. [A visible symbol worn by high-caste Hindus.] They are beaten for refusing to carry dead animals and eat carrion, or for walking through the village with socks and shoes on, or for not bowing down before the caste Hindus, for taking water in a copper pot while going out to the fields to ease themselves. Recently an instance has been noted where the Untouchables were beaten for serving chapatis at a dinner party.

You must have heard and some of you must have experienced such atrocities. Where beating is not possible, you are aware of how the weapon of boycott is used against you. You all know how the caste Hindus have made daily life unbearable by prohibiting you from getting work, by not allowing your cattle to graze in the jungles and prohibiting your men from entering the village. But very few of you have realized why all this happens. What is the root of their tyranny? To me, it is very necessary that we understand it.

The instances cited above have nothing to do with the virtues and vices of an individual. This is not a feud between two rival men. The problem of untouchability is a matter of class struggle. It is a struggle between caste Hindus and the Untouchables. This is not a matter of doing injustice against one man. This is a matter of injustice being done by one class against another. This struggle is related to social status. This struggle indicates how one class should keep its relationship with another class of people. The struggle starts as soon as you start claiming equal treatment with others. Had it not been so, there would have been no struggle over simple reasons like serving chapatis, wearing good quality clothes, putting on the sacred thread, fetching water in a metal pot, sitting the bridegroom on the back of a horse, etc. In these cases you spend your own money. Why then do the high-caste Hindus get irritated? The reason for their anger is very simple. Your behaving on par with them insults them. Your status in their eyes is low; you are impure, you must remain at the lowest rung. Then alone will they allow you to live happily. The moment you cross your level the struggle starts.

The instances given above also prove one more fact. Untouchability is not a short or temporary feature; it is a permanent one. To put it straight, it can be said that the struggle between the Hindus and the Untouchables is a permanent phenomenon. It is eternal, because the high-caste people believe that the religion which has placed you at the lowest level of the society is itself eternal. No change according to time and circumstances is possible. You are at the lowest rung of the ladder today. You shall remain lowest forever.

This means the struggle between Hindus and Untouchables shall continue forever. How you will survive through this struggle is the main question. And unless you think it over, there is no way out. Those who desire to live in obedience to the dictates of the Hindus, those who wish to remain their slaves, they do not need to think over the problem. But those who wish to

live a life of self-respect and equality will have to think over this.
. . .
What is religion? Why is it necessary? Let us first try to understand. Several
people have tried to define religion. But amongst all of these definitions, only
one is most meaningful and agreeable to all. 'That which governs people is
religion.' That is the true definition of religion. This is not my definition.
Mr Tilak, the foremost leader of the Sanatani [orthodox] Hindus himself is
the author of this definition. So nobody can accuse me of having interpolated
the definition of religion. However, I have not accepted it merely for
argument's sake. I accept it as a principle. Religion means the rules imposed
for the maintenance of society. I also have the same concept of religion.

Although this definition logically appears to be correct, it does not disclose
or clarify the nature of rules which govern a society. The question still
remains as to what should be the nature of the rules which govern society.
This question is more important than that of definition. Because the question
of which religion is necessary for man does not depend on its definition but
on the motive and nature of the rules that bind and govern a society. What
should be the real nature of religion? While deciding this question, another
question follows. What should be the relation between a man and society?

The modern social philosophers have postulated three answers to this
question. Some have said that the ultimate goal of society is to achieve
happiness for the individual. Some say that society exists for the development
of the inherent qualities and energies of man and to help him develop himself.
However, some claim that the chief object of social organization is not the
development or happiness of the individual but the creation of an ideal
society. There is no place for an individual in Hindu society. The Hindu
religion does not teach how an individual should behave with another
individual. A religion which does not recognize the individual is not personally
acceptable to me. Although society is necessary for the individual, mere
societal welfare cannot be the ultimate goal of religion. According to me
individual welfare and progress (individual development) should be the real
aim of religion. Although the individual is a part of the society, its relation
with society is not like the body and its organs, or the cart and its wheels.
[A well-known Hindu text described the different categories of castes as
different parts of the body.]
. . .
I tell you all very specifically, religion is for man and not man for religion.
To get human treatment, convert yourselves. Convert for getting organized.
Convert for becoming strong. Convert for securing equality. Convert for
getting liberty. Convert so that your domestic life may be happy. Why do
you remain in that religion which prohibits you from entering a temple?
Why do you remain in that religion which prohibits you from drinking water
from a public well? Why do you remain in that religion which prohibits you
from getting a job? Why do you remain in that religion which insults you
at every step? A religion in which man's human behaviour with man is
prohibited is not religion but a display of force. A religion in which the touch

of human beings is prohibited is not religion but a mockery. A religion which precludes some classes from education, forbids them to accumulate any wealth and to bear arms, is not religion but a mockery of human beings. A religion that compels the ignorant to be ignorant and the poor to be poor is not a religion but a punishment.

. . .

I also take leave of you in the words of the Buddha. Be your own guide! Take refuge in reason! Do not listen to the advice of others! Do not succumb to others! Be truthful! Take refuge in truth! Never surrender to anybody! If you keep in mind this message of the Buddha at this juncture, I am sure your decisions will not be wrong.

* * * *

Throughout Ambedkar's writings, cultural revolt is inextricably bound up with economic revolt and challenges to the linked power of caste and wealth in Indian society. The following examples spell out some of Ambedkar's perspective on the changes in political and economic institutions that would be needed for any real transformation of Indian society. The first is from his speech to a Study Camp of the All-India Trade Union Workers held at Delhi on 17 September 1943. The excerpt used here was published in the April 1982 edition of the Toronto journal The Outcry, *an occasional publication of the Ambedkar Mission, an association of Dalit immigrants to Canada and the United States.*

Labour Must Control Government

Dr B. R. Ambedkar

The first thing to do is to discard the mere establishment of trade unions as the final aim and object of 'Labour' in India. It must declare that its aim is to put labour in charge of the government. For this it must organize a Labour Party as a political party. Such a party will no doubt cover trade unions in its organization. But it must be free from the narrow and cramping vision of trade unionism. It must equally dissociate itself from communal and capitalistic political parties such as the Hindu Maha Sabha or the Congress.

The second thing for Labour in India is that without much knowledge there can be no power. When a Labour Party is formed in India and when such a party puts forth its claim to be installed on the *'Gaddi'* [throne] before the electorate, the question 'Is Labour fit to govern?' is sure to be asked. Labour will have to prove positively that it can govern better.

Let it not be forgotten that the pattern of a Labour government is more difficult than that of other classes. A Labour government cannot be a government of *laissez-faire*. It must be a government essentially based on a system of control. A system of control needs a far greater degree of knowledge and training than a *laissez-faire* government does. Here lies the importance of study and study circles.

Parliamentary democracy, it was believed, would bring about the millennium in which every human being would have the right to liberty, property and pursuit of happiness. This the parliamentary democracy had failed to achieve. The causes for this failure were wrong ideology and wrong organization. What had ruined parliamentary democracy is the idea of freedom of contract. The idea became sanctified and was upheld in the name of liberty. Parliamentary democracy took no notice of economic inequalities and did not bother to examine the result of freedom of control on the parties to the contract should they happen to be unequal. The result is that the parliamentary democracy, in standing out as a protagonist of liberty, has continuously added to the economic wrongs of the poor, the downtrodden and the disinherited class. It was the poor labouring classes who were responsible for the failure of democracy. They have shown a most appalling indifference to the effect of economic factors in the making of their lives. They have developed no ambition to capture government and are not even convinced of the necessity of controlling government as a necessary means of safeguarding their interests.

Their third besetting sin is the way in which they are led away by an appeal to nationalism. The working classes who sacrifice their all to the so-called cause of nationalism have never inquired whether the nationalism for which they were to make their offering would, when established, give them social and economic equality.

I am not opposed to trade unionism. But trade unions, even if they were powerful, would not be strong enough to compel capitalists to run 'capitalism' better. Unless trade unions aim at controlling the government, they would do very little good to the workers and would be a source of perpetual squabbles among trade union leaders.

* * * *

In the years before Independence, Indian political debate was marked by an optimism that now has a dreamlike quality. Major restructuring of economic ownership seemed not only possible but well within the range of routine legislative action. There was widespread support for nationalization of at least some types of industries and public services: the resources of Indian capital were limited, and there was little enthusiasm for sustaining a foreign presence in the Indian economy. There was also extensive political support for some level of land reform. Throughout much of India, a numerically insignificant strata of landed elites controlled vast tracts of land, a single landlord often owning several villages. Political parties of both the Centre and Left were dominated by the urban middle class, all competed for the political allegiance of increasingly restive tenant farmers, and all promised land reforms.

Ambedkar approached these issues from the perspective of the Untouchables, who had few possessions and far less property, not even tenancy rights. They would not benefit from land reforms that went no further than tenant farmers, who themselves exploited an already vast army of agricultural labourers. He conceded compensation, the real sticking point with leaders of the politically dominant Congress, but warned India against sanctifying private property. He then proceeded to focus on the issue of landless labour, and in doing so he confronted a spectre that increasingly haunts Indian politics and economics. The national government now finds itself facing an agricultural labour population that expands relentlessly as marginal cultivators slip into the ranks of the landless and impoverished. The single most effective policy innovation to date is the creation of a new census category that masks the statistical image but does not alter the reality. At the same time, much of the political Left finds itself constrained by the increasing conservatism of the larger and now landed ex-tenants on whom it originally built its rural organization.

The following excerpts are from States and Minorities, *a document that Ambedkar wrote in the form of a draft constitution and submitted to the Indian Constituent Assembly at the request of the All-India Scheduled Caste Federation. In it Ambedkar consciously broke with liberal tradition and included sweeping provisions for economic nationalization under the heading of 'Fundamental Rights'. The document itself is still very much alive; in the Introduction we noted the recent resolution on land nationalization by a Buddhist welfare association, and we will meet ideas derived from the work in later chapters on contemporary law and economics.*

Protection Against Economic Exploitation: A Fundamental Right

Dr B. R. Ambedkar (from *States and Minorities,* **1947: Article II, Section II – Remedies Against Invasion of Fundamental Rights; and Appendix I – Explanatory Notes)**

Clause 4: The United States of India shall declare as a part of the law of its constitution –

(1) That industries which are key industries or which may be declared to be key industries shall be owned and run by the State;

(2) That industries which are not key industries but which are basic industries shall be owned by the State and shall be run by the State or by Corporations established by the State;

(3) That Insurance shall be a monopoly of the State and that the State shall compel every adult citizen to take out a life insurance policy commensurate with his wages as may be prescribed by the Legislature;

(4) That agriculture shall be State industry;

(5) That the State shall acquire the subsisting rights in such industries, insurance and agricultural land held by private individuals, whether as owners, tenants or mortgagees, and pay them compensation in the form of debenture equal to the value of his or her right in the land. Provided that in reckoning the value of land, plant or security no account shall be taken of any rise therein due to emergency, of any potential or unearned value or any value for

compulsory acquisition;

(6) The State shall determine how and when the debenture-holder shall be entitled to claim cash payment;

(7) The debenture shall be transferable and inheritable property but neither the debenture-holder nor the transferee from the original holder nor his heir shall be entitled to claim the return of the land or interest in any industrial concern acquired by the State or be entitled to deal with it in any way;

(8) The debenture-holder shall be entitled to interest on his debenture at such rate as may be defined by law, to be paid by the State in cash or in kind as the State may deem fit;

(9) Agricultural industry shall be organized on the following basis:

(i) The state shall divide the land acquired into farms of standard size and let out the farms for cultivation to residents of the village as tenants (made up of groups of families) to cultivate on the following conditions:

(a) The farm shall be cultivated as a collective farm;

(b) The farm shall be cultivated in accordance with rules and directions issued by Government;

(c) The tenants shall share among themselves in the manner prescribed the produce of the farm left after payment of charges properly leviable on the farm;

(ii) The land shall be let out to villagers without distinction of caste or creed and in such manner that there will be no landlord, no tenant and no landless labour;

(iii) It shall be the obligation of the State to finance the cultivation of the collective farms by the supply of water, draft animals, implements, manure, seeds, etc.;

(iv) The State shall be entitled to —

(a) levy the following charges on the produce of the farm:

(i) a portion for land revenue;

(ii) a portion to pay the debenture-holders; and

(iii) a portion to pay for the use of capital goods supplied; and

(b) prescribe penalties against tenants who break the conditions of tenancy or wilfully neglect to make the best use of the means of cultivation offered by the State or otherwise act prejudicially to the scheme of collective farming;

(10) The scheme shall be brought into operation as early as possible but in no case shall the period extend beyond the tenth year from the date of the Constitution coming into operation.

Appendix I: Explanatory Notes

Clause 4: The main purpose behind the clause is to put an obligation on the State to plan the economic life of the people on lines which would lead to the highest point of productivity without closing every avenue to private enterprise, and also provide for the equitable distribution of wealth. The plan set out in the clause proposes the State ownership in agriculture with a collectivized method of cultivation and a modified form of State Socialism in the field of industry. It places squarely on the shoulders of the State the obligation to supply capital necessary for agriculture as well as for industry. Without the supply of capital by the State neither land nor industry can be made to yield better results. It also proposes to nationalize insurance with a double objective. Nationalized Insurance gives the individual greater security than a private Insurance Firm does, inasmuch as it pledges the resources of the State as a security for the ultimate payment of his insurance money. It also gives the State the resources necessary for financing its economic planning in the absence of which it would have to resort to borrowing from the money market at a high rate of interest. State Socialism is essential for the rapid industrialization of India. Private enterprise cannot do it and if it did it would produce those inequalities of wealth which private capitalism has produced in Europe and which should be a warning to Indians. Consolidation of Holdings and Tenancy Legislation are worse than useless. They cannot bring about prosperity in agriculture. Neither Consolidation nor Tenancy Legislation can be of any help to the 60 million Untouchables who are just landless labourers. Neither Consolidation nor Tenancy Legislation can solve their problem. Only collective farms on the lines set out in the proposal can help them. There is no expropriation of the interests concerned. Consequently there ought to be no objection to the proposal on that account.

The plan has two special features. One is that it proposes State Socialism in important fields of economic life. The second special feature of the plan is that it does not leave the establishment of State Socialism to the will of the Legislature. It establishes State Socialism by the Law of the Constitution and thus makes it unalterable by any act of the Legislature and the Executive.

Students of Constitutional Law will at once raise a protest. They are sure to ask: Does not the proposal go beyond the scope of the usual type of Fundamental Rights? My answer is that it does not. If it appears to go beyond, it is only because the conception of Fundamental Rights on which such criticism is based is a narrow conception. One may go further and say that even from the narrow conception of the scope of the Constitutional Law as comprising no more than Fundamental Rights the proposal can find ample justification. For what is the purpose of prescribing by law the shape and form of the economic structure of society? The purpose is to protect the liberty of the individual from invasion by other individuals which is the object of enacting Fundamental Rights. The connection between individual liberty and the shape and form of the economic structure of society may not be apparent to everyone. None the less, the connection between the two is real. It will be apparent if the following considerations are borne in mind.

Political Democracy rests on four premises which may be set out in the following terms:

(i) The individual is an end in himself.

(ii) That the individual has certain inalienable rights which must be guaranteed to him by the Constitution.

(iii) That the individual shall not be required to relinquish any of his constitutional rights as a condition precedent to the receipt of a privilege.

(iv) That the State shall not delegate powers to private persons to govern others.

Anyone who studies the workings of the system of social economy based on private enterprise and pursuit of personal gain will realize how it undermines, if it does not actually violate, the last two premises on which Democracy rests. How many have to relinquish their constitutional rights in order to gain their living? How many have to subject themselves to be governed by private employers?

Ask those who are unemployed whether what are called Fundamental Rights are of any value to them. If a person who is unemployed is offered a choice between a job of some sort, with some sort of wages, with no fixed hours of labour and with an interdict on joining a union and the exercise of his right to freedom of speech, association, religion, etc., can there be any doubt as to what his choice will be? How can it be otherwise? The fear of starvation, the fear of losing a house, the fear of losing savings, if any, the fear of being compelled to take children away from school, the fear of having to be a burden on public charity, the fear of having to be burned or buried at public cost are factors too strong to permit a man to stand out for his Fundamental Rights. The unemployed are thus compelled to relinquish their Fundamental Rights for the sake of securing the privilege to work and to subsist.

What about those who are employed? Constitutional Lawyers assume that the enactment of Fundamental Rights is enough to safeguard their liberty and that nothing more is called for. They argue that where the State refrains from intervention in private affairs — economic and social — the residue is liberty. What is necessary is to make the residue as large as possible and State intervention as small as possible. It is true that where the State refrains from intervention what remains is liberty. But this does not dispose of the matter. One more question remains to be answered. To whom and for whom is this liberty? Obviously this liberty is liberty to the landlords to increase rents, for capitalists to increase hours of work and reduce rates of wages. This must be so. It cannot be otherwise. For in an economic system employing armies of workers, producing goods *en masse* at regular intervals, some one must make rules so that workers will work and the wheels of industry run on. If the State does not do it the private employer will. Life otherwise will become impossible. In other words what is called liberty from the control of the State is another name for the dictatorship of the private employer.

How to prevent such a thing happening? How to protect the unemployed as well as the employed from being cheated out of their Fundamental Rights to life, liberty and pursuit of happiness? The usual remedy adopted by democratic countries is to *limit* the power of government to impose arbitrary restraints in the political domain and to *invoke* the ordinary power of the legislature to restrain the more powerful individual from imposing arbitrary restraints on the less powerful in the economic field. The inadequacy, nay, the futility of the plan has been well established. The successful invocation by the less powerful of the authority of the legislature is a doubtful proposition. Having regard to the fact that even under adult suffrage all legislatures and governments are controlled by the more powerful, an appeal to the legislature to intervene is a very precarious safeguard against the invasion of the liberty of the less powerful. The plan follows quite a different method. It seeks to limit not only the power of government to impose arbitrary restraints but also of the more powerful individuals – or to be more precise, to eliminate the possibility of the more powerful having the power to impose arbitrary restraints on the less powerful by withdrawing from him the control he has over the economic life of people. There cannot be the slightest doubt that of the two remedies against the invasion by the more powerful of the rights and liberties of the less powerful, the one contained in the proposal is undoubtedly the more effective. Considered in the light of these observations the proposal is essentially a proposal for safeguarding the liberty of the individual. No Constitutional Lawyer can therefore object to it on the ground that it goes beyond the usual scope of Constitutional Law.

So far the plan has been considered purely as a means of safeguarding individual liberty. But there is also another aspect of the plan which is worthy of note. It is an attempt to establish State Socialism without abrogating Parliamentary Democracy and without leaving its establishment to the will of a Parliamentary Democracy. Critics of State Socialism, even its friends, are bound to ask why make it a part of the Constitutional Law of the land? Why not leave it to the legislature to bring it into being by the ordinary process of law? The reason why it cannot be left to the ordinary law is not difficult to understand. One essential condition for the success of a planned economy is that it must not be liable to suspension or abandonment. It must be permanent. The question is how this permanence can be secured. Obviously it cannot be secured under the form of government called Parliamentary Democracy. Under the system of Parliamentary Democracy, the policy of the legislature and of the executive is the policy of the majority for the time being. Under the system of Parliamentary Democracy the majority in one election may be in favour of State Socialism in industry and in agriculture. At the next election the majority may be against it. The anti-State Socialism majority will use its law-making power to undo the work of the pro-State Socialism majority and the pro-State Socialism majority will use its law-making power to do over again what has been undone by their opponents. Those who want the economic structure of society to be modelled on State Socialism must realize that they cannot leave the fulfilment of so fundamental a purpose to the exigencies of ordinary law which simple majorities – whose political fortunes are never determined by rational causes – have a right to make and unmake. For these reasons Political Democracy seems to be unsuited for the purpose.

What is the alternative? The alternative is Dictatorship. There is no doubt that Dictatorship can give the permanence which State Socialism requires as an essential condition for its fructification. There is, however, one fact against Dictatorship which must be faced. Those who believe in individual freedom strongly object to Dictatorship and insist upon Parliamentary Democracy as a proper form of government for a free society. For they feel that freedom of the individual is possible only under Parliamentary Democracy and not under Dictatorship. Consequently those who want freedom are not prepared to give up Parliamentary Democracy as a form of government. However much they may be anxious to have State Socialism, they will not be ready to exchange Parliamentary Democracy for Dictatorship even though the gain by such an exchange is the achievement of State Socialism. The problem therefore is to have State Socialism without Dictatorship, to have State Socialism with Parliamentary Democracy. The way out seems to be to retain Parliamentary Democracy and to prescribe State Socialism by the Law of the Constitution so that it will be beyond the reach of a parliamentary majority to suspend, amend or abrogate it. It is only by this that one can achieve the triple object, namely, to establish socialism, retain Parliamentary Democracy and avoid Dictatorship.

The proposal marks a departure from the existing Constitutions whose aim is merely to prescribe the form of the political structure of society, leaving the economic structure untouched. The result is that the political structure is completely set at naught by the forces which emerge from the economic structure, which is at variance with the political structure. Those who want socialism with Parliamentary Democracy and without Dictatorship should welcome the proposal.

The soul of Democracy is the doctrine of one man, one value. Unfortunately, Democracy has attempted to give effect to this doctrine only so far as the political structure is concerned by adopting the rule of one man, one vote, which is supposed to translate into fact the doctrine of one man, one value. It has left the economic structure to take the shape given to it by those who are in a position to mould it. This has happened because Constitutional lawyers have been dominated by the antiquated conception that all that is necessary for a perfect Constitution for Democracy is to frame a Constitutional law which would make government responsible to the people and to prevent tyranny of the people by the government. Consequently, almost all laws of Constitution which relate to countries which are called Democratic stop with adult suffrage and fundamental rights. They have never advanced to the conception that the Constitutional Law of Democracy must go beyond adult suffrage and fundamental rights. In other words, old time Constitutional Lawyers believed that the scope and function of Constitutional Law was to prescribe the shape and form of the political structure of society. They never realized that it was equally essential to prescribe the shape and form of the economic structure of society, if Democracy is to live up to its principle of one man, one value. The time has come to take a bold step and define both the economic structure as well as the political structure of society by the Law of the Constitution. All countries like India which are late-comers in the field of Constitution-making should not copy the faults of other countries. They should profit by the experience of their predecessors.

* * * *

Shortly after States and Minorities was written, the Constituent Assembly began work on the Constitution, and Ambedkar, a member of the Assembly, was appointed to the constitutional drafting committee. The vast majority of the Assembly proved far more interested in the economic rights of those who had some property than those who had none. The final document included a general commitment to the ideals of economic democracy in a non-juridical section on 'Basic Principles', but it was private property that was protected under 'Fundamental Rights'. In his summary statement to the Assembly on 25 November 1949, Ambedkar defended the Constitution as the best compromise of which the Assembly and its generation was capable, and emphasized the relative ease with which the Indian Constitution could be modified by succeeding generations. He then went on to restate his belief in the critical importance of social and economic democracy, and did so in words that are repeated with increasing frequency and urgency by the contemporary Dalit movement. This particular selection appeared in the August 1983 issue of The Oppressed Indian (Delhi).

The Future of Parliamentary Democracy

Dr B. R. Ambedkar

What we must do is not to be content with mere political democracy. We must make our political democracy a social democracy as well. Political democracy cannot last unless there lies at the base of it a social democracy. What does social democracy mean? It means a way of life which recognizes liberty, equality and fraternity as the principles of life. These principles — liberty, equality and fraternity — are not to be treated as separate items in a trinity. They form a union of trinity in the sense that to divorce one from the other is to defeat the very purpose of democracy. Liberty cannot be divorced from equality, equality cannot be divorced from liberty. Nor can liberty and equality be divorced from fraternity. Without equality, liberty would produce the supremacy of the few over the many. Equality without liberty would kill individual initiative. Without fraternity, liberty and equality could not become a natural course of things. It would require a constable to enforce them. We must begin by acknowledging the fact that there is complete absence of two things in Indian society. One of these is equality. On the social plane, we have in India a society based on the principle of graded inequality, which means elevation for some and degradation for others. On the economic plane, we have a society in which there are some who have immense wealth as against many who live in abject poverty.

On 26 January 1950, we are going to enter into a life of contradictions. In politics we will have equality and in social and economic life we will have inequality. In politics we will be recognizing the principle of one man, one vote and one vote, one value. In our social and economic life we shall, by reason of our social and economic structure, continue to deny the principle of one man, one value. How long shall we continue to live this life of contradictions? How long shall we continue to deny equality in our social and economic life? If we continue to deny it for long, we will do so only by putting our political democracy in peril. We must remove this contradiction at the earliest possible moment or else those who suffer from inequality will blow up the structure of political democracy which we have so laboriously built up.

2. Social and Economic Realities

*In spite of significant changes triggered by the pre-Independence struggles,
today's Untouchables still face a harsh reality. It is this world that both fuels
and blunts the continuing liberation movement. Untouchables and two allies
describe this world in the following articles, editorials and poetry. The first,
Neerav Patel's 'self-introduction', captures much of the spirit and substance
of change and resistance. Patel is a young Untouchable poet from the north-
western state of Gujarat, the scene of massive and protracted anti-Untouchable
riots since 1981. A selection of his poetry was published in 1980 by the
cultural wing of the Dalit Panther organization that has played an important
role in mobilizing Untouchable resistance to attacks during the riots.*

Self-introduction

be my guest someday, sawarna [high caste Hindu].
if you want to feel the pangs of woe
come in the guise of an untouchable.
see, yonder is the way to our village from the city.
avoid that tallest mansion —
our young girls are seduced there customarily.
that landlord is the king of our village —
he would not spare even a young bitch!
don't ask for water from the public water-pots.
do you know
how to drink water with the bowl of your palms?
and don't ask for my address there —
somebody may call you names.
here live brahmans,
      kanbis,
      kolis,
      potters, blacksmiths and others.
yes, cross that hillock beyond the boundary,
and there appear huts buried under the tamarind trees,
or there may be two or three dogs licking bones.
dark and half-clad bodies:
yes, sawarna, they are my kith and kin —
mother is roasting beef at home,
father is rinsing hides in the tanning-pit.

this is my uncle
tailoring a leather bag for kanbis.
sister-in-law is peeling the aval stems.
and nanki has gone with a pitcher to fetch water from the tank.

that's all, sawarna.
don't cover your nose with the scented handkerchief,
you may suffocate,
you may nauseate at the sight of squabbles.

but see,

here i am reading pablo neruda
lying on the charpai under the neem tree.
i feel some times a lone man myself
on this island of ours.
my father said, sawarna —
your hic-cup was cured by the salty waters of our tanning-pit
in your childhood.

we can love each other
if you can shed your orthodox skin.
come and touch, we will make a new world —
where there won't be any
dust, dirt, poverty, injustice, oppression.

> Neerav Patel, *Burning at Both The Ends* (Ahmedabad: Dalit Panthers, 1980)

As the very existence of Dalit poetry like this indicates, the Dalit struggle for education that began in the years before Independence has continued. Education has generated many of the resources that feed the liberation movement — information about rights that returns to illiterate villagers via literate sons; the ability to tap the financial resources of those who find paid employment; the literary skills that link scattered local Dalit movements. At the same time, education is still a struggle for most Dalits. A recent survey by the Indian Council of Social Science Research showed 60 per cent of the fathers of Scheduled Caste college students were village labourers; 47 per cent of their fathers were illiterate and another 34 per cent were self-educated or had only primary education (Shah, 1982). The following two articles translate these statistics into human terms and underline the critical importance of the government scholarship programmes initiated by Ambedkar. The fact that so many students' families must still go into debt to supplement limited aid is a reminder of Untouchable reality rarely understood by the dominant society.

The author, M. B. Chitnis, was a higher caste educator, part of a multicaste team assembled by the late Dr Ambedkar. At different times Chitnis served as an administrator at both Marathwada University and Milind College, the institutions described here. Both schools are in Aurangabad, a provincial city in western India, and became the focal point of anti-Untouchable riots in 1978 that were triggered by Untouchable efforts to rename Marathwada

University for Dr Ambedkar. Conditions today remain much as they were when this survey was conducted, and the Namantar *(Naming) issue remains a smouldering symbol of linked caste and class conflicts.*

An Educational, Social and Economic Survey of Milind College Students

Shri M. B. Chitnis, *Milind College Annual*, **vol. X (1973)**

An educational, social and cultural survey of 1,030 students of Milind College of Arts was conducted in the month of January 1972. This survey covered 47 per cent of the students enrolled in the college during the year 1971-2. The total enrolment in that year was 2,193. Of the students covered by the survey 705 were from pre-university class and 324 from F.Y. [First Year] Arts. The composition of the students of the Milind College of Arts in 1971-2 and 1972-3 was:

	1971-72
Scheduled Castes ['Untouchables']	1977
Scheduled Tribes	34
Denotified and Notified Tribes	108
O. B. C. & E. B. C. [low-ranked castes]	71
Non-Scheduled Castes	3

The remarkable feature of the composition of the students is the proportion of 3 per cent non-Scheduled Caste and Tribe to 96 per cent Scheduled Caste and Tribe students. To understand this unique phenomenon of congregation of large number of Scheduled Caste and Scheduled Tribe students in this college a short review of the growth of the college will not be out of place. Milind College of Arts is a sister institution of Milind College of Science and Dr Ambedkar College of Arts and Commerce. These three institutions are a result of the bifurcation of the original People's Education Society's [PE Society] College of Arts, Science and Commerce founded in 1950 in Aurangabad by Dr B. R. Ambedkar. The aim and object of the PE Society was to promote higher education amongst poor and middle classes in general and Scheduled Castes in particular. In the year of its establishment i.e. 1950, PE Society's college had a total enrolment of only 125 students, of whom 12 belonged to Scheduled Castes. Collegiate education was in its initial stage then in Marathwada, a region with a population of five million and three colleges with about 375 students on their rolls. This was mainly due to the unprogressive feudal regime which Marathwada suffered for 600 years. Before 1950 there was only one college in the entire region situated in Aurangabad, teaching 125 to 150 students up to intermediate level in arts and science. Marathwada turned a new page in its educational progress in 1950 with the advent of private enterprise in the educational field. By the year 1958, which saw the inception of Marathwada University, the number of colleges had grown to eight and of the students to 2,012. The establishment of the university has given such an impetus to higher education in the region that during the current year 1972–3 there are 82 colleges with the total enrolment of 42,000 in eight different faculties.

Multiplication of colleges in a town like Aurangabad has brought to the fore some social problems which education was supposed to solve but which the growth of education has on the contrary accentuated as never before. This problem is the polarization of student population according to castes and communities in centres with multiple colleges as in Aurangabad. In 1958 when there were only two colleges, one run by Maharashtra government and the other by People's Education Society, the composition of the PE Society's college was two Scheduled Caste to six non-Scheduled Caste students. The character of the People's Education Society's college was thus cosmopolitan. After fifteen years, i.e. in 1972–3, the composition of the students of PE Society's colleges of Arts, Science, Commerce and Law, with total enrolment of 6,150, was 90 per cent Scheduled Castes and Scheduled Tribes and hardly 10 per cent non-Scheduled Castes. The reason for this polarization on the basis of castes is that caste prejudices are still a very potent factor in Indian society and not because the organizers and the teachers belong to one community, namely, Scheduled Castes. The caste composition of the governors of the PE Society is cosmopolitan and so is the teaching staff. The physical plant, scientific equipment, libraries, play grounds and the examination results of the colleges are in no way inferior to other colleges in the town. The root cause of this segregation of the Scheduled Castes and Scheduled Tribes students and their congregation in the PE Society's college is, therefore, to be sought not in any other educational deficiency but still deeper, in the very socio-religious tradition of Indian society.

If we classify the students according to the economic status of their families we find that majority of them belong to the lowest rung of society. Here are some of the astonishing results of an economic survey undertaken in the year 1971–2, which included about 50 per cent of the students.

(a) Seventy-three per cent of the students' families belonged to the category of 'landless workers'.

(b) These landless workers had to remain unemployed for an average of 3.8 months during the year.

(c) The average daily wage rate of a male landless worker was Rs. 2.50 and that of a female worker was Rs. 1 only.

(d) The parents of the 52 per cent of the Scheduled Caste students had to raise loans from the village money-lenders, at exorbitant rates of interest, to finance the education of their wards.

(e) Those Scheduled Caste families who owned some landed property belonged to the category of 'small farmers'. Their average land-holding was 4.9 acres of dry land.

As their employment is uncertain and at subsistence level only, the plight of these families and the students hailing from them during the current year of scarcity could be seen from the survey published elsewhere in this issue of the journal.

Education: out of 1,030 students covered by the present survey, 824 students were the first in their families to take collegiate education.

College education among Scheduled Castes and Tribes is vastly on the increase in the country, particularly in Maharashtra, where during the current year 42,000 students belonging to Scheduled Castes, Scheduled Tribes, Nomadic Tribes, Denotified Tribes are taking post-matric education. The figures for the entire country for the Scheduled Caste students in 1951-2 was 1,604. It rose to 157,000 in 1970-1. The corresponding figures of Scheduled Tribes are 575 and 29,000 respectively. During the year of survey [1972] 7,000 students were studying in Marathwada colleges; in the current year [1973] the number has gone to 10,000. On an average one-fifth of the total population of Marathwada University hails from the backward classes. Though education has become widespread, the Scheduled Caste student has during his early educational career still to surmount age-long prejudices of his educator. Eighty per cent of the 1,030 students in the survey had to sit outside the classrooms in their primary stage owing to the observance of untouchability in the villages where they began their educational career. Encouragement from their school teachers in their education, though on the increase, has still much headway to make. Only 40 per cent of the students replied that they received encouragement from their teachers; 28 per cent said that they were definitely discouraged by their teachers. Nearly 15 per cent said their teachers showed an indifferent attitude; 11 per cent of the students did not reply to the question about encouragement by their teachers They had also to face opposition from the non-Scheduled Caste students and their elders whenever they sought to exercise their natural right to receive education on equal footing. Some 529 students, i.e. 51.3 per cent, experienced this kind of discriminatory treatment from their caste Hindu classmates.

Life in school, which should promote more and more social fusion, still resists change. Seventeen per cent of the students had no friends in the communities and religions other than their own. Out of the 83 per cent who had friends outside their own castes, 10 per cent had Brahman friends, 30 per cent Maratha, 12.5 per cent other Hindus, 2.5 per cent Christian, 15 per cent Muslim and the remaining 30 per cent had them from sub-castes of the Scheduled Castes other than their own. Only 40 per cent of the friends from the caste Hindus invited them to their houses; 60 per cent cultivated friendship only in the school and never dared to invite them to their houses owing to their own and their parents' prejudices. Of the students who invited them to their houses, 47 per cent did not play with them, 62 per cent did not take tea with them and 71 per cent did not dine with them. They felt greater affinity and friendliness mainly with students of their own communities. Only a few are intimate towards persons of other castes and communities as would be seen from the following figures:

11.5% were intimate towards Marathas.

4% towards the Brahmans.

18% towards the other Hindus.

4% towards the Christians.

6% towards Muslims.

56% towards other sub-castes of the Scheduled Castes.

Though almost 85 per cent of the parents and guardians of the students are illiterate, they showed interest in the educational progress of their wards. Seventy-five per cent of the students said that their parents very often made inquiries about their progress in their studies, while 29 per cent said that their parents were indifferent. Parents of only 46 per cent were in a position to purchase books for them; 54 per cent had to make do with the notes dictated in the class by their teachers or had to borrow books from their classmates.

Economic Progress

It is a general belief that the cooperative movement has made a great headway in rural areas, but that is not so in respect of the Scheduled Castes. Only twenty-eight students, i.e. 2.8 per cent, had a relation who was a member of a co-operative society. Of them only twenty could obtain loans from a society, i.e. 98 per cent did not get any loan from the co-operative societies. Only 2.5 per cent have benefited from the scheme of loans from the nationalized banks.

Families of 824 students, i.e. 80 per cent of the total, are landless labourers; fourteen of them, i.e. 1.7 per cent, are recipients of lands distributed by the government under schemes for landless labour.

Decentralization of power down to the village level has helped to elevate relations of seventy-two students, i.e. 7 per cent of the total number, to membership in the Grampanchayats or Municipalities. This is due to the reservations for the Scheduled Castes in the composition of these institutions. Of these seventy-two, four are the Sarpanch, and three hold membership in a Zilla Parishad.

To the question, whether they would prefer to serve in the town or village, 48 per cent of the students said that they preferred jobs in urban areas and 52 per cent in rural areas. Of those who preferred to serve in the town, instead of in the village, 75 per cent did so because of the severity of the practice of untouchability in the villages, and 25 per cent preferred town to village because the village did not provide the necessary amenities for a good life and recreation.

The Scheduled Castes, being mostly landless labourers, have got to be more mobile than other village communities and transfer residence from one village to another, whenever the practice of untouchability by the village orthodoxy becomes unreasonable or whenever opportunities of jobs dry up in the village. During the last fifteen years, 20 per cent of the families left their original villages. Of them 65 per cent left on account of severity of observance of untouchability and 35 per cent for better work prospects elsewhere. Twenty per cent of the families have at least one member in permanent or semi-permanent service: 11 per cent in government service, 3 per cent in semi-government service, 4 per cent in co-operative societies, 3.9 per cent in the armed forces, and 1.7 per cent in the police force.

*The particular scarcity described below has gone and has been replaced
periodically by others, with relief activities sometimes more efficient and
sometimes much the same. This brief survey is useful primarily as an
indicator of Untouchable student experience and family status that is more
common than is usually recognized.*

Survey of Impact of Scarcity Conditions on Milind College Students

Principal M. B. Chitnis and Prof. D. D. Kamble
Milind College Annual, **vol. X (1973)**

The severity of the present famine and scarcity conditions in Maharashtra
have been severely affecting the students of our college. To probe the extent
of it we conducted a survey of 686 students of the PUC class. Of these, 606
students reported that scarcity works have been started in their villages and
they participated in these works during October vacation. The works were of
the following types:

1.	Building of new roads	156
2.	Tanks	32
3.	Minor projects	5
4.	Bunding	157
5.	Breaking of metal [road stones]	250
6.	Desilting of tanks	42
7.	Deepening of wells	41
		683

Not all the students and their relatives could get continuous work on these
scarcity projects, though they were prepared to undertake any manual work.
All these works were started by government, excepting two which were sponsored by private agencies. Some of the works have been completed and the
villagers are anxiously awaiting the start of similar new works, as the possibility
of the usual employment on the farm has completely dried up. Though the
works are government controlled, the wages for work are not paid regularly.
In most of the cases the wages were delayed as follows:

	Centres
Payment per week	227
Payment fortnightly	225
Payment monthly	231

In spite of complaints to government officers in charge of the projects, payment of wages continued to be irregular. No social or political leaders helped
to redress these and other grievances. At certain places wages were paid in
kind and at others in cash.

In cash: 471
In kind: 162 (food articles)

Though government had fixed daily wages at Rs. 2-50 for males and Rs. 2 for females, actual receipts by the workers varied from centre to centre: from Rs. 2-50 to Rs. 2 for male workers, and from Rs. 2 to just 80 pice [cents] for female workers.

Grain shops are not necessarily located near the scarcity work centres. Workers have to depend upon the government centres and the co-operative society's shops or private shops situated at a distance. The survey shows the distribution of grain shops according to the following agencies:

Government grain shops	138
Co-operative societies' shops	60
Private shops	270

The students complained that many of the government and co-operative society shops pleaded shortage of stocks of grain, and they were very often obliged to purchase grain from private shops at black market rates. As a result of this scarcity of grain, the students and their families had to reduce their daily intake of food in terms of Bhakari [coarse fried bread] as follows:

reduction by one-quarter	186
reduction by one half	212
reduction by three-quarters on some days	83

They ate Bhakaris when they had work and received their wages. On the days of unemployment, they almost starved themselves and had to subsist on Kannya, that is, rough ground-bajra and fried grams.

The parents of most of the students, being extremely poor, having no savings either in cash or ornaments or luxury articles, had to sell tin from the roof of their huts, cooking utensils, poultry, cattle and goats. The information regarding such sales is as follows:

Those who had to sell:

tins	45
utensils	98
cattle	96
poultry	117
goats	63

236 pawned their utensils and some sundry articles with the village Savakars (money-lenders).

Parents of the students who have large families and only one or two grown-up able-bodied members in the family who can work on scarcity centres tried to persuade them to give up their college career and help them in supplementing their earning. Out of 683 students, 444 were asked by their parents to give up college and join them on scarcity work.

Some students reported that families of their relations had left the villages owing to non-availability of work near their villages. Their number is 361.

It is not only the non-availability of food grains that has characterized the scarcity condition of Marathwada. Scarcity of water has also affected a number of villages, particularly the communities to which our students belong. namely Scheduled Castes, Tribes, etc. It is reported that out of 683 villages, only in ten villages are the Scheduled Castes permitted to utilize common wells. At 114 villages, there are separate wells for the Scheduled Castes; only 14 of them have adequate supply of water. The remaining have to fetch water from tanks, ponds in the *'nallahs'* and canals. Starvation has led some people to kill stray cattle and subsist on their flesh. Some students reported that deaths have occurred amongst Scheduled Castes in the villages of Dhawala and Navgan Rajuri in Bhir district, and Aundha Nagnath in Parbhani district, which in their opinion are the areas worst affected by famine.

* * * *

As the author of the following article points out, most Untouchables throughout India are still trapped in poverty at the bottom of the nation's vast agricultural sector. The author, a Dalit economist, is equally concerned with the pervasive linkage of social, economic and political-administrative power that undermines even ameliorative programmes. This article is part of a longer paper presented to the conference on "Minority Strategies: Perspectives on Race and Untouchability" held in New York City in 1983.

Role of Development Schemes for Scheduled Castes and Tribes: Do They Work?

Dr R. M. Ambewadikar*, **Department of Economics, Marathwada University**

Indian Weaker Sections: One of the Third World countries, India is the seventh largest and the second most populous country in the world. The main occupation of this country is agriculture. Slightly less than 80 per cent of the population is rural and engaged in agriculture and allied activities.

Landless labourers, marginal farmers (holding less than one hectare), small farmers (holding between one and two hectares), and rural artisans form the poorest strata of society. A majority of them live in rural areas where hardcore poverty is found. Of the 350 million people subsisting below the poverty line in the country, around 300 million are found in the rural areas.

The economic profile of the small and marginal farmers is distressing. It is estimated that in 1971–2 (the date of the most recent national survey), nine-tenths of the small cultivators' households received an annual average

*The author is grateful to Dr V. V. Borkar, Professor and Head, Department of Economics, Marathwada University, Aurangabad for his valuable suggestions in this paper.

income of less than Rs. 2,000/- and half of the small cultivators' households less than Rs. 1,000/-. The budget of the small cultivator household is, therefore, almost always unfavourable, the deficit ranging from 5 per cent to 27 per cent. Thus the large majority of the very small landholders are in perpetual debt. The average total assets of 'small cultivators' in India is Rs. 2,573 only. This puts his credit-worthiness at a very low level.

People from the Scheduled Castes (Untouchables) and Scheduled Tribes form a large proportion of these suppressed categories. The majority of the Scheduled Castes and Scheduled Tribes, who form about one-fourth of the total Indian population, subsist below the poverty line and besides face problems peculiar to them. Continuing to pursue traditional occupations they are unable to avail of the fruits of economic growth and participate fully in the process of modernization. The population of the Scheduled Castes in India is about 100 million. They have very few assets and are generally dependent upon agricultural labour, leather work and other low-income occupations.

Of the total working population of Scheduled Castes, 52 per cent are agricultural labourers and conversely 33 per cent of all of India's agricultural labourers are Scheduled Castes. The few cultivators amongst Scheduled Castes are sharecroppers or subsistance farmers. Others mostly pursue traditional occupations and are unable to avail themselves of the new employment opportunities. Their literacy level is only 14.7 per cent as compared to the all-India level of 33.80 per cent (excluding Scheduled Castes and Tribes). Female literacy among them is as low as 6.44 per cent against an all-India female literacy level of 22.5 per cent (excluding Scheduled Castes and Tribes). In spite of their adverse conditions, they contribute significantly to the sustenance and growth of the production system of the country. The practice of untouchability against Scheduled Castes creates a special handicap for them; even the few educated groups amongst them are unable to compete for various job opportunities. The Scheduled Tribes still remain largely outside the mainstream of development, mainly because of their relative isolation and their exploitation by outside agencies. A large portion of bonded labourers are also Scheduled Castes [SCs] and Scheduled Tribes [STs].

In the case of both SCs and STs, social and economic impoverishment are the main causes of their backwardness. In spite of constitutional directives and a number of legislative and executive measures by the government, their situation has not improved perceptibly owing to the lack of genuine support. Although special programmes were formulated in the five-year plans for the upliftment of weaker sections in general, the economic base of SCs and STs continues to be extremely weak.

While a number of special programmes aimed at ameliorating the conditions of the weaker sections in general have been sponsored by the government, not a single agency has been created specifically for the economic development of the Scheduled Castes (Untouchables). Some of the special programmes implemented for weaker sections in general are: Intensive Agricultural

Development Programme (IADP), Drought-Prone Areas Programmes (DRAP), Crash Scheme for Rural Employment, Small Farmers' Development Agency (SFDA), Marginal Farmers' and Agricultural Labourers' (MFAL) development agency, Integrated Rural Development Programme (IRDP), Regional Rural Banks (RRBs), Farmers' Service Societies (FSSs), Tribal Development Agencies, etc. Of these programmes, SFDA and IRDP have been selected for detailed discussion in this paper, as they focus on rural weaker sections among whom SCs and STs are concentrated.

Small Farmers' Development Agency: The All-India Rural Credit Review Committee (1969), which tried to evaluate the progress of the Crop Loan Scheme and the Scheme of Outright Grants introduced for the benefit of small farmers on the recommendation of an earlier panel, namely the Committee on Co-operative Credit (1960), found that the performance was hardly inspiring despite a few noticeable bright spots. The flow of credit continued to be biased in favour of large and medium farmers; the weaker sections received very little support even from the co-operatives primarily meant for them. The committee, while emphasizing the need for speedy and complete restructuring, recommended the creation of special agencies for the first time in India for small and marginal farmers and agricultural labourers, namely Small Farmers' Development Agencies (SFDAs) and Marginal Farmers' and Agricultural Labourers' (MFALs). Eighty-seven projects of these two development schemes were operating for the benefit of the weaker sections in rural areas since 1971. On the recommendation of the National Committee on Agriculture (NCA) in 1973, two major changes were initiated during the Fifth Five-Year Plan period (1974–5 to 1978–9). First, the number of projects (agencies) was enhanced from 87 to 160 spread over 200 districts all over India. Secondly, the programmes for small farmers, marginal farmers and agricultural labourers were combined to make 160 composite SF/MFAL projects. These composite projects were called SFDAs; one was assigned to each selected district to reach a target of 50,000 beneficiaries within 5 years. A person holding land between one and two hectares was to be considered as a small farmer and one holding less than one hectare a marginal farmer. Those benefiting under the category of agricultural labourers include persons earning a major part of their income by expending wage labour on farms. They include, apart from those having no other means of livelihood, marginal farmers and rural artisans such as carpenters, blacksmiths, cobblers, potters, etc.

The SFDAs were to be managed by the government officers of high rank, elected members of Parliament and State Legislative Assemblies and local bodies, and one or two members from small farmers and/or agricultural labourers. They were to be administered by the Deputy Collectors and a small team of technically suited officers.

Objectives of the SFDA scheme were to – (1) help increase the output of small farmers by enthusing and educating them for undertaking intensive cultivation and provide facilities such as supply of credit and other inputs and marketing of produce, (2) provide facilities for developing subsidiary occupations like animal husbandry, dairying, farm forestry for the target group, (3) supply credit, raw materials and service to the artisans and craftsmen with a view to upgrading their skills and modernizing their trades, and (4) encourage production by artisans through the small village industries agency for sale within the rural community.

Critical Evaluation

Evaluation of the performance of SFDAs made by a number of expert panels reveals the following features:

1. Identification of Target Groups: The studies made by the Reserve Bank of India (RBI) and the Project Evaluation Organization (PEO) of the Planning Commission of India revealed that all the participants were not identified exclusively from the originally defined target group of small and marginal farmers, but also from larger farmers with holdings of 3.00 to 3.20 hectares (RBI on MFAL; and PEO on SF, MF and AL). Lands owned by these farmers in other villages were also not taken into account for judging their status (RBI on SFDA; and ASCI (Hyderabad) on SFDA of Hassan district). The findings of the PEO and Administrative Staff College of India (ASCI), Hyderabad, reveal that the Village Level Workers (VLWs) misused their discretionary powers under the powerful influence of big landlords. Tenants were excluded from the list in almost all the agencies. Even supervising officers who noticed the discrepancies appeared to be helpless in the matter. PEO observed that a substantial number of farmers were identified wrongly. Very little attention was paid to the identification of the agricultural labourers, many of whom are Untouchables. In several projects, this group was not identified at all (RBI on SFDA). The factors responsible for slow progress of agencies and wrong identification of target groups were certainly casteism, lack of sympathy for the poor, and influence and pressure of the caste Hindus and better-off sections on the officials of the agency.

2. Coverage of Beneficiaries: Up to the middle of 1980, a total of more than 168 lakh [168,000] familes were identified in 168 SFDAs. This amounted to coverage of a little more than one lakh [100,000] families per agency. This was more than the targeted strength. Of these, nearly 73 lakhs (43.2 per cent only) were enrolled as members of different co-operative societies. The study of MFALs of ten districts conducted by the RBI in 1973, revealed that till 1972 no agricultural labourer (a category that would include large numbers of Untouchables) was enrolled as a member of any primary agricultural co-operative credit societies (PACSs) in six out of the ten districts, though the MFAL was started there in 1969 for doing this job (RBI on MFAL, p. 210). The reasons for this were traced to sociological factors, conservative attitudes and to efforts to retain power balance. Most PACSs managed by the big landlords felt that they would lose a source of cheap labour if these people became economically independent (ibid, p. 190). On the whole, no determined efforts were made to enrol agricultural labourers as members in PACSs.

Out of the 168 lakhs of identified potential beneficiaries, about 80.33 lakhs (47.8 per cent) have so far been covered under one scheme or the other of the programme. Almost 62 lakhs (77 per cent of identified and 77.5 per cent of beneficiaries) were assisted in one way or the other in improving their agriculture. The next group includes those assisted under the schemes in the animal husbandry sector such as help in starting dairy, poultry, piggery, etc. Under these schemes a mere 9 lakh families (5.3 per cent of the identified and 11.2 per cent of the beneficiaries) have been assisted. Almost an equal number have been helped to improve or expand their irrigation facilities. Thus almost 99 per cent of the beneficiaries are from agricultural pursuits. Apart from the above three groups of schemes, assistance under other schemes have reached only a small number, i.e. 1 per cent only.

3. Expenditure on Programmes: Government assistance under these schemes has been devoted mainly towards the payments of subsidies and financial grants to organizations, besides administrative expenses. Total expenditure incurred on 87 agencies during the Fourth Plan (1969–74) was to the tune of Rs.4,153.48 lakhs, which comes to Rs.47.74 lakhs per agency. Total expenditure after the end of the Fourth Plan up to June 1980 was of Rs. 19,198 lakhs on 161 agencies, which came to Rs.114.27 lakhs per agency. The all-India average expenditure per beneficiary comes to about Rs.290.

The major component of the above expenditure was in the form of subsidies to beneficiaries mostly linked with capital investment loans of medium and long term, extended by either co-operatives or commercial banks.

4. Disbursement of Loans: Since inception of the scheme to June 1980, a total amount of over Rs.406 crores (4,060,000,000) have been disbursed as either medium- or long-term loans. The per capita loan comes to Rs.506. Since around 30 per cent of a term loan represents the subsidy, about Rs.152 out of Rs.290 (average expenditure per beneficiary) might have been utilized towards subsidy per borrower.

It is clearly seen from the disbursement of credit by the co-operatives and the commercial banks that there is a rising trend in the figures of disbursement of loans by both the agencies, after the Fourth Plan period. This was partly because of an increase in number of projects in the Fifth Plan and partly because of a real fillip to SFDA activities. However, one can observe that a gradual decline in this respect occurred during the recent three years ending 1979. The decline is more in co-operatives than in commercial banks. This was due to the shortfall in the performance of co-operatives, which were specially meant for weaker sections. This was also due to the slow-down of the SFDA activities in general. The commercial banks have given a better performance than co-operatives at every level.

Thus one can see that on the whole the performance of SFDAs in respect of financial assistance is on the decline. This can be attributed partly to the exorbitant rate of interest charged to the borrowers and/or unsatisfactory terms regarding repayment. Overdues in co-operatives in rural areas are as high as 50 per cent. Owing to this unsatisfactory position, credit disbursement is declining.

5. Co-operativization of the Poor: The performance of the agencies in bringing the identified persons into the co-operative movement was not at all encouraging, though the co-operative movement was primarily meant for the poor. In nearly 50 per cent of the SFDAs, half of the identified persons were not members of co-operatives which were specially meant for them. The percentage varied from as low as 8 (ASCI, Hyderabad, on SFDA) to 98 (PEO on SFDAs). The RBI had revealed in its report that in more than one-third of the districts, less than 25 per cent of the identified persons were enrolled as members in co-operatives. Participation in co-operatives by the marginal farmers and agricultural labourers was the lowest.

The main reasons for low membership of the weaker sections were domination of co-operatives by better-off sections, casteism, lack of sympathy for the poor, low credit worthiness, indifference by the poor due to bad past experience, lack of adequate knowledge, etc.

6. Response by the Co-operatives: The performance of credit co-operatives was not up to the desired level. The position was bad in most of the agencies. The RBI study reveals that in 50 per cent of the Central Co-operative Banks the amount of loans shared by the small farmers was below 20 per cent. It was less than 10 per cent in eleven Central Co-operative Banks out of nineteen. The financial assistance in the form of share capital contribution, managerial subsidies, risk fund contribution, etc., by the agencies produced good results in only a few projects (RBI on SFDAs).

The main factors responsible for the poor performance in this respect by the co-operatives were the inadequate funds with the co-operative banks and diversion of funds to the dominating better-off sections, besides low membership of weaker sections.

Various studies revealed that agricultural labourers, including the many Untouchables, were not in receipt of required credit. The PEO has observed that of the total loans invested in SFDAs and MFALs, the amount used to benefit the agricultural labourers was insignificant (1 per cent only). Of the amount advanced, the share of co-operatives was negligible. In several project areas, agricultural labourers had absolutely no access to co-operative credit. Marginal farmers and agricultural labourers are mostly in need of consumption loans which are not extended by the PACSs in villages.

Performance in Respect of Individual Programmes
The SFDAs and MFALs had undertaken programmes such as intensive agriculture, minor irrigation, dairying, poultry, piggery, sheep- and goat-rearing and rural works programmes for the benefit of the target groups in rural areas. The role of agencies in these programmes is discussed below.

1. Intensive Agriculture: Owing to inadequate infrastructure facilities, the agency could not do much in this respect. A major shift in the cropping pattern in most of the project areas is not in evidence. Not enough efforts were extended by the agencies to prepare well-suited crop rotations and persuade farmers to adopt them. Nor were special efforts made for adoption of new techniques of cultivation and for multiple cropping.

2. Minor Irrigation: The achievements by the agencies varied considerably from below 10 per cent to above 80 per cent; the achievement of most of the agencies ranged between 26 and 75 per cent (PEO; RBI; and ASCI on SFDA and MFAL). The programmes did not make much headway due to fragmented and small holding and hilly topography.

3. Dairying: Though the programme of supply of milch cattle had been taken up by all the agencies, it was of significance in only a few project areas. As reported by several studies (PEO and RBI on SFDAs), most of the SFDAs achieved more than 50 per cent of their target, but the situation with MFAL programmes, whose potential beneficiaries were mostly Scheduled Castes and Tribes, was not encouraging. Thus the agencies took care only of farmers in supplying milch cattle and not the category of landless agricultural labourers in which Untouchables are concentrated.

Some of the problems often faced by the agencies were inadequate market facilities, high cost and non-availability of cattlefeed, absence of breeding facilities, unsatisfactory health coverage, non-availability of high yielding milch cattle, and lack of co-ordination with the programmes of government departments. In spite of these handicaps, dairying emerged as one of the relatively successful components of the programmes.

4. Poultry: Most of the agencies introduced poultry schemes, but only in a few agencies did it make satisfactory progress. The performance of SFDAs was relatively better than MFALs in this field also. Main factors for slow progress were high price of feed and low price of eggs, non-availability of breeds, inadequate marketing arrangements and lack of veterinary aid.

5. Piggery, Sheep- and Goat-Rearing: Only in a few projects were these schemes introduced. In these projects the beneficiaries were covered in very small numbers. In a few projects the piggery scheme failed due to the adverse attitude of participants to this occupation, high cost of feed and lack of good market. Sheep-rearing was quite popular in some areas due to availability of plenty of grazing fields and lower cost of maintenance. The performance was poor in the case of goat-rearing. Heavy casualties occurred due to improper health care and lack of veterinary facilities.

6. Rural Works Programme: The Rural Works Programme relates to the construction of godowns [storage sheds] and market yards, community wells and devices for lift irrigation, provision of custom services to the farmers and other rural works programmes designed to generate employment opportunities for marginal farmers and agricultural labourers during the slack season.

These programmes were undertaken by most agencies much later than the other above discussed schemes, and consequently the progress in this respect was limited, though the entire expenditure was to be met from the agencies' funds. Some agencies placed much emphasis on these programmes, even neglecting subsidiary occupations. Road construction and minor irrigation were the most common items in this programme. A complete picture of employment to agricultural labourers and marginal farmers is not available. However, as observed by the PEO the percentage of identified agricultural labourers provided with employment under this scheme ranged from 0.4 to 19.0, and for marginal farmers from 0.2 to 6.2

Proportion of Beneficiaries of SCs and STs
Data on the number of Scheduled Castes (SCs) and Scheduled Tribes (STs) identified, enrolled as members and benefited by one scheme or the other are available for 150 SFDAs surveyed out of 168 existing in the country as of May 1980 (NIRD, Hyderabad, *Rural Development in India*, p. 28). SCs and STs are about 23.7 per cent of the Indian population, but in the identified categories they are 16.6 per cent, in enrolment of membership 13.5 per cent, and in beneficiaries 18 per cent only. Thus they are not taken at least in existing proportion for various benefits by the other sections. The expenditure incurred on these two classes in 1979--80 was 13.3 per cent of the total for the agencies. Out of a total 7,198,721 beneficiaries, 7,078,883 (98.3 per cent) were from agricultural pursuits such as improved agriculture, minor irrigation and animal husbandry. In village industries and other occupations (from the tertiary sector) there were only 11,160 (1.7 per cent) beneficiaries. Thus the SFDAs were working for small and marginal farmers only, and not for landless agricultural labourers (among whom Untouchables are concentrated) and rural artisans. Rural works programmes were beneficial to landless labourers, but they were not undertaken except in a few instances.

Defects in the Working of SFDAs
Following were the prominent defects in the working of the SFDAs:
1. Trying to cover under one scheme all weaker sections, including small farmers and marginal farmers, was not calculated to promote efficiency in implementation. Merging SFDAs and MFALs was again improper, because the issues relating to the different classes are hardly likely to be identical. The problems and needs of the different categories of the rural poor — such as small farmers, marginal farmers, agricultural labourers, Scheduled Castes, Scheduled Tribes, Notified Tribes, Denotified Tribes, non-farm workers and rural artisans — are different and require specific programmes to be chalked out for meeting them. Even among the Scheduled Castes and Scheduled Tribes, there are poorer and indigent sections, neglected and suppressed sections. Identical programmes for the upliftment of all the weaker sections will not yield results.
2. The members of better-off sections, such as landlords, managed to infiltrate the target groups of weaker sections to usurp the benefits bestowed by these agencies by producing false certificates issued by the colluding bureaucrats. Naturally, to accommodate them the genuine poor were elbowed

out. The entire set-up is such that even among the poor, the relatively better placed were more readily covered and indigent sections tended to be ignored.

3. The landless labourers, who were amongst the poorest of the weaker sections and generally hailed from the Untouchable communities, actually received negligible or no benefits from the agency. The benefits of the agency were denied to these people by operating their schemes — such as rural works programmes, goat- and sheep-rearing, and poultry schemes — rarely or too late.

4. The commercial and co-operative banks did not exhibit any inclination or enthusiasm to finance the schemes of the weaker sections in general and that of Scheduled Castes and Scheduled Tribes in particular. The Reserve Bank of India stipulates that at least 20 per cent of the total outstanding credit should be loaned to the weaker sections. There is also a scheme for outright grants for the benefit of these sections, which also has not been operative for the most part. The co-operative banks, which are dominated by the better-off classes, have played an even smaller role in helping the poor than the commercial banks. The assistance received by SFDAs from all financing agencies has been declining.

5. The contribution of the concerned government departments such as Revenue, Agriculture, Animal Husbandry, Co-operation, Fisheries, etc., towards the smooth operation of the agencies was insignificant.

6. Infrastructural facilities comprising marketing, storage, transport facilities, feed stocks, veterinary hospitals, banking, post office, etc., were woefully inadequate for subsidiary businesses like dairy, animal husbandry, poultry, etc., which adversely affected their progress.

7. The implementing officers of the agencies were generally drawn from the better-off classes who lacked knowledge of the intricacies of problems at grass-roots level and genuine sympathy for the lowly. Perhaps public-spirited officers belonging to weaker sections might have given a better performance.

8. Last but not least, representatives of Scheduled Castes and Scheduled Tribes were not taken on to the managing committees of the agencies. Members of Parliament and State Legislative Assemblies generally hailing from better-off sections dominated these committees and tried to manipulate the agencies to promote their vested interests.

Conclusions

As experienced by the agencies, the problems of weaker sections in rural areas are complicated and they need closer attention on a long-term basis than attempted by the agencies. A thorough examination of eligibilities, needs, constraints and assistance required is needed, if the rural poor are to be helped. Obviously this cannot be accomplished by a small team of three or four officers to cover about 50,000 people, and that too within five years. A systematic individual-centred and broad-based approach is essential.

The indicators used for measuring the performances of programmes have all been statistical indices like number of potential beneficiaries identified, number of these covered under some subsidy scheme, amount spent,

Cover design of *Audit,* by Pralhad Chendwankar (Bombay: Abhinav Prakashan, 1976).

equipment distributed, etc. While all these are essential for monitoring the desired activities, these are only indirect indicators and are not necessarily able to show the change in incomes and the quality of life of beneficiaries.

Lastly, the programmes primarily meant to help the poorest tended to be helpful to the relatively better-off among the said weaker sections. The highly skewed power structure in the rural areas ensures to the relatively better-off sections a lion's share of any facilities available.

* * * *

Patil

When Patil sent
    for me, I went
'Siddown', said, yet
ground was wet.

Threw at my head
Torn sacking jute
still there I stood
quite mute.

Brought black water
in a cracked tea cup.
Saw dirt in it
Said, 'No tea thanks.'

Patil cracked betelnut
yelled, 'why aint this runt
bloody scum, dancing on boards
to fill its gut?'

Paunch-scratching, spewed
forth filth-abuse
I went on standing mute
rooted still within my boots.

Wonder now, why did I stand
hand't eaten no fodder
at his father's hand.

Pralhad Chendwankar, *Audit* (Bombay: Abhinav Prakashan, 1976; translation by Guari Deshpande and Eleanor Zelliot)

A Patil is a village official, invariably a major local landowner from one of the higher castes. Chendwankar is an Untouchable poet from the western state of Maharsahtra, and like other Dalit writers has used his art to describe and protest the experiences of the average Dalit.

Below the ranks of marginal farmers and agricultural labourers are India's debt-bonded workers. Debt bondage is illegal, but it is also a reality for many, including a disproportionate number of Untouchable families. A 1978 national survey by the Gandhi Peace Foundation estimated 2,600,000 debt-bonded labourers in agriculture alone, of whom 62 per cent were Untouchables and another 25 per cent tribals. In the following short excerpts from his book, Dr N. D. Kamble, who is from a Dalit family, describes his recent study of bonded labour in a district of south-central India. Anger, and horror at the ability of some to destroy the independent spirit of others, blend with scientific research and an argument for land nationalization as a long-term solution.

Bonded Labour in India

Dr N. D. Kamble

Preface

After the introduction of the concept of ownership, exploitation of man by man started. The property relationship was such that one who owned it dominated one who did not, and in the process the latter was made a slave by the first. The present bonded labour system is the same slave system which existed for centuries together in India. It is not only the culmination of the debtor-creditor relation into a slave and master relation, it is also an outcome of the unequal social-economic system prevailing in India. The system provided a built-in mechanism for continuation of exploitation of the under-privileged sections by the privileged sections of the society. The caste system functioned as a transmission belt to pass on such slavery from one generation to another.

The system was glorified by giving it the religious colours of Karma theory and Varnashrama Dharma. The seat of power and the legal system also perpetuated the evil of this system. Consequently, it continued without interruption, in one form or the other. For the first time in India, the British restricted the slave system by passing the Bengal Regulations Act in 1806, but allowed forced labour by Act VI of 1825. Unfortunately, section 6 of the Madras Compulsory Labour Act 1858 even legalized forced labour. However, the Indian Penal Code 1862 banned the bonded labour system and made it a punishable offence. Many state governments passed laws banning the bonded labour system like Kamia Agreement Act, 1920, of Bihar; Money Lender Act, 1938, of Bihar; Debt Bondage Abolition Regulation Act, 1940, of Orissa and Madras; Bombay Money Lenders Act, 1946; Article 23 of the Constitution of India made bonded labour a punishable offence. Rajasthan Agricultural Relief Act, 1954, and Sargari Abolition Act, 1961; Lacadives, Minicoy and Amindivi Islands Revenue and Tenancy Regulation Act, 1965; Bonded Labour Abolition Act of Kerala, 1972; Scheduled Castes/Tribes and Denotified Tribes Debt Relief Ordinance of Uttar Pradesh, 1974, were some of the important acts passed in response to the constitutional provisions against bonded labour. Yet this evil practice continued. Hence, the President of India promulgated the Bonded Labour System (Abolition) Ordinance, 1975, in order to wipe out the evil of the bonded labour system.

In response to this ordinance, bonded labourers were released for a short while, but due to lack of alternative sources of living many of them again became bonded labour. Nearly 3 per cent of the households, mostly from landless households and from lower castes, were bonded labourers. By and large, bonded labourers stay in the farms or in the places desired by their masters. They are confined to one place; consequently they are cut off from the changing outside world. Many of them did know about the ban on the bonded labour system and yet could not take advantage of it due to fear of their master and lack of alternative sources of living.

Bonded labourers are paid nominal wages. Moreover their family members cannot take remunerative jobs elsewhere without prior permission of their masters, who normally would not grant permission as they get free work even from them. Thus their poverty aggravates and forces them to borrow from their masters at exorbitant rates of interest. Normally all contracts between master and bonded labour are oral, and even in written agreements most of the masters take undue advantage of the illiteracy of the bonded labourers and enter excess amounts in the agreements. Consequently, a bonded labourer cannot clear off his debt during his lifetime and he is forced to renew his bondage throughout his lifetime. After his death the bondage is passed on to his children. This is why even children below ten years of age are working as bonded labourers. Children are made to believe that accepting liability of bondage of their father is a sacred duty. Thus the bondage is passed on generation to generation. Bonded labourers can be mortgaged, purchased or exchanged by their masters.

The remedy lies in providing minimum productive assets to the bonded labourer before he is released. To stop ugly practices like this all productive assets should be owned and operated by the society and not by an individual or a group of individuals.

Survey Methods
To know the household and economic conditions of the bonded labourers and the mechanism of the operations of the system, as currently practised, a survey was conducted.

Selection of the survey villages: Tunkur district in Karnataka state was selected for the present study. According to the Census of India, 1971, there are 2,725 villages spread over 10 talukas of Tunkur district. Out of 2,725 villages, 2,454 villages are inhabited. Out of these inhabited villages, 20 villages, constituting 0.75 per cent of the total villages, were surveyed, as listed in Table 3.1. These villages were randomly selected from all talukas in proportion to their number in each taluka. After selecting at random these 20 villages, each village was visited to identify the number of bonded labour households in them.

Selection of households: After visiting the selected 20 villages it was found that . . . 10 villages reported having 36 bonded labour households. All these bonded labour households are taken for the present study.

Methodology: Besides personal interviews with each bonded labourer, a structural questionnaire was also introduced to elicit information from the bonded labour households. However, more emphasis was laid on the personal

Table 3.1
Selected Villages

Takula	Sl. No.	Villages	Village Code No.	No. of Households No. of Bonded Labourers	No. of Masters
Tumkur	1	Doddagolla Halli	04	1	1
	2	Kuruvelu	07	4	3
	3	Doddanaravangala[a]	031	–	–
Tiptur[a]	4	Nonavinakere[a]	118	–	–
	5	Kadushettyhalli[a]	120	–	–
Kunigal	6	Vanigerakaval[a]	219	–	–
	7	Hulivana	225	1	1
Pavagada	8	Devalakere	301	5	5
Chickanaya-kanahalli	9	Navile[a]	403	–	–
	10	Tarabenahalli[a]	409	–	–
Turuvekere	11	Kallanagattihalli[a]	502	–	–
	12	Kodihalli[a]	514	–	–
Gubbi	13	Herur	623	2	2
	14	Kunaghatta	629	7	5
Sira	15	Devarahalli[a]	702	–	–
	16	Ranganahalli	709	2	2
Madhugiri	17	Thondoti	801	1	1
	18	Dodderi	824	17	16
Korategere[a]	19	Bhaktarahalli[a]	911	–	–
	20	Kambadahalli	909	–	–
Total	*20*			*40*	*36*

[a] No bonded labour households.

interviews than the structural questionnaire because of the delicate nature of the problems and the involvement of the bonded labourer in supplying information which might be disliked by his master and therefore might put him in a serious situation. Since the study was sensitive to the socio-economic structure of villages, sufficient care was taken to see that the bonded labourers were not harassed on account of their giving information. As far as possible the interviews were taken when their masters or the family members of the masters were away.

The survey found forty bonded labourers from thirty-six households belonging to the Scheduled Castes (Untouchables); Artisan, Lingayat and Vokkaliga castes; and the Muslim community. Of the bonded labour households, 50 per cent were Untouchable families, although Untouchables are only 13 per cent of the population in the state in which the study was conducted.

Master-Slave Relationship

Master's Occupation: It will be interesting to know something about the occupation of the masters of the bonded labourers. It was generally expected that the money-lenders-cum-landlords who could not cultivate their lands themselves would trap poor landless agricultural labourers or marginal farmers and make them bonded labourers, for working on their agricultural lands. However, it is not only the landlords, but even businessmen and men in services who keep bonded labourers. According to Table 3.2, 14 per cent of the bonded labourers' masters were businessmen and the remaining 86 per cent were landlords. Businessmen while they are in business cannot cultivate their lands so they prefer bonded labourers to free agricultural labourers.

The impact of tenancy reforms was marginal, as most of the landlords distributed their lands among their family members, relatives and even to fake members, so as to escape from land reforms. There were some cases in Bihar where lands were recorded even under the names of animals; such dodging of the government was possible because of their collusion with government officials.

We also found such fake transfers in the sample villages. However, we found that on records for official purposes the lands were distributed among the members of the landlords' family and their relations, though all the documents as well as lands were retained by the landlords. Thus in reality the lands are owned by the landlords themselves. Such landlords got hold of the cheapest labour, like bonded labour, and cultivated their lands.

Social and economic status has a very high correlation with political position in rural as well as urban areas. For example Table 3.2 shows that out of the total number of masters, five masters (constituting 12 per cent) were chairmen of the village Panchayats, and seven masters (constituting 18 per cent) were members of the village Panchayats. Thus political power and

Table 3.2
Particulars of Masters

Bonded Labour's Status	Master's Caste				Master's Occupation			Master's Official Panchayat[a] Position		
	Ling-ayat	Vok-ka-liga	Mus-lims	Total	Agri-cul-ture	Busi-ness	Total	Chair-man	Mem-ber	Total
Former	–	10	–	10	9	1	10	3	2	5
Current	6	22	2	30	26	4	30	2	5	7
Total	6	32	2	40	35	5	40	5	7	12

[a] The Panchayat is now the officially recognized unit of local government.

economic power are going hand in hand. In such a situation how can a bonded labourer go against the master or think of coming out of the clutches of bondage? Politicians are boasting that they have released bonded labourers and some of them say that the landlords are not responding to them. In reality, in such situations both landlords and politicians are one and the same. How is it possible to introduce change against the landlords who are also politicians? The tragedy of execution of such reformative laws lies in the dual personality of the law-makers. When *executors* of the laws are also *victims* of the laws, then it is not surprising if they do not execute such laws. Thus the makers of laws, executors of laws, and the persons against whom laws are made, by and large are the same people. Hence, such laws normally become only decorative pieces of the legislatures.

Caste of Bonded Labourer and His Master: The caste factor in India plays an important role in determining intercaste relations, so also in determining the relationship between the bonded labourer and his master. If a bonded labourer belongs to his master's caste, he is likely to get relatively less harsh treatment than a bonded labourer belonging to a caste lower than that of his master. It is normally found that a bonded labourer belongs to a caste lower than that of his master, and at times to the same caste as the master. But there was not even a single incidence where a bonded labourer belonged to a higher caste than his master.

Payments to Bonded Labour: The bonded labour system, as known today, has been aggravated by poverty and inequality. Most of the poor and under-privileged people are made bonded labourers of one type of the other, in one place or the other. For many centuries such evil practices in India were systematized and legalized for the benefit of a few privileged and rich people. Since political and economic powers were concentrated in a few hands of socially privileged sections they managed to create, pass and execute certain laws protecting their own interests but detrimental to the interests of the under-privileged masses. Even religion came to their rescue in providing myths for strengthening the system. Even non-payments of wages or remuneration were supported by the socio-religious laws rather than condemned by them: for example, nothing belonged to the Sudras [labouring castes], and if anything

Table 3.3
Payment of Wages to the Bonded Labourer

Bonded Labour's Status	Payment time			Monthly Wages (Rs.)						Goods		
	Mon-thly	Year-ly	Total	50-100	100-200	200-300	300-500	500 & above	Total	Grain	Cloth	Total
Former	7	1	8[a]	—	3	—	4	1	8	—	6	6
Current	21	9	30	5	10	8	7	—	30	1	20	21
Total	21	10	38	5	13	8	11	1	38	1	26	27

[a] Two persons worked for food only.

was possessed by them it could be calmly taken away by the privileged higher castes without any fear (*Manu Smriti*, Chapter VIII, Verse 417). Such laws were continued in different forms with modifications according to the necessity of changing circumstances.

In the present study nearly one-fourth of the bonded labourers are paid once a month, but not in cash. Some of them are paid in grain or clothes, but charged according to the will of the master. Many times, in the agreement, the bonded labourer is given for every year, one pair of clothes, sometimes a pair of shoes and food grains to sustain him, but these were always inadequate to support his family. Nearly 97 per cent of the bonded labourers were paid below Rs. 500 per annum while one-seventh of them were paid only Rs. 50 to Rs. 100 per annum, which comes to only 28 paise per day, which is not sufficient even to have a cup of tea in a hotel. Such a nominal wage is nothing but total exploitation of the bonded labourers. Some were not paid at all. Is it possible to remain at least alive at such a low wage level? In such conditions how can a weak bonded labourer revolt against such a tyrannical system? For raising one's voice against any tyranny, minimum strength is required; that too is absent. If this is so, how can a bonded labourer dream of freedom? Only out and out help from outside, for his complete liberation, will help, rather than passing half-hearted laws and making legal provisions practically beyond their reach. Moreover, the judicial system is costly, and it can be misused by money and other powers. The poor bonded labourer cannot afford to hire a pleader to defend himself. It is unlikely that even the guilty will be punished with the help of a good pleader, but of course such so-called good pleaders charge exhorbitant fees. Only the rich can afford to pay it. Hence the poor have to submit meekly like animals to the tortures of the exploitative socio-economic system.

Table 3.3 further shows that most of the bonded labourers who are still working get coarse clothes from their masters which do not last even for a few months; as a consequence they have to forego even clothes for the rest of the year. Since food grains are not given to all of them they have to buy food grains from outside or force their family members to work elsewhere for food grains. As a result most of them work only for food grains or only for food. Such acute poverty leading to exploitation and oppression is a blot on a democratic society. It needs to be wiped out early, not by hypocritical slogans of *'Garibi Hatao'* (remove poverty), but by taking positive steps.

It is in the interest of the country to relieve them of bondage and poverty. They are underfed; hence, their working capacities are low, they are exposed to diseases, and their life is short. Their poverty prohibits them from taking treatment, and contagious diseases spread in society. Landlords/masters of bonded labourers bother about extracting work around the clock from bonded labourers, and not about their living conditions. It is striking to note that two bonded labourers were working only for food and nothing else. It is like feeding a bullock for extracting work. In such a situation what can a bonded labourer give to his family? It is no wonder if his family is also exploited and oppressed by the cruel elements in society. This type of exploitation of human labour is not different from slavery. The bonded labourers are treated like cattle; hence, this system should be condemned by all means.

Out of forty bonded labourers from thirty-six households, thirty bonded labourers are still working; ten were released in response to the President's Ordinance, but because of the absence of alternative occupations, they again preferred to be bonded labourers. Neither the bonded labourers themselves nor their masters reveal the fact of their being bonded, because neither did the bonded labourers want to face the risk of unemployment and starvation nor did the masters want to lose their bonded cheap labourers. Thus the system of bonded labour, in spite of its legal abolition, is continuing. In the absence of subsistence, bonded labourers cannot but remain bonded labourers. There is no point in releasing bonded labourers and throwing them on the roads without subsistence or an alternative source of living. Many of them did not like being bonded labourers, but cannot help being so because of the lack of an alternative source of livelihood. Many of them prefer to be half fed and over-exploited rather than be free without any source of living.

Years of Bonded Labour: All the bonded labourers under study were under bondage for more than two years. In fact, one Scheduled Caste and one Vokkaliga bonded labourer were bonded for more than ten years, which reflects their exploitation for a long period by the landlords. Out of forty bonded labourers, sixteen were bonded for two to four years, eleven were bonded for four to six years, seven were bonded for six to eight years, four were bonded for eight to ten years and two were bonded for more than ten years. The contract of a bonded labourer can be broken by repayment of the entire debt by the bonded labourer after borrowing from another landlord. This means while getting rid of one landlord, the bonded labourer becomes bonded to another landlord. Thus the bondage continues in the same manner except with a change of master. The borrowed money could hardly be repaid, resulting in their perpetual bondage.

Place of Residence: Since the master of the bonded labourer wants to extract work round the clock, he keeps him in a place from which his services would be easily extracted. For this reason practically all bonded labourers were residing either in their master's houses or on their farms. Generally, the bonded labourers are required to reside on their master's farms by constructing themselves thatched huts. A large number of the bonded labourers, particularly those belonging to Scheduled Castes, were residing on the landlords' farms. Such physical location of huts of the bonded labourers on the landlords' premises enables the landlords to command services from bonded labourers and their family members at any time, mostly without payment. Thus the exploitation of bonded labour is not confined to the labourer himself, but it also covers both old and young, men and women members of his family. Often, family members of the bonded labourer feel obliged to work for the landlord even without his command. Their residence on the farm helps to protect the farm produce from being stolen or grazed by cattle or destroyed by mischievous social elements. The benefits derived by the landlords from the bonded labourer and his family members are many. Bonded labourers are not only labourers on the farm of the landlords, but they also work in the houses of the landlord and elsewhere at the command of landlords.

On the basis of observations made earlier, it may be stated that the bonded labour system very definitely exists, in spite of passing laws against it, because of collusion between the masters of bonded labourers and executive machinery which seems to be sympathetic towards the masters. The social system is such that the masters are also socially privileged high-caste men who have economic power and access to political power. Loopholes in the law help the masters rather than the serfs. The bonded labourers are so weak that they cannot take advantage of legal provisions. Moreover, they do not have alternative sources of living even if they are released from bondage, so they are compelled to continue as bonded labourers.

The hammering of bondage since childhood on the bonded labourer kills his imagination and aspiration for freedom. Even if he is released from bondage he may not appreciate the value of freedom; on the contrary, he may prefer bondage to a free climate because of his acclimatization. Surprisingly, bondage is sometimes treated as an ornament by some of them. Some of them take pride in the richness and power of their masters. While talking, many of them refer to their landlords as 'My master' and 'My owner' and 'My sir', etc. Even their children and wives use similar honorific words for their landlords. Thus even while talking in normal conversation, they consciously or unconsciously accept slavery and help to strengthen the system instead of challenging it. Even if someone talks about freedom from bondage, bonded labourers themselves do not appreciate it and some of them feel it an insult to their masters and treachery on their part. One who tries to convince them to get rid of the bondage is disliked by some bonded labourers. Nevertheless, some of them feel like getting rid of the bonded labour system, but they have to accept it because of their helplessness. Day-to-day living in a village becomes practically impossible for them if they leave their masters, because the masters are economically powerful and socially belong to higher castes, so they can declare a total boycott of bonded labour families. In some villages, bonded labourers sided with their masters to please them, even against their bonded labour fellows who were released.

This was precisely because they have to remain in the villages. Otherwise their fate would be like those released bonded labourers who were compelled to leave their native places and go elsewhere for work. One family which left the village and went to Hospet City for work in an iron ore company feels happier in spite of its being uprooted from the village. It is because the family members get better treatment and much higher wages than they were getting in their native village. However, the family being away from relations at times feels sorry because of absent kith and kin. Particularly females and old people feel very badly about leaving the places of their ancestors where kith and kin resided for generations, while youths feel happy after leaving the bondage and village. From this point of view, the younger generation

Home of a New Delhi sweeper, Ram Pyari, with her son in foreground and the home of one of her employers in the background. (B. Joshi)

seems to be more awakened than the older one.

* * * *

Flight to the cities has indeed become a common alternative to social and economic oppression in the small world of India's villages. Untouchables are not alone in this voluntary 'diaspora', but a recent survey of 'jhuggi/ jhompri' *(shanty) dwellers in the capital city of Delhi showed 65 per cent were Untouchables (Majumdar, 1983). The following commentary and exhortation appeared as an editorial in* Dalit Voice *(1–15 April 1983), a fortnightly newspaper that is published in Bangalore, a city in south-central India. Articles and letters to the editor come from Untouchables and other minorities who write from points as distant as Calcutta; Birmingham, England; and Three Rivers, Texas.*

Bombay: Whose Grandfather's Property?

J. R. D. Tata's speech in reply to a special reception accorded by the Mayor of Bombay has received very wide publicity for two reasons. He once represented India's richest business house, now occupying the number 2 position after the Birlas overtook the Tatas. Secondly, he gave expression to something that is very much worrying India's entire ruling class: that the bigger Indian cities are exploding with over-population because of the exodus of the poor and destitute from the countryside, and life in the metropolis is becoming unbearable to the rich and leisured class. Hence the flow into Bombay, Calcutta, Delhi, Madras and Bangalore must be stopped. If possible the urban slum and pavement dwellers, beggars, etc., must be forcibly evicted and bundled out mercilessly.

JRD might not have spoken these very words but he meant exactly this when he said 'the Government's failure to tackle the problems of Bombay was not due to inefficiency or ignorance but a misconceived populist posture and partly no doubt to safeguard votes from the masses'. Bombay, which he described as his much-loved home, had become a victim of unending influx from the rural areas. 'As the millions who poured into Bombay in the last 30 years came in a legitimate search of employment and a better life for themselves and their families than rural India could give them, our politicians claimed that no democratic Government could prevent them from coming into the city' (*Times of India*, 12 March). He said the influx perhaps could have been reduced if from the beginning the people had discovered that they would not be allowed to occupy and build hutments on any open ground with impunity. The bulk of the Bombay slum dwellers had well paid jobs. He felt sorry that in the distorted interpretation of social justice, they were allowed to enjoy all these benefits virtually free. It is deplorable to find that this misconceived idea now finds sympathy even among our judges.' Tata demanded a control on the population of Bombay or else it 'will become the greatest collection of slums by the turn of the century'. Tata only asked the government to pack up the poor, but Antulay, then Chief Minister of Maharashtra, actually hounded them out and was stopped only by a sane judge of the Bombay High Court in a rare gesture towards the poor. This is what Tata meant when he criticized 'the distorted interpretation of social justice finding sympathy even among judges'. When the courts side with the poor, the ruling class never likes it.

Since Tata has raised a very important issue of checking the city population which affects Dalits, OBCs [low-ranked but non-Untouchable castes] and minorities, we want to deal with it here. Tata is echoing what India's ruling class sincerely feels. We respect Tata and acknowledge his contribution to India. But this is a disastrous policy for Dalits. The government may any time re-enact Antulay. Already under different names such as city beautification, slum clearance, urban development, etc. the different governments are virtually driving the poor beyond the city limits. The urban rich often complain that the poor are creating all sorts of problems by occupying gardens, playgrounds, any open space, and dirtying the area. This is true. All of Calcutta is fast turning into one vast slum. Bombay is following. If Calcutta is already a dead city, Bombay is dying.

Why this exodus from the villages? In Trombay (suburb of Bombay), we visited a vast slum (Cheetah Camp) exclusively of Tamil Dalits and Muslims from Tamil Nadu's southern-most district. In Dharavi, considered Asia's largest slum, it is again the Dalits and Muslims who live cheek to jowl. Why are these two large persecuted minorities of India becoming urban slum-dwellers? As more and more people of India are slipping below the poverty line, these two communities, the poorest of the destitute, will naturally be the first to be affected when pauperization grows. Muslims have already become an urban community. But does Tata know why Dalits are making a beeline for the cities? Being mostly landless agricultural labourers, they find it impossible to live in villages. Not only are more and more Dalits losing their lands and becoming farm workers, the rapid rural decay is making it difficult for them even to get jobs as landless labourers. That means starvation. In many villages, aggressive landlords are boycotting local farm hands and bringing labour from outside as a punishment. On one side starvation, but more than that their very life, their little property and the honour of their women are in danger. It is no longer possible for the poverty-stricken, unarmed Untouchables to live in villages. Hundreds of Dalits who fled to Bombay during the 'Marathwada Caste War' [a series of anti-Untouchable riots in 1977] have not yet returned even after so many years. There are one hundred and one reasons why the Dalits prefer the city.

It may be an animal existence, miserable in the congested, dirty slums, but in the villages even the very existence of the Dalits is threatened. Dalits and Muslims have realized this and hence for the past three decades they have migrated to the cities. As insecurity and pauperization increase in the countryside, this trickle will turn into a flood. And it is a healthy sign. No power on earth can stop this natural process. Not even one hundred Tatas. We have long been advocating the shifting of Dalit population to bigger cities. We call upon Dalit organizations and leaders to take up this work seriously and make it an organized mass migration, come what may. Every Dalit employed in cities must try to shift his entire family if not the entire Dalit population of his village to the city. Always prefer bigger cities, not small ones. Since Dalits are in a minority in every village, with minor exceptions, their very existence is threatened. How can they think of organizing themselves under such circumstances? Therefore if the widely-scattered Dalits are brought together in cities, it becomes easier to educate, agitate and organize. Number is strength. Dr Ambedkar [an Untouchable leader] had spoken about India's stinking 'village republics' — the cesspool of caste politics. Where [high-caste] Hindus are in brute majority, Dalits have no salvation. Therefore he demanded the organized shifting of Dalits to bigger cities. Transfer of Dalit population from the jaws of Hindu hounds should be undertaken in a very big way. The ruling class will put forward one hundred and one obstacles. We must fight it out. Who is Tata to say that the poor should be thrown out of Bombay? Why is he silent about the villages turning into war camps, the landed gentry becoming warlords? It is to escape from them that Phoolan Devi, a Dalit girl, rightly turned into a dacoit [robber]. We want more such Phoolan Devis.

The bluff of land reform and distribution of surplus lands to the landless has been called. Nobody talks about it today. Not even the Marxist governments of Bengal and Tipura. When there is no attraction for the Dalits to stay on in villages, what right has Tata to say the poor have no right to enter Bombay? Does he mean to say that the cities must be reserved as the pleasure house of the parasites? He must know that the urban boom is the result of rural decay for which the ruling class is directly responsible. In the name of slum clearance, city beautification, urban ecology, etc., the ruling class is only trying to throw out the poor to make way for the rich. We know this. The ruling class has no plan to cure the disease, the poverty of India. On the other hand, it is foolish enough to mistake the symptom for the disease (or it is just to fool us?) and spend all its time and energy curing the symptom of this creeping paralysis. The urban slums are boils on the body of the dying, decaying society of India. But the ruling class wants to cure the boil, its symptom, not the disease. We shall not allow this nonsense. We are as much part of this country as any of the elite. It is we who shall decide, not Tata. We shall resist this nonsense with all our might. We have any number of tree-lovers, animal-lovers, cow-lovers, nature-lovers. But alas, no human-lovers in India. Whose grandfather's property is Bombay, to say that the poor should be thrown out?

* * * *

Where mobility has come for Untouchables, it is largely through special access programmes to scholarships, scarce seats in higher education, and employment in public sector industry and civil service. (No significant anti-discrimination policies apply in the private sector.) These programmes have been some antidote to the pervasive effects of limited family backgrounds and to prejudice that blocks Untouchables who do have skills to compete as equals. An antidote — but a limited one. The number of jobs in the organized sector is limited, and Untouchable access is still greatest at the level of menial and semi-skilled jobs. In 1980, official figures showed Scheduled Caste representation in central government public industries as follows: Class A jobs, 2.9 per cent; Class B, 5.1 per cent; Class C, 18.0 per cent; Class D (exclusive of sweepers), 22.4 per cent. Representation in central government ministries/departments at corresponding job levels was 4.9 per cent, 8.5 per cent, 13.4 per cent and 19.4 per cent. (Indians officially classified as Scheduled Castes are 15 per cent of the population.)

In spite of continuing limitations in the search for more-than-menial jobs, the appearance of a few Untouchables so outrageously out of place as to compete for skilled jobs or higher education has triggered increasingly violent resistance, including months of riots in several states in 1985. The pattern was set during three months of riots in Gujarat in 1981, which began with hostility to Untouchable medical students and then engulfed private sector factory workers (not covered by the special reservation policies) and Untouchable villagers. Subsequent studies showed that Scheduled Caste and Tribe students together held only 507 (11 per cent) of a total of 4,500 medical school seats at the time of the riots, though they constitute 21 per cent of the state's population (Desai, 1981). Throughout the state, there was a close correlation between the incidence of violent attacks and Untouchable mobility through any channel, including rural co-operatives or small businesses (Bose, 1981).

Some observers have pointed out that one significant development during the riots was Dalit mobilization of effective resistance in some urban areas. However, a representative of the People's Union for Civil Liberties has reported that as of late 1983 no legal action had been taken against those accused of the murder of Untouchables during the riots (Yagnik and Bhatt, 1984).

The following description of the riots and Untouchable losses was made available to the editor a few months after the riots by an Untouchable elected official, and was used by Dr Laxmi Berwa, an Untouchable human rights activist, in testimony to the United Nations in 1982 on behalf of a coalition of Untouchable organizations from India and Western countries. The data have been cross checked with reports of both the People's Union for Civil Liberties, a national association with a predominantly higher status Indian membership, and the Bharatiya Depressed Classes League, a national Untouchable organization. The human details of the attacks form a protest poetry of their own.

Caste War in Gujarat: A Report from the Field

The caste war in Gujarat started as a result of agitation by medical students of B. J. Medical College (Ahmedabad) for removal of 'carry forward system' of unfilled seats reserved for Scheduled Castes and Scheduled Tribes students. Later on they extended their demand to total abolition of reservation system from education and services too. In 1978 the government had implemented a 'roster system' in postgraduate courses which includes carry forward and inter-changeability of SC [Scheduled Caste, i.e. Untouchable] and ST [Scheduled Tribe] seats.

The agitation started from B. J. Medical College on 4 January 1981. On 5 January 1981 the agitating students resorted to stoning, damaged college furniture and raised slogans to abolish the reservation system for SC and ST. On 12 January, these students hijacked four Ahmedabad Municipal Transport Service buses and also resorted to stoning the students of Dental College, who were not in support of their agitation. On 22 January 1981, three government vehicles, including two jeeps of the Public Health Department, were set on fire by the agitating students in B. J. Medical College campus. On 22 January 1981, the agitating caste Hindu students tried to prevent the non-clinical students from entering the college. On 24 January 1981, the SC and ST students were beaten by the agitating students while they were going to attend a conference at B. J. Medical College. On 26 January 1981, the caste Hindu agitating students addressed a caste Hindu meeting in 'Asarwa Chakla' and thereafter attacked the Harijan [Untouchable] Chawl [tenement building], Aryoday Mill Chawl, with burning missiles and lethal weapons.

On 28 January 1981 the government of Gujarat closed State Medical Colleges. Agitating students went to the High Court of Gujarat but their petition was rejected. The Division Bench of the High Court, comprised of Judges Justice M. P. Thakkar and Justice R. C. Anand, held a bench on holiday and appealed to agitators as follows: 'We appeal to the medicos to withdraw their agitation against reservation which could result in disintegration of the country. Doctors have to heal the wounds of the society and not to cause them.'

On 5 February 1981, the agitating caste Hindu miscreants attempted to topple the statue of Dr B. R. Ambedkar [the late Untouchable leader] at Sarangpur Darwaja (near Ahmedabad Railway Station) and the statue's spectacles were knocked down. Thereafter riots followed on a large scale.

Many riot-hurt areas, listed below, have a high density of 'Dalits' (SCs): Rajpur, Gomtipur, Omnagar, Chamanpura, Meghaninagar, Girdhar Nagar, Pritampura, Baliya, Limbi, Asarwa-Hasipura, Nirmalpura Chawl, Fulchand Chawl in Saraspur, Naroda and Behrampura, Majoor Gaon, Gitamandir Road, Ramapir Tekra, Vaday, Ranip, Rupa Pari of Dariyapur and Patni Sheri.

Attacks on Dalits were from five Ps: Pocket, Public (mostly the Patel community, a high caste), Press, Police and Politicians. All these Ps were in the hands of the Patel community, who are the landlords in all areas of Gujarat state.

The press, instead of giving the correct situation, twisted the matter in police reports and published the news 'Harijan mobs attack on caste Hindus'; 'Police were forced to open fire and burst tear gas shells to disperse attacking mob of Harijans', etc.

Incited by this 'news', caste Hindus attacked and murdered Harijans, and threw stones on Harijans. Police too rushed to Harijan streets and chawls and severely beat the Harijans.

In Girdharnagar-Pritampura, police opened fire. In Girdharnagar-Parsini Chawl, police rushed into the chawl, dragged the Harijans and beat them severely with lathis. In Meghani Nagar, the Harijans were beaten by caste Hindus. In Bhimraonagar, the police opened fire — one dead. In Ganpatnagar, police beat innocent Harijans. The Tirupati Society of Harijans in Ranip was attacked by caste Hindu Patels and burnt. In Rajpur-Gomtipur, police fired and created a scene of terror to crush Harijans. One young boy (SC) died. From Shivanand Nagar, Harijans fled their houses and their furniture was burnt by caste Hindus. Baherampura, Majjorgaon, police beat up Harijans of the chawls and resorted to firing — death of two Harijans. Police and caste Hindus entered Saraspur-Nirmalpura and beat Harijans. Five persons were stabbed to death on the road by caste Hindus in the presence of police. Saraspur-Fulchand chawl, Harijans fled the locality. One Harijan social worker was murdered with a knife by caste Hindus. Saraspur-Vankarvas — New Cloth Market was attacked by caste Hindus and Harijans were severely beaten. In Bharadia police beat up Harijans. Women and children were not spared.

The following is a list showing the incidents of atrocities on Harijans by caste Hindus during the agitation.

Statement showing the incidents of atrocities on Harijans [Untouchables] by caste Hindus during the agitation in Gujarat.

S.E.No.   INCIDENTS

Harijan Colonies (Bastis) burnt
1.	Jogeshwari Society, Asarwa, Ahmedabad	15 huts
2.	Tirupati Society, Rani, Ahmedabad	12 tenements
3.	Shivanandnagar, Amaraiwadi, Ahmedabad	25 houses
4.	Nadia Chawl, Asarwa, Ahmedabad	16 huts
5.	Siddharth Society, Kalol Dist., Mehsana	Almost whole of the society
6.	Detroj Village, Ta.[a] Viramgam, Dist.Ahmedabad	42 houses
7.	Uttersanda Village, Dist. Kaira	25 houses
8.	Pij Village, Ta. Nadiad, Dist. Kaira	16 houses
9.	Surat City, Dist. Surat	68 huts
10.	Mehsana, Dist. Mehsana	MP's factory office
11.	Nadiad City, Dist. Kaira	4 houses
12.	Badarkha Ta., Dholka, Dist. Ahmedabad	13 houses
13.	Viramgam City, Dist. Ahmedabad	2 shops
14.	Ranip (Sabarmati)	13 huts
15.	Trania	Harijans fired on
16.	Vehelal	Harijans fired on and stones thrown on them
17.	Torna	Houses

[[a] 'Ta.' refers to Tahasil; 'Dist.' to District. Both are local administrative units.]

Harijan Colonies Looted and Robbed
1. Sangam Society, Meghaninagar, Ahmedabad
2. Fulchand Chawl, Saraspur, Ahmedabad
3. Rupapari, Dariapur, Ahmedabad
4. Bharadia Vas, Khanpur, Ahmedabad
5. Shahpur, Vankar Vas, Ahmedabad
6. Jogeshwari Society, Asarwa, Ahmedabad
7. Medawali Chawl, Shahibaug, Ahmedabad
8. Manjushri Mills Chawl, Girdharnagar, Ahmedabad
9. Kadiawali Chawl, Balia Limbdi, Ahmedabad
10. Pritampura Society, Shahibaug, Ahmedabad
11. Kadjodra Village, Ta. Dehgam, Dist. Sabarkantha
12. Sanoda, Ta. Dehgam, Dist. Sabarkantha
13. Kalol City, various societies and shops
14. Modasa City, District Sabarkantha
15. Baroda City, Baroda, various residential areas
16. Dehgam Parixit Society, Dist. Ahmedabad
17. Detroj Village, Ta. Viramgam, Dist. Ahmedabad
18. Umreth Dottas and subbed Harijans
19. Jadar: looted, set fire. Migrated to Jujal village.

List of Incidents of Atrocities on Harijans
Migrated (Hijrat) to camps of Harijans due to atrocities as detailed above.
1. Fulchand Chawl, Ahmedabad. 200 Harijans migrated. Jagjivanram Society, Saraspur, Ahmedabad.
2. Sanoda village Harijans migrated to Chamunda Chawl, Ahmedabad.

3. Shivanand Society and surrounding Harijans migrated to Rajpur, Gomtipur, Ahmedabad. 700 persons.
4. Nadia huts, Asarwa, Ahmedabad. Migrated to their various relatives at various places.
5. Detroj Village Harijans migrated to Kunkvai Village Camp. 600 persons.
6. Tirupatti Society, Harijans migrated to Majurgao and to other places. 105 persons.
7. Surat City, Surat. 60 families of Harijans were shifted elsewhere because their huts were burnt.
8. Jadjoom Village, Ta. Dehgam. 100 persons were shifted to their relatives.
9. Siddharth Society, Kalol. Families of this society were shifted.
10. Uttarsanda Village, Dist. Kaira. Houses are burnt and families moved elsewhere.
11. Pij Village, Ta. Nadiad. Families are moved elsewhere in Dist. Kaira.
12. Ranip. 23 huts of Harijans shifted to Ahmedabad city.

Boycotts of Harijans
1. Gojaria, Dist. Mehsana
2. Jotana
3. Langhjoj
4. Unjha
5. Chanasma
6. Ladol
7. Kathalal, Dist. Kaira
8. Biliya, Dist. Mehsana
9. Sojitra, Dist. Kaira
10. Jetalpur, Dist. Ahmedabad
11. Lali, Dist. Ahmedabad

In these villages the Harijans are deprived of the right to work and social gathering.

Casualties and Injuries of Harijans
1. Stabbed to death: 6 persons, list attached herewith.
2. Injured (Medical cases in Shardaben and Civil Hospital only. Cases elsewhere in Ahmedabad city and Gujarat state — details not available.)

Persons Killed by Hindus and by Firing of Police
1. Amrutlal Kalidas Solanki, Rajpur, Ahmedabad   31-1-1981
2. Narsinhbhai Mafatlal Harijan, Bhimravnagar, Asarwa, Ahmedabad   6-2-1981
3. Amrutlal Ukabhai Harijan, Vijaynagar, near Ved Mandir, Ahmedabad   22-2-1981
4. Bhanjibhai Narsinhbhai Parmar, Gurjarnagar Co-op. Society, Saraspur, Ahmedabad   22-2-1981
5. Bechar Bhagvanbhai, Bharatnagar, Gitamandir, Ahmedabad   22-1-1981

Persons Killed by Caste Hindus
1. Somchandbhai Maganbhai Solanki, Nirmalpura Society, Saraspur, Ahmedabad   5-2-1981
2. Narsinhbhai Parshottambhai Parmar, 19, E.S.I.S. Quarters, Bapunagar, Ahmedabad   7-2-1981

3. Shankarbhai Narsinhbhai Leua. Vijaynagar, Kankaria Road
   Ahmedabad   22-2-1981
4. Baluram Sadhu, Khadawali Chawl, Rakhial, Ahmedabad   3-3-1981
5. Karsanbhai Amrabhai Harijan. Rajpur, Gomtipur,
   Parsottam Modi's Chawl, Ahmedabad   26-2-1981
6. Gobarbhai Kuberbhai Makwana. Thuleta, Ta. Virgamgam,
   Dist. Ahmedabad   5-2-1981
7. Lallubhai Limbabhai Parmer, police driver.
8. Vasantlal Parmer. Patan, Dist. Mehsana.

List of Injured Persons
1. Dhanjibhai Kalidas Harijan. Rajpur, Kundawali Chawl,
   Ahmedabad   28-1-1981
2. Govindbhai Narsinhbhai Harijan. Amaraiwadi slum
   quarters.   29-1-1981
3. Tribhovan Govindbhai Makwana, Khadawali Chawl,
   Rakhial, Ahmedabad   30-1-1981
4. Babubhai Motibhai Chavda, Topi Mill Musa's Chawl   31-1-1981
5. Manuhbhai Devjibhai Nadia, Rajpur Jethabhai's Chawl,
   by police   31-1-1981
6. Somchandbhai Becharbhai. Rajpur, Khadawali Chawl,
   by police   31-1-1981
7. Chhaganbhai Govindbhai Parmar, Rakhial Khadawali
   Chawl, by tear gas   31-1-1981
8. Shashikant Manilal Mekwana. Rajpur Ghanchi's Chawl,
   by police firing   31-1-1981
9. Premjibhai Ganeshbhai Chamar. Jhulta Minara,
   Gomtipur   31-1-1981
10. Hargovindbhai Ishwarbhai Vankar. Ashoknagar Co-op.
    Society, Ahmedabad   31-1-1981
11. Jethabhai Nagarbhai Harijan. 625, Nava Bapunagar,
    Ahmedabad   31-1-1981
12. Bhagwanbhai Narandas Parmer. Rajpur, Kundawali
    Chawl, Ahmedabad   31-1-1981
13. Bhanubhai Sendhabhai Harijan. Rajpur, Kundawali
    Chawl   1-2-1981
14. Maganbhai Mithabhai Parmar, Kisanlal's Chawl,
    Rajpur, by acid   1-2-1981
15. Dhanjibhai Aljibhai Gehel. Sabarmati Municipal Driver 2-2-1981

*This portion of the report continues through 112 separate incidents of
injury in the urban Ahmedabad area, and concludes with a note that data
from other regions had not yet been compiled.*

3. The Enemy Within

One Day I Cursed That Mother-Fucker God

Keshav Meshram, in *Vidrohi Kavita* (Poetry of Protest) (Pune: Continental Prakashan, 1978; trans. Jayant Karve and Eleanor Zelliot with Pam Espeland).

One day I cursed that mother-fucker God.
He just laughed shamelessly.
My neighbour — a born-to-pen Brahman — was shocked.
He looked at me with his castor-oil face and said,
'How can you say such things to the
Source of the Indescribable,
Qualityless, Formless Juggernaut?
Shame on you for trying to catch his dharma-hood
in a noose of words.'

I cursed another good hot curse.
The university buildings shuddered and sank waist-deep.
All at once, scholars began doing research
into what makes people angry.
They sat in their big rooms fragrant with incense,
their bellies full of food,
and debated.
On my birthday, I cursed God.
I cursed him, I cursed him again.
Whipping him with words, I said
'Bastard!'
'Would you chop a whole cart full of wood
for a single piece of bread?
Would you wipe the sweat from your bony body
with your mother's ragged sari?
Would you wear out your brothers and sisters
for your father's pipe?
Would you work as a pimp
to keep him in booze?
Oh Father, Oh God the Father!
You could never do such things.
First you would need a mother —

one no one honours,
one who toils in the dirt
one who gives and gives of her love.'
One day I cursed that mother-fucking God.

Dalit poet reading to a Dalit gathering in Maharashtra. (E. Zelliot)

* * * *

Dalit activism currently extends from small groups organizing agricultural labourers to the fragile beginnings of independent journalism, but underlying all of these tactics is the conviction that the most important struggles are those within the minds of both the oppressed and their oppressors. There are significant differences within the movement, but not over the need to break free of high-caste psychological domination and rethink self and society. The result is direct and immediate Dalit confrontation with the world of the mind and the institutions that feed the mind — the traditional priesthood, its modern academic reincarnation, the glossy high-caste/high-class world of the popular media. Concurrent with efforts to mobilize against overt oppression and exploitation there have been efforts to repossess culture and self, to work out independent Dalit values and standards through independent cultural institutions.

Not surprisingly, literature and theatre − some of it highly sophisticated, some designed for direct mass communication − have played an important part. The following selections convey some part of the bitterness, frustration and hope that mark the Dalit cultural movement. The first is by the founder and editor of Asmitadarsh *('Mirror of Identity'), one of the earliest Dalit literary magazines. Dr Pantawane is also professor of Marathi at Marathwada University. The article was first presented to an international conference on racism and untouchability in New York City in 1983.*

Evolving a New Identity: The Development of a Dalit Culture

Dr Gangadhar Pantawane (1983)

The colossus of contradictions has existed in India for centuries − the Untouchables. They were named *Atishudras*, Broken men, *Antyaja, Antyevasin, Avarn*, Scheduled Castes, non-Hindus, Downtrodden, Protestant Hindus, *Harijans* − and now *Dalits*. Can there be such a thing as Dalit culture? The so-called superior people of India have never accepted the Dalits and Dalit culture. Instead they have always praised the traditional culture, that is, Hindu culture. Hindu culture and social organization was originally idealized as the way to promote the organic unity of society, but in practice the result was the supremacy of one class over the other, and a system of graded inequality that prevented the servile communities from rising. It is precisely this graded inequality and untouchability that have been the first and foremost sources of Dalit culture in India . . .

[After a description of the late 19th Century origins of Dalit value change, Dr Pantawane turns to the present.]

Today's Dalit literature is a literature of the depressed, oppressed and suppressed people of India, and as such it is one of the most significant developments in modern Indian literature. Still today it is asked, Who is Dalit, and what is Dalitness? Can there be a Dalit literature? A few years back the word 'Dalit' was not accepted even by some of the Dalit writers themselves. They preferred to use the term 'Protest Literature'. But now the term 'Dalit' is accepted with pride, and the concept of 'Dalit literature' is recognized in the university syllabus.

What is Dalit? To me, Dalit is not a caste. Dalit is a symbol of change and revolution. The Dalit believes in humanism. He rejects the existence of God, rebirth, soul, sacred books that teach discrimination, fate and heaven, because these have made him a slave. He represents the exploited men in his country. A very determined Hindu social system was developed to destroy him as a human being. Human dignity was insulted and he fell prey to unavoidable circumstances. His lifeless body had to face the agony of pain, but the burden of alienation has been the source of rebirth for thousands of people.

Dalitness is essentially a means towards achieving a sense of cultural identity. The inferiority complex based on 'to be Dalit' has now disappeared.

Now Dalitness is a source of confrontation. This change has its essence in the desire for justice for all mankind. In this sense, Dalitness is a matter of appreciating the potential of one's total being. Thus individual, culture, social burden and Dalitness cannot be isolated. In this context the answer to the question 'Who am I?' has a new cultural dignity, and in the writings of Dalits this is repeatedly reflected. J. V. Pawar, a Dalit Panther poet, says

> I have become an ocean
> I stand erect, I roll like the ocean

Another promising Dalit poet, Waman Nimbalkar, expresses it this way:

> On the horizon I will erect
> the rainbow arch of mankind
> I am conscious on my resolve
> The worth of the blood of Eklaya's broken finger
> I will not bastard my word
> I stand today at the very end
> of the twentieth century
> (trans. Jayashree Gokhale)

For this new Dalit individual, social and cultural freedom have come because of his self-elevation and self-identification.

The values and philosophy of the late Dr Ambedkar form the backbone of the contemporary Dalit movement and its literature. Ambedkarism is a modern and democratic approach to civilisation which leads to man's emancipation. It is a symbol of equality and the urge for humanism. It is a thirst for unending knowledge. It does not believe in blind faith, and incarnations of God. It is especially important to remember this because some students and critics of the Dalit movement have linked today's Dalit literature with the literature of Chokhamela and other Untouchable 'saints' of the 13th Century *bhakti* movement. I have high regard for Chokhamela, who was a pioneer among Untouchable writers, but I must clarify humbly that the sorrows and agonies expressed by Chokhamela do not protest the barriers of the social system or try to destroy the wretched casteism. He complained about pollution, but he never spoke against the Hindu mind and the Hindu culture which created the heinous conditions he had to face. Why did he not blame God for the concept of pollution, if God is the creator of the earth and human beings? On the contrary, his last resort is God Vithal, who may end his sufferings, he blindly believes. In many poems Chokha states that his low caste is a result of his past deeds. To my mind, his asking 'who is pure on this earth?' is not a protest but merely a complaint. And, needless to say, God and his dieties never bothered about his complaint. How then can he be called a protestant? It was impossible for him to revolt against the social structure and he never insisted upon this. Today's Dalit literature rejects the degraded Hindu social set-up. Dalit writers relentlessly expose the inhumanities and prejudices of caste society and instil a new social and cultural consciousness.

Ambedkar is also a key source of the political and economic perspective that marks Dalit literature. Ambedkar proclaimed while dedicating the Constitution to the nation that he would fight for his nation to the last drop of blood, but at the same time he warned his countrymen that they should not be satisfied with political democracy alone. On the contrary they would have to gain social and economic democracy in order to strengthen political democracy. Without this, political democracy would be in vain. Dalit writers know the promises enshrined in the Indian Constitution. They also know that the promises given in the Constitution remain unfulfilled. All the provisions by Dr Ambedkar in the Constitution regarding abolition of untouchability, rights against exploitation and equal rights for Indian women, are known to Dalit writers. But they are disillusioned when, even after thirty-five years of Independence, Indian Dalits still confront atrocities. Even now houses are burned and Dalit women are raped and stripped naked and paraded through the streets of a town. How can Dalit writers praise Indian democracy? Some have described such democracy as mockery.

Dalit literature is designed to reveal such experiences. These experiences are new to Indian literature and to the written cultural history of India. Why is this so? Because most of the writers in India have come from the higher strata of the society. Some middle-class writers have protested, but usually their protest was against strictures of literary form rather than content. Very few non-Dalit writers have written on and about the life of Dalits, and most of these wrote out of mere sympathy. Mere sympathy does not produce revolutionary literature. There are only a few exceptional writers who have put their heart and soul together in depicting the deep sorrows and sufferings of Dalits: Premchand in Hindi; Mulkraj Anand in English; Keshao Deo in Malayalam; Shripad Mahadeo Mate, Madhu Mangesh Karnik, G. T. Madholkar and Aroon Sadhu in Marathi.

Unrelieved suffering has been the reality of Dalit experience. Because Dalit writers cannot forget their people's past, and because Manu, the ancient architect of Hindu social laws, has been a crucial part of both past and present, Manu is a recurrent theme. Baburao Bagul and Bandhumakdao, the short story writers, and Keshav Meshram, Trymbak Sapkale and Jyoti Lanjewar, the poets, all stress the same thing: Manu, the prejudiced law-giver, is still alive in a variety of forms. Though the modern Indian Constitution has thrown him away, he is not dead. He lives in the textbooks of schools and colleges, he lives in the minds and hearts of thousands of Hindus and in their day-to-day actions. The major part of the Indian society is still under the dominion of Manu. In the 19th Century, Jyotiba Phule and Gopalbaba Walankar had already suggested burning the Brahmanical 'Manusmriti' text, and in the 20th Century Dr Ambedkar set it on fire at the hands of G. N. Sahasrabuddhe, a Brahman associated with him. It was a radical move. This historical incident is one about which Dalit writers cannot be indifferent. One of the Dalit poets denounces Manu and his heirs this way:

Cover of collection of poems, *Julus,* by P.M. Shinde. Aurangabad: Asmitadarsh Press, 1972.

82

O heirs of Manu
for millennia we have watched
our own naked evening
In half a dozen huts on the village
boundary
Our countless bodies have been burning,
set afire by your feeble thoughts.

Under Manu's code, the segregated people were for centuries denied the right to read and write. This fact always burns in the minds of Dalit writers, and they attack the tradition vehemently. How can they forget that Manu ordered the privileged class *'No cha shudraya matim dadyat'* ('Do not allow the lower classes to learn'). But today the Dalits have risen through education and they are producing a literature of their own. The days have changed because of the policies of the British, the emphasis Dr Ambedkar gave to education, and the Indian Constitution.

However, change has not been easy. In spite of the powerful expressiveness of today's writers, their voices were long unheard. Dalit writers had to work for a long time with great confidence and integrity before their efforts finally reached readers through the development of independent Dalit literary journals like *Asmitadarsh* ('Mirror of Identity'). Jean Paul Sartre's observation that 'Man is nothing other than what he makes himself' is profoundly true of the Dalits and their literary movement.

A growing number of Dalit short story writers have described the humanity, pride and vitality of their Dalit brethren. In the poems of Namdeo Dhasal, Daya Pawar and others, the image of the Dalit is of changing, revolutionising, reforming, improving. Dalit literature as a whole rebels against the assumptions of Hindu ideologies and rejects the attitudes and behaviour of Hinduism which were obstacles in the path of self-respect and freedom for Dalits. It also rejects the concept of God. Nietzsche said that 'God is dead' but Dalit literature denies the existence of God completely. [The Buddhism that is a common component of the Dalit cultural movement is explicitly atheistic, but the growing number of Dalit Christians and Muslims who have become part of the Dalit cultural movement would constitute an exception to this particular point.] The passionate rejection of traditional Hindu culture is reflected in this poem by a new Dalit poet, V. L. Kalekar:

No! No! No!
A triple rejection
To your economic, social, political, mental, religious, moral and
    cultural pollution.
you ever-living, ever-luminous suns!
Your very touch brings a contagious disease.
But I am a new sun
Independent, self-luminating,
    Possessed of a new spirit
I reject your culture.
I reject your Parmeshwar centred tradition.
I reject your religion based literature.

   . . .
   I have taken into account the unceasing battles.
   I may bend but I won't break.
(Translated by Jayashree Gokhale-Turner)

Another important aspect of Dalit literature is self-criticism or self-protest. It is always easy to protest against our enemy, but it is a very difficult thing to protest against ourselves. Dalit writers have a serious perspective on human affairs and feel their responsibility for change, so they do not hesitate to attack inferiority and superiority complexes among themselves. The attack on inferiority complexes helps to break down the slave-psychology, which is an ingrown problem. Superiority complexes are a somewhat different matter. Some peculiar tendencies arose in the Dalit community which compelled the Dalit writers to pen such portraits. In the British period a few Dalits could get butlers' jobs at the residences of high-ranking British officers. Due to this close association with Britishers, some Dalit families imitated their habits, dress and style of conversation. This change made them keep aloof from the society in which they had lived for years. The tendency to be superior to their own community was strengthened. The same thing had happened in an earlier period with a group of people who followed the cult of Chakaradhur in the religious rebellions of the 13th Century. They called themselves Mahanubhavaas ('great souls'), and supposed themselves superior to their brethren. At present some of the Dalits who hold higher posts in government presume themselves to be superior to their fellows. Such people try to maintain the stylish standards of high-caste people. But their futile imitations of high society do not allow them to mix freely with their own community, and this leaves them in an isolated position in society as a whole. These people impose the same behaviour on their children and the tragic result is that they try to conceal their caste and are alienated from the masses. Hence this superiority complex is a subject on which Dalit writers today sternly criticize their own brothers.

Dalit writers also have not spared the political leaders who have exploited innocent followers for their own political advantage. The very sad attitude of many Dalit leaders has been exposed satirically in many poems. Namdeo Dhasal calls these leaders 'dogs' who cease their barking and shut their mouths at the bidding of non-Dalit political powers.

The conversion of many followers of Dr Ambedkar to Buddhism in 1956 was an historical event of unique significance in the Dalit movement, and it often figures in our literature. Dr Ambedkar had declared in 1935 'Though I was born a Hindu, I do not intend to die a Hindu', and he embraced Buddhism in 1956. In the interim period he asked the Hindus several times to become introspective and consider whether they must not cease to worship the past and instead recognize that nothing is eternal. He strongly advocated annihilation of caste and the reforming of Hindu religion, suggesting some solutions on how this could be done. However society never responded positively to his revolutionary thoughts, so he embraced Buddhism as a way of life with five lakhs [500,000] of his followers. The reaction of the orthodox people in

India to the conversion was shock and outrage, but to the Dalits and Dalit writers it was a new life and a new outlook.

The writings of Dalits in the 1960s and onwards give the impression of a bird who has been freed from the cage of eternal bondage. The poets often use the folk stories about Buddha and Aryastya and many symbols pertaining to Buddhism. The impact of the conversion is constantly revealed in Dalit poetry, in short stories, novels and plays. A new Dalit poet, Harish Bansode, says:

We have begun a new life
We have found our own temples
Regained our lost faith
All are equal here

Recently Dalit playwrights have also entered the picture and have begun to portray the problems of today's Dalit in their writings. In non-Dalit plays the image of the Dalit and the interpretation of his life are distorted. Well-known Marathi playwrights Vijay Tendulkar and Jayawant Dalvi have portrayed the Dalit in just such a distorted manner. In their recent plays, *Kanyadan* ('Marriage', literally 'the gift of a daughter') and *Purush* ('Man'), both writers insist that the Dalit is inferior and uncultured. Dalvi especially has interpreted his Dalit 'hero' as an escapist and a brute. Siddharth, a Dalit Panther leader, loves a Brahman girl, but he is not faithful to her. Though the hero has a postgraduate degree, he never speaks in the standard language. Needless to say the leading Marathi playwrights have projected a Dalit image of weakness and folly in their plays.

Against this background Dalit playwrights have played an important role. They do not compromise with the old path of Hindu culture or with the new path of 'Established' society. Through the medium of theatre and street plays these writers are depicting effectively the inner and external conflicts in Dalit life and Dalit society. In Maharashtra, some of the leading figures are Datta Bhagat, Rustom Achalkhamb, Prakash Tribhuvan, Ramnath Chavan, Prabhkar Dupare, Bhagwan Sawai, B. S. Shinde and Texas Gaikwad.

The potential contribution from Dalit women writers to Dalit literature is significant. From the outset, the writings of Dalit women reflected self-experience and burning indignation. Muktabai, an Untouchable girl who read her essay on the problems and sufferings of Untouchables in the school established by the great reformer Jotiba Phule, in 1852, was the first example. After a period of a century or more Dalit women have awakened and are again giving literary expression to their deep feelings. Kumud Pawade, Jyoti Lanjewar, Urmila Pawar, Hira Bansode, Sugandha Shende, Surekhad Bhagat, Asha Thorat, Aruna Lokhande, Susheela Mool and Meena Gajbhiye are examples from Maharashtra.

Kumud Pawade is by profession a lecturer in Sanskrit, once considered a language of God that the lower castes were not allowed to learn or even to hear. But the times have changed and a Dalit woman teaches Sanskrit to students from the higher castes. Mrs Pawade has published several articles on culture, social education and women's problems. She already has a book, *Antahsphot* ('Inner Burst'), to her credit. The writings of Mrs Aruna Lokhande, Mrs Asha Thorat and Sugandha Shende are impressive and self-disciplined. Atrocities on Dalit women, the problems of non-educated women and the ugly outlook of educated and advanced Dalit women towards non-educated women are some of the subjects of their writings. Mrs Thorat also has been doing research on Dalit folk literature.

The Dalit woman is a Dalit amongst Dalits. She has suffered much and she is still suffering. She must walk through the burning desert of casteism in search of some oasis. Mrs Bansode says it is due to casteism that Dalit women are being dishonoured and molested. In one poem she lodges a complaint in the people's court hoping for justice, but at last she attacks the inhuman game of the oppressors:

> This complaint of mine
> is against the orthodox culture
> which has imprisoned us in a sealed room,
> which has given us the charity of life completely boycotted.
> Where the wind treats us as strangers,
> where the monsoons give us only famines
> where the water plays with us
> the most inhuman game of mirage.
> We are rejecting this
> unclean and poisonous life.
> And to escape from these cruel curses
> will you give me
> a bright and auspicious moon?
> My countrymen, to your court
> I have brought a complaint.
> Will you give me justice?

(Translated by N. G. Bhavar)

Regardless of the particular writer or literary form, Dalit literature is, ultimately, a declaration of independence. It is impossible to understand the revolutionary quality of Dalit literature without understanding the people to whom it is addressed. Dalits do not write to please non-Dalits. The literature was not intended for this; its foremost purpose was to address directly the Dalit people. It speaks for them and to them. Dalit poetry is a weapon for them while at the same time it draws upon them for strength. Dalit literature is part of the people. The writers express themselves without fear and shame. In this respect there is a close relationship between Dalit literature and Black Literature. Dr J. M. Waghmare, a Dalit literary critic, has depicted significant similarities among both sets of writers. He says that both Dalits and Blacks are in search of their own cultural identity. The experience of both is based on social and cultural inequality. Both write out of social commitment. The language of both is a language of cultural revolution. Uniqueness and creative vitality are basic features of both literatures. The Dalit writer is honest to his life and to his experiences. His vision and experience cannot be translated honestly into art by euphemisms. It is a natural outburst of feelings and thoughts which were suffocated for centuries.

Dalit literature has now gained its own reputation in the sphere of Indian literary history. To spread this literary movement, conferences of Dalit writers are being organized by *Asmitadarsh* and similar organizations every year in various parts of the land. The Dalit writer is confident of building his temples for tomorrow, standing freely on top of the mountain.

* * * *

One of the groups associated with all phases of the Dalit movement is the Dalit Panthers. The Panthers began in the late 1960s in the slums of Bombay, as young Dalit activists developed a confrontational style to mobilize their neighbourhoods against discrimination and violence. Many of the original participants were young poets, and cultural activities continue to be an important part of the Panther programme. The original organization fragmented, but both style and name have spread to Dalit communities in other language regions. The following selection is from a book of poetry, Burning from Both Ends, *published by the Dalit Panthers of Gujarat state in 1980. This particular branch has been active in organizing both agricultural and urban labourers, but the book is consciously addressed to a different audience — the high-caste world of the English-speaking elite. Included here are the publisher's and the poet's introductions, and a small selection of the poems themselves. Another poem from this book appears in Chapter 3.*

Burning from Both Ends
Neerav Patel

dalit panthers' cultural wing

dalit panthers is an organization of the downtrodden masses, it represents the disillusioned generation — conscious of its plight, sufferings, aspirations, struggle. because they are young and oppressed, they become bitter at the latent and blatent exploitation of the capitalist system. naturally their reaction is militant. they assert themselves more vehemently, to be treated at par with the rest of the human race. the *dalit panthers'* cultural wing does this in its own way. *dalit theatre* and *dalit literature* are the two major activities they are presently engaged in.

on this auspicious day of 14 april 1980, being the 89th anniversary of dr. babasaheb ambedkar, we present with pride and pleasure our young panther poet, *neerav patel*, as the *dalit panthers' poetry series no. 1*. some of his poems were previously published in our journal, *panther*, and the *dalit* poetry magazine, *akrosh*.

. . .

    ramesh chandra parmar, president; dalit panthers, gujarat.

o where are you, my midas;
those people refuse to touch me!
they do not allow me to forget for a moment that i am neerav patel, alias
harijan. i wonder why and how i am a *harijan*! because i don't dress like *them*,
speak like *them*, behave like *them*? because my father and his father were
harijans? no, i know this silly sequence ends somewhere in the past, for
everybody is born as adam and eve — naked, free and equal. i would rather
like to die than dwell upon the plea that nobody can select one's parents.
yes, it is because of them only that i am a *harijan*.
i wish i could call myself in algebraic sign, like n^p: no clue to clan, colour or
creed!
i know little of english and less of poetry. having been born in a *harijan*
ghetto, nursery school or k.g. are still fascinating dreams of a deprived
childhood. no girl in jeans is my companion. i overhear the yankee accent
and mannerism at the elite campus of st. xavier's, and read every piece of
paper written in english that comes my way — be it a folio from a bank ledger
or an ad for cosmetics. an eavesdropping *ekalavya*!
prof. bhambhi consoles that i am a poet potentially, though ill-equipped. but
i don't wait for miracles. for i can't afford this. i am burning from both the
ends. i am afraid, before i get perfection in the medium or art, i might get
killed or commit suicide. let my successor weed out the slips. meanwhile you
may take it as a poet's privilege.
i wish i could attack and appeal at the same time! the urban intelligentsia is
insensitively unaware of the *harijan* experience and problem.
they have tortured me for too long. i have deliberately decided not to give a
glossary of our *desi* [countrified] diction. at least to tease them, to annoy
them. yes, a childish revenge! i shall be glad if you are not one of *them*. oh,
i forget my father's advice — when one is modest by birth, one is expected
to be modest. here are then a few originals and several translations from
gujarati. my anguish and my agony. now bear with me —
    neerav patel, ambedkar jayanti, 1980.
. . .

post mortem

they failed to find any musk from his navel.
his skin was dissected layer by layer by layer
but did not yield a single sheet of gold.
oh, his skin was simply made of flesh & fibres!
from his big belly
they could not discover the precious gems —
(he was supposed to have eaten throughout his life.)
not a page of holy scriptures was found from his coiled brain.
and neither could they collect a drop of proverbial
suryavanshi bravery from his large liver.
nor did they find the nectar earned by his holy deeds
from his poisonous heart.
he was cut to pieces
but they did not find his 6th sense.
yes, from his chest was found a pretty heart of wolf.
from the tips of his fingers were found the roots of claws.
from his crystal-clear denture

were found trident teeth.
from his beautiful eyes were found the crocodile's tears
and from his orthodox veins was found frozen alcohol.
yes, that was the post-mortem
of a mummy of an *aryakumar* [high caste big shot].

journalistic apathy

it's neither glossy nor glamorous.
not chic, not debonair.
like a surrealist's imagination of anatomy
it's clumsy, distorted and nauseating.
but the bleeding wound on the forehead
is hot red
as the deep romantic chasm
in the centre-spreads of mod mags.
it was just hopping on the ground
like the slaughtered head of a chick —
before a moment
the eyes were aglow with tears,
(alas, they are dead as dumb-bells).
the sensuous lips are turning muddy brown
like drought-hit earth.
the luscious cheeks are getting dried hollows
like a rotten apple.
it never claimed headline or hotline —
the teleprinter went on tick-ticking the sports-flashes,
the camera feasted on the nude beaches.
the poor head of a *harijan*!
it is as compassionate as the
wrinkled face of mother teresa.
darkness has settled like dust
upon the sad face of agony —
it craves for lime light,
miss anees jung —
make it a cover page agony.

jasumati, my black jasmine

whenever you come with broom and dust-bins in the street
you cease to be the black jasmine
grown upon the dark dung-hill
outside the boudaries of our village.
the red sun blossoms upon your face
upon your bosom
and in your heart.
vultures wearing sacred threads[1] take rounds
of ganges[2] [the sacred river] and you.
when you stoop to sweep,
the black berries under your nylon blouse
peep to the sunny embrace of the earth.

you, *jasumati*, suddenly become jasmine
again for a moment:
the dried paste of honey upon your black lips
begins to moisten.
had it been midnight
the fireflies would have kissed them
in search of juicy buds —
your cups dripping brew.
instantly you become a feast for the zooming vultures.
— a nasty joke,
— a quick and sudden hug,
— a slap upon your heavy buttocks.
you are cornered like an easy prey.
they enjoy the delicious,
most touchable flesh of an untouchable girl.

you moan and become mother —
mother of a bastard.
they button up their trousers and take a plunge in the ganges.
they defile you, dear *jasumati*
like a crow defiles with his dirty bill.
and the kid is thankless too,
like his father.
drinks your milk and
pisses upon you.
you stink
and become untouchable and outcast
cursing is no good, darling.
— your sigh may extinguish a star in heaven.
— your shrill may slice the moon.
— or the sun may breed more spots in his heart
like the patient of a chest disease.

i love you, dear *jassu*,
although you are no more virgin —
i know you should conceive
many more bastard christs in your womb
for you are born mulkraj anand's *bakha's* daughter.[3]

and you know i am helpless and hapless
with the cut-off thumb bleeding since time immemorial;[4]
with no bow, no arrow of my ancestors.
i could kill birds and bears,
deer and doves,
i could fell oak and break rock
but i cannot kill the killers,
the culture-clad vultures.

i love you, *jasumati*,
like *arjuna* loved his stripped-off bride[5]
— with foggy eyes,
    swollen throat,
    closed fists,
    dropped head,

and interred legs.

i swear i never gambled upon you, dear *jassu*,
nor my forefathers did.
how can we poor untouchables afford such luxury?
i love you
and love you more than ever.
you are chaste like the water of the ganges
where holymen wash their bottoms ceremoniously.

i love you *jasumati*
my black jasmine grown upon the dark dung-hill
outside the boundaries of our village.

[1. 'sacred thread': worn only by high-caste Hindus. 2. 'ganges': sacred river
believed to remove ritual pollution. 3. 'bakha's daughter': character in the
modern anti-untouchability novel by Anand. 4. 'cut-off thumb': reference to
Ekalavya, the low-caste figure in an ancient myth who was ordered to cut off
his thumb to avoid defeating a high-caste hero in archery. 5. 'arjuna': mythical
high-caste hero who gambled away his wife.]

* * * *

*Oral communication is central to the Dalit movement in ways that do not
translate easily to a collection of written works. The many who cannot afford
books and the many more who cannot read can always listen; songs and oral
poetry and popular drama are therefore an important part of meetings and
demonstrations. There is a long-standing Indian tradition of injecting social
and political commentary into the familiar forms of religious morality plays
and folk entertainment. Modern higher-caste practitioners have ranged from
Congress nationalists in the Independence movement to a variety of
contemporary Marxist street theatre groups. My own first encounter with
the Dalit use of this tradition was some years ago in the sweeper colony of a
north Indian town, where educated young men from the community used
the annual pageant for the saint Balmiki to popularize such ideas as civic
rights and women's education. The contemporary Dalit theatre movement
now uses many of the conventions of modern Indian cinema and theatre,
but the goal is the same – entertainment in the service of wholly
unconventional mass education.*

*The following excerpts also illustrate the importance of the growing cadre
of college-educated Dalit activists who serve as multilingual bridges between
the uneducated of slum and village and a new national Dalit communications
network that centres on a variety of Dalit periodicals. The first three pieces
are from* Dalit Voice, *an English-language biweekly that is published in the
Kannada-speaking state of Karnataka and is regularly translated into the
Tamil language of the neighbouring state of Tamil Nadu. One of the reader/
correspondents we meet here is from the western Marathi-speaking state of
Maharashtra, another from the predominantly Hindi-speaking capital city
of New Delhi. The fourth and final section is part of a personal*

*communication from B. S. Shinde, director of the Dalit Rangabhoomi
Theatre, and includes an extended description of one of the theatre's plays.
The name of this enterprise,* Rangabhoomi, *is a word of many meanings; it
can mean simply 'theatre' – or it can mean 'battle ground'.*

Letter to the Editor of *Dalit Voice*

Dalit Voice, 1-15 August 1983

B. S. Shinde, Pune: I appreciate the revolutionary material in *DV* which is
inspiring young Dalits and minorities. I was inspired by your editorial on the
Mandal Commission, which made me write a Marathi play, *Ayog*, which was
well received. It shows how the OBCs [Other Backward Castes, a scant notch
above Untouchables] hate Dalits but during the famine both starve and come
to work together. Both face the same exploitation. A lady social worker
proves this on the spot. Then both demand an inquiry commission which,
when appointed, takes its own time. The OBCs and Dalits, fed up by the
delay, demand on-the-spot justice. This is the plot of my play inspired by
DV . . .

Notice to Readers of *Dalit Voice*

Dalit Voice, 1-15 August 1983

Ahwan Theatre
Educate!   Unite!!   Revolt!!!
We have taken our first revolutionary step by forming a Dalit theatre in Delhi.
We intend to use the powerful media of theatre to take to every corner of
India the message of Dalit fight to transform the present oppressive society
into an egalitarian one.
    We call upon those committed to the removal of oppression to join our
group. We would especially welcome those with talents in the various aspects
of theatre craft.
    We request you to send in your poems, dramas, short stories on Dalit life.
We request those interested to join our movement to awaken those dormant
spirits that are oppressed and repressed to action.
    Ahwan Theatre

Dalit Stage Comes of Age

Dalit Voice, 1-15 April 1984

Pune: The first All-India Dalit Drama Convention was held here from 24 to

B.S. Shinde, teacher, playwright,
and president of Dalit
Rangabhoomi, Pune.
(Dalit Rangabhoomi)

27 February, the noted Dalit dramatist, B. S. Shinde, presiding. Mohan Dharia, ex-Minister, welcomed the participant drama troupes from various parts of Maharashtra, Delhi, Madhya Pradesh. The convention was inaugurated by Mrs Geetabai Gaikwad, wife of the late Dadasaheb Gaikwad, a noted reformer. It began with a folk ballad on Dr B. R. Ambedkar. She offered flowers to a model of a monument in memory of those Dalit activists who have died in the Dalit political, social and cultural movements.

Shinde in his presidential address said the stage is a powerful media to educate the masses. Babasaheb (Dr Ambedkar) used the media to rouse the sleeping Dalits. Many troupes are working in various parts of India and the conference wants to bring them together in a Dalit movement. It was announced that an independent Dalit Natya Parishad (federation) would be established. Five seminars were held on various aspects of the stage and eighteen plays were staged. The topics discussed included women's problems, children's theatre, street plays, folk arts, criticism-aesthetics and expectations.

Many noted writers, thinkers and artistes took part in the discussion. Dr Ratanlal Sonagra, V. B. Deshpande, Baba Oak, Rao Saheb Kasbe, Sujata from Ahwan Theatre in Delhi, Sharma from Janwadi Manch in Ratlam (Madhya Pradesh) were contributors. Dalit playwrights Avinash Dolas, Datta Bhagat, Amar Ramteke, Premanand Gajvi, Arun Kumar Ingale, B. S. Shinde, Texas Gaikwad, Mrs Shilpa Mumbriskar, etc. took an active part. A big procession of artistes and writers was led out at the end. It was a cultural procession with many floats and bands of musicians.

Dalit Rangabhoomi presents . . .

Kalokhachya Garbhat (**'In The Womb of Darkness'**)

Written by Shri B. S. Shinde
Produced by Shri Texas Gaikwad

The following synopsis of Dalit Rangabhoomi's first play, produced in 1979, was provided by the playwright, B. S. Shinde. The central village in the play serves as a composite setting for a series of real events of the post-Independence era, and for the shifting Dalit mood that has accompanied these events. Tatya and the Patel are composite characters built up from real individuals. Sidram Sakat, the young Dalit who publicly murders his father's known killer when the police and courts fail to punish him, is a direct quotation from life and is still in prison.

1. The narrator introduces a group of Dalits, addressing the audience directly [to explain] that these people were exploited by the higher classes, when they were unaware of their rights. They have now been awakened by Dr B. R. Ambedkar. Don't go by their torn clothes and poor life. They are volcanos. If you try to suppress them they will revolt. Beware! Behold! They are the sparks of tomorrow's revolution.

2. The Hindu religious penal code, Manusmriti, and all the Puranic myths say that Dalits and Shudras are not human beings. Their mere touch, why even their shadow, pollutes the three higher classes. So a young Dalit asks Mahatma Phule [a 19th Century social reformer] whether this is true. Did God make this? Mahatma Phule replies that this is not true. All human beings are equal in all respects. God and religion are the creations of man. So man is more powerful than so-called gods and religion.

3. Dalits were supposed to do all sorts of dirty jobs — sweeping village roads and latrines and drains, carrying away dead animals — without expecting any payment. The Shastras [classical Hindu texts] supported this. But awakened Dalits are refusing to do this. Tatya Sonawane, a Dalit village leader who advocates this refusal, is beaten by the village Panchayat committee members. He is warned that if he wishes to live in the village peacefully, he has to do all that the committee tells him. Tatya says 'Even if you kill me I won't do this or allow other Dalits to do it.'

4. When all the Dalits refuse to do their jobs for the village, the caste Hindus become furious and take the law into their own hands. The Dalits

are not allowed to purchase anything from the village market, not even salt and oil. [The social boycotting described here is a traditional form of coercion banned by the Constitution but still commonly enforced.] Dinakar, a son of Tatya Sonawane, gathers all the Dalits together and carries them in procession to the Panchayat committee's office to ask them why they have closed the market to them. Before they reach the Panchayat office, they become the target of a deadly attack by caste Hindus armed with stones and sticks. The Dalits try to maintain peace and order. Suddenly someone rushes into the mob and stabs Dinakar, the peace-loving young Dalit leader. Seeing Dinakar's pitiable condition, his young Dalit friend Sada bursts into tears and abuses the caste Hindus, warning them that he will take revenge

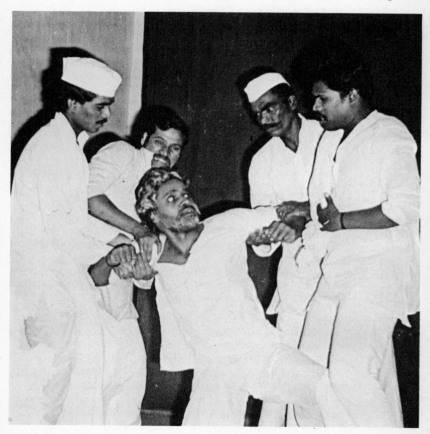

A Dalit Rangabhoomi presentation of *Kalokhachy Garbha* (In the Womb of Darkness). Here Tatya Sonewane, a Dalit leader, is bullied by higher caste villagers trying to enforce traditional Dalit behaviour in the village. Actors Avinash Ambedkar, Prakash Khude, Anant Mumbriskar, Arun Gaikwad, and Alhat. (Dalit Rangabhoomi)

against this injustice. But Dinakar, before breathing his last, makes him take an oath that he will not do anything that is unlawful but will fight for his rights in a parliamentary way.

5. Sidram Sakat, son of Daaji Sakat, a Dalit, enters a Hindu temple in his village with his friends. Caste Hindus see him and they beat him like a dog. His father rushes to the scene and rescues him. Being a submissive and innocent Dalit who is unaware of Dr Ambedkar's message, he begs the caste Hindus to excuse his son for polluting the temple by his presence. The caste Hindus warn Daaji that they will not tolerate misbehaviour by his son hereafter. No Dalit is allowed to cross the steps of their temples. Daaji surrenders and agrees to behave as they wish.

6. Caste Hindus thrust all the dirty jobs on Daaji because he is submissive and innocent, and his life continues to be in danger. He comes to Tatya Sonawane, the strong Dalit leader, for advice. Sonawane advises him to be strong and bold. None can harm him if he joins with other united Dalits.

7. Dalit women usually collect firewood from the nearest forest for their daily needs. On this occasion two Dalit women are carrying a load of firewood on a summer day and feel thirsty. They rest under the shade of a tree. They happen to see a well in the field of a caste Hindu farmer. No one is watching them. They come near the well and are about to touch the water in this tank meant for animals when the farmer comes out of his home and abuses them for 'polluting' the water. He calls out his men, strips the women naked, and beating them with a whip takes them to the Panchayat office. None dare to stop him . . .

8. This news spreads throughout the state. Hearing of this brutal treatment to Dalit women, young Dalits from the cities rush to the village. They pour in in hundreds and form a furious procession. They hold a meeting where they condemn the ruthless inhuman treatment by caste Hindus and demand an enquiry commission. The incident gives birth to growing young Dalit leadership.

9. Sattapa Patel's son Sankar, a law college student in the city, secretly marries the daughter of Tatya Sonawane, the village Dalit leader. When Tatya finds this out he takes her to the Patel's house and asks him to accept her publicly as his daughter-in-law. The caste-spirited Patel flatly refuses to accept her and instead orders his men to remove Tatya's eyes in public because he dared to stare at him and speak to him boldly in spite of being a Dalit. Tatya is blinded. But blind Tatya continues his fight for his rights.

10. Jobless and landless Dalits acquire lands for farming from the government. The Patel gets disturbed. He thinks that if Dalits become owners of land he may not get cheap labourers, so he plans a conspiracy with the help of his aristocratic friends. They destroy the Dalits' crops and burn eleven Dalits who came to protect their crops.

11. On hearing this bad news, that eleven young Dalits were burnt alive, blind Tatya bursts into tears. A Socialist Brahman leader visits them and expresses his sorrow over this mishap and advises them that Dalits should now join his Socialists. Tatya condemns him and tells him that no one can bring

equality to this land without breaking down the caste and class feeling taught by the orthodox mentality. 'You high-caste socialists talk about economic equality but you don't want to break the caste system. Go away. We don't need your kind of equality. We will find our own way.'

12. Tatya Sonawane continues his movement. The caste Hindus become uneasy. During this period the District School Board offers a grant of Rs. 100,000 to construct a school building. The villagers demand land from the Dalits for the construction site. The Dalits agree to give their piece of land for the school building on condition that the school be named for Dr Ambedkar. All the villagers accept this condition but afterwards they name the school for the village deity. The Dalits challenge this and this time all the caste Hindus become furious and burn the Dalit locality when the Dalits are sleeping. Only Daaji escapes. He tries to save the life of his friend Tatya, but a gang of caste Hindus catches him and tortures him to death. His son, Sidram Sakat, eventually takes the law into his own hands and kills the Patel in a public place. He himself surrenders to the police and says 'Your judicial system could not spare a bit of justice to me when my father was killed. So I have killed my father's killer.'

* * * *

Rise People
(Popular movement song, translated by Gail Omvedt)

> Rise, people, rise up now, break the chains of caste
> Throw off the corpse of slavery, smash the obstacles,
> > Rise people —
> We may be Maratha, Mahar, Brahman, Hindu, Muslim, Christian,
> Humanity is one, all are brothers.
> Why is a drop of water fenced in with thorns?[1]
> Why are men prohibited even from spitting?
> Hurl away the oppression of cunning priests,
> > Rise people —
> The tears of dalits have filled the wells of history,
> The cream of generations swallowed the hypocrisy of fanatics,
> The sun of self-respect has been enflamed,
> > Burn up caste
> Crash, smash, throw away the walls of hatred,
> Reduce to ashes this age-old school of the blind,
> > Rise up people —
> This man by tradition has looted that man,
> The stigma stuck by culture has burst into flame,
> The eternal culture that was offended even by the
> > touch of our shadow,
> The deformity of purity which crushed humaneness,
> The volcano that was cast outside the village has erupted,[2]
> > Rise up people —

[1. I.e., Why segregated wells? 2. Untouchables who are routinely segregated outside the main village residential areas.]

Marathwada Is Burning

(Popular movement song in traditional epic ballad style, translated by Gail Omvedt)

Know the time, defeat it,
O harness the cart of unity
    Marathwada is burning, Marathwada is burning,[1]
      Marathwada is burning.

One Pochiram Kamble, sweating to fill his stomach,
Became the enemy of the village — Jai Bheem was on his lips.[2]
Accosted in the fields, tied with a rope,
His hands and feet branded, then thrown in the fire
He burned fiercely, the son of Bheem,
    This is the creation of casteism,
    Marathwada is burning —

One daughter-in-law of Bansode, toiling in other's fields,
Sitting in front of the hearth of darkness,
Indebted to the whole village.
She was only a Mahar [a Dalit caste], but a mine of beauty
As if gold was in the house of the poor.
Her bangles were broken; what tyranny![3]
    Who will avenge this?
    Marathwada is burning —

The Mahar boys in school studied and went ahead,
They refused to carry away the dead cattle, the work of their forefathers.
At the time of exams a conspiracy was hatched,
One was charged with theft, beaten in the village square,
And so was absent from the exams,
And on top of this abused as a 'Dhed' [derogatory caste term].
    Marathwada is burning —

One went outside the village, his body was wasted with toil,
He collected pennies one by one.
He too was looted.
We see all this with open eyes,
Still we live our lives
By our own hands we feed the fire that burns the corpse.
We the people of Bombay and Pune,
How hollow is our pose,
We gossip about revolution but live the lives of eunuchs.
Oh — beat, smash, cut, break
Whatever comes in our way,
    Marathwada is burning, Marathwada is burning,
      Marathwada is burning!

[1. A region of the western state of Maharashtra that erupted in widespread anti-Dalit violence in the 1970s. 2. 'Jai Bheem', a common Dalit salutation referring to Dr Ambedkar; hence an Ambedkarite who rejected traditional Dalit status. 3. The breaking of a woman's glass bangles is a common symbol of rape.]

4. Grassroots Organizing

There is very little distance between Dalit art and Dalit reality. Grassroots efforts to organize in defence of rights and self-respect are indeed hazardous, and yet the efforts persist and expand. Most attempts are still localized and ad hoc – a group of neighbours mobilize to resist some specific form of oppression in their daily lives. This type of effort is possible even for people who have very limited resources, but it is also very vulnerable to repression. Even when Untouchables are able to find allies in the local population or the machinery of the state, they are easily – and often – isolated at critical junctures in any struggle for rights.

This pattern is clearly visible in the following terse account of the official Commissioner for Scheduled Castes and Tribes.

Murder of Scheduled Caste Persons in Dharampura Village of Bhojpur in Bihar State

Report of the Commissioner for Scheduled Castes and Scheduled Tribes 1977–78, vol. 1

As per newspaper reports four Scheduled Caste persons were killed and four others, including three women, injured, when a group of armed men belonging to upper castes attacked them on 20 October 1977 in Dharampura village of Bhojpur in Bihar State. The Commissioner got this matter investigated through the Zonal Director, ex-officio Deputy Commissioner for Scheduled Castes and Scheduled Tribes, Patna. It was revealed that the incident took place during the day on 20 October 1977 when most of the villagers had gone to a nearby village to celebrate Durgapuja. Meanwhile two persons came to the house of Scheduled Caste persons and informed them to go to the Mahantji [hereditary Brahman temple priest, in this village also a major landlord] for amicable settlement regarding a sharecropping dispute. The Scheduled Caste persons were reported to have replied that they would do so after some time. However after about twenty minutes a mob of about sixty persons led by the Mahantji of the village temple came and attacked the Scheduled Caste persons. In the raid two Scheduled Caste persons died of gunshot wounds. The mob caught hold of two Scheduled Caste persons and dragged them to a nearby house and put them to death. In all, four Scheduled Caste persons were murdered and four others (one male and three females) were injured.

It was further revealed that persons belonging to various communities such as Scheduled Castes, Ahirs [a non-Untouchable peasant caste], etc., had been cultivating about 180 acres of land belonging to Mahantji for the last twelve years. The Mahantji is reported to have purchased a tractor in 1974 and made efforts to remove the sharecroppers from the land. The sharecroppers filed a petition in the court in June/July 1975 for protection of their interests and continued cultivating this land. [State law provides security of access to land for those who have sharecropped for an extended period.] At harvesting time the Mahantji also filed a suit against fifty-five persons and the matter was reported to be pending with the police. The police inspector at Buxar is reported to have submitted an investigation report against the sharecroppers stating that they had forcibly harvested the crops. The sharecroppers were reported to have complained to the SDO about the report of the police inspector. The SDO conducted a further inquiry into the matter and also constituted a tripartite agrarian dispute settlement board as provided under the Bihar Bataidar Act. As regards action taken [after the attack], the Chief Minister of Bihar is reported to have visited this village and sanctioned an amount of Rs. 5,000 in respect of each person killed in the course of this unfortunate happening. Out of forty-four persons accused in this case, forty-three had been arrested and only the Mahantji was absconding. However, on 28 October 1977 the Mahantji was reported to have got himself admitted to Patna Medical College Hospital with effect from some date prior to the incident. The case is *sub judice*.

* * * *

Local efforts do not always remain isolated, however. Improving education and communication facilities have increased the number of Dalits who are involved in extended protest networks, especially in urban areas. The following article, by a non-Dalit author, describes the activities and growth of a multi-caste coalition of slum-dwellers in the northern state of Bihar. Throughout India, urban shanty towns have a disproportionately high population of Untouchables, and of young people of a variety of castes whose education far outstrips their job opportunities. They are especially likely to be home to people from the needed/despised Untouchable sweeper castes, who have an established tradition of building social-cum-labour unions around their profession. In this article we meet a variety of groups that are evolving and coalescing around their struggle for survival on the economic fringes of Bihar's capital city. Typically, their efforts have brought them into conflict with the linked power of economic interests, established political parties (in this case, both the ruling Congress (I) and one of the Communist parties, the CPI), and the police. A shorter version of this article originally appeared in India Now, *a publication produced by the Indian People's Association of North America. The author is an engineer by profession who also serves as a journalist with* India Now.

Patna: Revolt in the Slums

Pradip Sen (Montreal, 1983)

Seven pigs snort and grunt as they emerge from an open drain. They are carrying the carcasses of dead crows in their mouths. They brush past a two-year-old child, sitting half-naked next to the drain, snot dribbling from its nose. The temperature is about 4°C. An elderly woman rushes up and takes the child into a straw shack open on three sides. Another child wriggles out from a pile of ash that is still warm. His back is bent and his legs curved like a cross-bow. He rests his body against the ash to keep it warm. I am sitting on a bench talking to Ganauri Azad and Shyam Prasad, President and Secretary of the Rickshaw-Thela Chalak Mazdur Sangh (Rickshaw and Handcart Workers' Union) of Patna city. We are sitting on Rajindernagore-Baisali settlement corner. The police station is 200 yards away.

'In February '82, the people from the thana (police station) came and started demolishing our shacks. This is their "green belt" for Patna city. They want to clear us out and beautify the city. We fought back with whatever we had in our hands. We had to retreat one block. How long can we fight?' said Shyam Prasad. 'We are back again now, but we have no shacks. Nothing. They took everything. We are living under the stars.'

The cold is intense. My head is covered with a shawl. It is one o'clock in the afternoon, but everyone's teeth are chattering from the cold. Mr Jagannath Mishra, the Chief Minister of Bihar, has declared 'What cold wave? Only some sick people have died.' Even official figures have put Bihar's death toll due to the cold at over 400. Everywhere I went in Patna, district committee members of the Bihar Kisan Sabha reported numerous deaths due to exposure, and that it was worse in adjoining districts.

Ganauri and Shyam are both rickshaw pullers, who live on this corner. Right now they have no shacks to live in. So they sleep on the footpath, next to a big government building. They are the main organizers of their union. There are 40,000 rickshaw pullers in Patna district. 'The three existing unions belonging to the CPI, CPI (M), and Congress (I) only visited us during the elections. We have our own fighting union' said Ganauri. An old woman who had been selling tea (she had sold only Rs.1 worth of tea all morning) and was watching me, suddenly came up to me and said, 'No roof, no house, even the house owners have built fences around their houses, so we cannot sleep on the footpath outside their houses. Where will we go? My children were born here. Where will we go?'

Ganauri, who is a Harijan [Dalit] youth, is also on the National Executive of the Indian People's Front [a progressive movement formed by people disillusioned with the major political parties]. When the IPF organized its huge rally on 15 October 1982 (both *Aryabarta* and *Nation*, daily newspapers, claimed that more than 100,000 poor people from the city and adjoining areas joined this rally against the Bihar Press Bill) the Rickshaw-Thela Chalak Mazdur Sangh had mobilized a large number of their members. Their main slogan was '*Chalak hai Malik*' ('The puller is the owner of the rickshaw').

I went to the office of *Samkaleen Janmat*, a Hindi magazine that is a little over a year old and is doing excellent work in reporting Bihar-wide mass struggles, as well as India-wide issues. While I was there, the three editors — Nabyendu, Srikanth and AgniPushp — were busy replying to innumerable letters that had come in from grassroots organizers of various movements in Bihar and Uttar Pradesh. It was here that I met Krishnadeo Prasad Jadav, Honorary Secretary of the Bihar Jhuggi-Jhopri Bashi Sangha (BJJBS), a major affiliate of the Indian People's Front in Bihar. The General Secretary of BJJBS is Dinesh Singh, a Harijan fish-seller who is also an organizer amongst the rickshaw pullers. The growth of the BJJBS is a reflection of the serious opposition to the nationwide attempts by the central government and their cohorts in the states artificially to 'Beautify' all major urban residential areas, resulting in heroic organized resistance put up by slum dwellers all over India. The Jama Masjid-style demolitions of Sanjay Gandhi have now become a daily affair in India, where slum-dwellers are fighting back, block by block, reorganizing their battle lines and repitching their tents in a continuous battle to put down their stakes as citizens of India. *'Mai bhi bharatbashi hun. Yeh mere desh hai. Garib ke izzat ke sowal hai'* ('I too am an Indian citizen. This is my country and the poor must have their dignity').

There are 85,000 *jhuggi-jhopri* (slum) dwellers in Patna district along with 35,000 footpath dwellers. There are forty-five main bustees in Patna . . . and there are people engaged in eighty-five different professions living in these slums. The majority of slum dwellers are either municipal sweepers or domestic workers (*dais*). The slums are in the main mud-walled shacks, extremely clean and well maintained with small, narrow alleys, giving them an ancient city-like structure. One — Purba Lohanipur — even has its own version of a town square and a town meeting room, complete with donated upholstery, and one large gym-type shack where public programmes can be held. One afternoon while I was there young children were being gathered together for their regular *khichuri* [rice and lentil porridge] lunch, a communal arrangement. There is, of course, no water or electricity, and there are no sanitation facilities. The government does not believe these people exist, although without their services there would be no municipal services in Patna city.

Twenty years ago the Communist Party of India (CPI) would organize the slum-dweller's struggles against landlord threats and evictions. But nowadays, except at election time, no political party has attempted to assist them. In any case, how effective can an outsider be as an organizer?

In 1976, during the Emergency, the Congress (I) started its 'beautification' programme. 'Beautification' means destroying the decades-old slum-metropolises and erecting single-family dwellings to house mainly non-poor government workers. In 1977, when the Janata government came to power, the Karpoori Thakur Ministry even passed a new act to prevent the bulldozing of slums. But in no time they themselves started smashing up bustees with the help of their political cadres. Mandiri bustee was evicted and three other bustees were smashed. In 1979, the local CPI member of the state legislature, Ramesh Singh, was allotted the Lohanipur bustee area by the government and in no time he mounted a campaign to evict the dwellers so that he could build houses for business and rental purposes aimed at middle and upper income sectors of society.

It was in 1980 that slum-dwellers began a sustained, organized drive to shore up all their resources, link up with other bustees, and forge a network for their own defence. Kishori Das, born and brought up in the slums – his father was a rickshaw puller and his mother served as a housemaid – began organizing the Lohanipur bustee-dwellers against police and *goonda* [hoodlum] attacks. Kishori, who had already passed his MA and LLB while living in the slums and while organizing his people, made sure that they were aware of their rights as citizens of India.

Meanwhile, other college students and intellectuals had formed the Rashtriya Nava Nirman Sangh (RNNS) to go and work in the bustees, principally to organize an anti-alcohol campaign and focus on the main enemies of the bustee-dwellers, the police and *goondas*. Organizers went to all forty-five bustees and as a result were able to unite seventeen existing local organizations in an expanded RNNS. Their main slogan was and continues to be '*Jis jamin pur hum basha gherey hain, woh zamin hamara hai*' ('Where we have built our houses, the land belongs to us'). In November 1980 they showed their organizational strength and unity when 5,000 slum-dwellers went in a procession to the District Magistrate's house to demand ration cards. Ration cards had been introduced principally so that the poor could be assured of food, as hoarding had become endemic. The District Magistrate refused the cards, stating that without 'holding numbers' (given to individuals who have land in their names and therefore addresses) no ration cards would be issued. The poor responded with *dharnas* (sit-ins) and *gheraos* (passive resistance encirclements of buildings), and they actively resisted attacks by police and political gangsters aimed at intimidating them. Eventually 45,000 ration cards were made out to the slum-dwellers. This was a major victory and reflected the genius and tenacity of poor people's grassroots organization, led and organized in most cases by poor, illiterate citizens.

After this important victory, the central focus of their struggle was directed at the government-inspired eviction programmes which were invariably life-and-death struggles against the police and CPI *goondas*. The complete turnaround by the CPI is reflected in that party's becoming landholders in the slums. This convinced the slum-dwellers of the CPI's hypocrisy. 'If you are not an all-weather friend and fighter, you are no friend', as one slum organizer put it.

The battle against eviction centred around Lohanipur bustee. The Indian People's Front office is situated in the heart of this slum. Ramesh Singh, the CPI legislator, and his gangsters accompanied by the police, raided the bustee several times. They always swooped down on the bustee in the afternoon when the majority of men had left for work and it was left to the women and children to defend their homes. The raids were initiated with warrants of arrest and followed with physical assaults, breaking of utensils and demolishing and firebombing of shacks.

Kishori Das, the convenor of what is now the BJJBS, took me to Purba Lohanipur where I met Shanti Debi, the woman who led the resistance in June 1981 against the police-*goonda* onslaught. The June incident at Purba Lohanipur assumed major proportions when, day after day, members of the RNNS (later reorganized as the BJJBS) mobilized a tremendous retaliation movement. Reporters from major national dailies descended on this god-forsaken hole to interview Shanti Debi and photographs of her after she was brutally beaten up in police custody were flashed all over the country. The Bihar Assembly was in an uproar. Opposition members made political capital out of the situation. The net result was that in July 1981 the government cancelled the allotment to Ramesh Singh in the face of the determined struggle of the bustee-dwellers. Now the entire plot of land is not registered in anyone's name. This second victory of the RNNS galvanized it into action on other fronts. Struggles to set up schools were initiated. The Kamgar Mahila Sangathan (Women Workers' Group) also came into existence with Madhuri Debi as President and Jhugni Debi as Secretary, both Harijan working women from the slums.

At the IPF office, I also met Dhir Singh Balmiki, General Secretary of the Patna Nigam Mazdoor Sangh, another constituent of the IPF. Dhir Singh is a Harijan whose father, a sweeper, hailed from Uttar Pradesh. Dhir Singh himself started as a sweeper at the age of thirteen. Now he is thirty years old. The organization is a sweepers' and cleaners' union. The majority of the 7,000 municipal workers in Patna are from the lower castes. Dhir Singh is also an important office bearer of the BJJBS, since he himself was born and has always lived in the slums. In March 1981 in Nayagram bustee the drunken son of the local Deputy Superintendent of Police rammed his jeep into a narrow alley and ran over a baby. The Sangh members immediately surrounded the jeep and would not release it for seven days, in spite of repeated attempts by the police to retrieve it. Finally, the District Magistrate agreed to the demands of the people to give a job to the unemployed father of the baby who was killed. The Congress (I) then appeared on the scene, promising to follow through on the demand if the bustee would be renamed for Sanjay Gandhi. They promptly went about hanging up pictures of Indira and Sanjay. This infuriated the people who tore down the pictures and instead renamed the bustee after Shaheed Bhagat Singh [a radical nationalist hanged by the British before Independence]. Immediately, clashes commenced with the Congress (I) and numerous attempts were made to set the slum on fire.

At the same time, *jhopris* [slums] in the Gaya area of Bihar were also being organized. Under the aegis of the Nagar Bikash Sangh an anti-alcohol campaign had started. This Sangh later joined the RNNS. At the same time, similar work had started in Nawada, Nalanda, Motihari and Rajgir, and it was as a direct result of co-ordinating all these struggles around the state that the RNNS was transformed into the Bihar Pradesh Rastra Nava Nirman Sangh. At the same time other groups were also active in both rural and urban

Bihar, including the Chatra Yuva Sangharsh Vahini, a break-away Jayaprakash Narayan style organization that has done grassroots organizing amongst the peasantry of Bodh Gaya. The Bihar Kisan Sabha was especially effective in developing committees in practically every nook and corner of Bihar. A member of another organization remarked that the 'Kisan Sabha is in practically every village in Bihar and is expanding its base constantly.'

On 22 and 23 March 1982, a *Sammelan* (conference) of the All-Bihar Jhuggi-Jhopri organizations was held. Eighty-seven delegates attended the conference and this is where the RNNS formally became the Bihar Jhuggi-Jhopri Bashi Sangh (BJJBS). A secretariat and a council were elected and the closing ceremony was marked by a massive torchlight procession. In June the *Times of India* remarked that all these organizations were part of an elaborate network, painstakingly constructed by the Naxalites over the years, and they were undoubtedly 'casting a shadow' all over Bihar.

The *jhuggi-jhopri*-dwellers' struggle has now taken root in all urban areas of Bihar. Every day there are reports coming in of clashes in Arrah, Madhubani and Nawada. Krishnadeo Prasad Jadav, the BJJBS honorary secretary, told me that 'it is fast becoming an India-wide phenomenon. Very simply, on one hand are fascist-type bureaucrats concerned only with beautifying cities, and on the other hand are the poor people of India defending their right to survive.' When the IPF organized its 15 October demonstration against the Bihar Press Bill [legislation that was designed sharply to restrict freedom of the press, a bill that became a popular symbol of repression], *roti* [bread] was made assembly-line style in the *jhopris* to supply the peasants who came from all over Bihar to join the demonstration. This showed the strong solidarity that is being forged through struggles of town and rural poor people.

From Lohanipur I went to Kankarbagh Thana, the colony that had just been renamed Shahid Bhagat Singh Colony. I met Tota Chowdhury, a young man in his twenties, who is the Patna district secretary of BJJBS. I also met Hiralal, who is the local branch secretary and owner of a tea shop in the middle of an open field. We sat down in his tea shop and talked of local activists. Tota explained the history of the local struggle in their colony.

It was Hiralal who summarized the feelings of India's wretched of the earth.

> We are citizens of India. Allot land to us — we will pay rent; we don't want to do anything illegal. We also want to make this town beautiful; give us water, electricity, schools for our children. But without alternate arrangements no bulldozer can move us from here. We will do *satyagraha* [civil disobedience], we will even do *atmadaha*, and we will fight back with whatever we have until our last drop of blood is taken away by the government.

More than 110 years after the Paris Commune, a bedraggled mass of people in a different land under a different sky, shivering and starving in the cold, straining almost severed sinews, are putting up new barricades in the streets of Patna. The cobblestones are coming loose, while a determined mass of

Indian citizens attempt to storm the heavens.

* * * *

Song of The Republic and The Dog
Namdeo Dhasal, 1973[1]

> Dog, leashed dog,
> He howls and barks from time to time.
> This is his constitutional right.
> He lives on stale crumbs.
> His mind is calloused with endured injustice.
> If at a rebellious moment it becomes unbearable
> and he jerks at his leash, tries to break his chain,
> then he is shot.
>
> In the crowded streets
> the drums of bunkus freedom are played.
> Friends, I ask an uncircumcized boy
> the meaning of democracy,
> 'do you have any inkling of it?'
> I ask the mother with the wornout old patched sari
> the worth of breast milk.
> I ask the man who works like an ox
> about fulfilment, prosperity, deprivation.
> These riddles have turned my mind helter-skelter
>   'Red carriage with green handles
>   widowed prostitutes sit inside'[2]
> Do you know, do you know what it is?
>
> He whose heart has become stone
> and his skin a rhinocerous hide
> and he is hanging stuffed with sawdust in a museum
> now only can his head remain
> cool, cool, expansive, and peaceful.
> How terrible, how terrible the age is,
> the thieves' age.
> We can't even chat about crops and water.
> The dark empire of hunger, the guts which have run dry,
> the ferocious python which wanders in them.
> We are not even allowed to weep.
> Liberty, equality, fraternity,
> the banyan tree of private property —[3]
> everything is equal before the law.
>   'Eat, drink, and be merry,
>   Go to hell'
> O how strange is this age, this dark age.
>
> We live to drink tea in hotels.
> We touch cup to cup, saucer to saucer.
> We search the railway timetable for a two hour journey.
> We try to fill up the Kumbhamela[4] of our existence
> with many colours and many fashions.
> After excessive tension we gather in public gardens.

We play the rythmic flute of our breaths.
The two children of poverty,
One white, one black.
Sea-saws are played on in sovereign gardens.
Dry tombs are impressed on the screen of the mind.

The laudatory songs of democracy are forced down.
Hybrid, hybrid —
What bastard brought this to us?
It won't take root in flesh
It won't mix in blood
It won't flower or give fruit
It won't give shade to the weary and tired
It no more fits the body than a ready-made shirt.

The gaping wounds on the body will not vanish.
We are becoming homeless.
We are becoming orphans.
Leaving our houses to the winds we are returning
to the burial grounds.
We dig up the bones of forty-two generations.
We sell them for four annas [a few cents] a kilo.
We fill the belly of the skeleton.
In the nation which spewed 'golden smoke'[5]
the market place of bones is flourishing.
We have become fakirs of fate.
Golden sparrow, golden sparrow,
golden birdseed, golden cage.
We are being sold.
How white are these travellers[6]
How white are these beggars
How white are these hunters
In their hands the white hunted rabbits.
On the table spread with a nice cloth they have placed their prey.
They pull out the daggar — swish, swish —
they pierce the rabbits' genitals
The geyser of blood gushes forth.

My mind is turning into blood-bathed doves.

The messengers of peace are dashing along the path of the sky.

The song emerges from the chaos, the song of the Republic:
    'Give alms, the eclipse is over,
    Give alms, the eclipse is over.'[7]

[1. Dhasal, one of the founders of the Dalit Panthers movement, was born and raised in the slums of Bombay. The English translation used here is by Vidya Dixit, Gail Omvedt, Jayant Karve, Eleanor Zelliot and Bharat Patankar, and was first published in the *Bulletin of Concerned Asian Scholars*, vol. 10, no. 3 (1978).
    2. A Marathi riddle. The answer is 'watermelon', but its use here is to emphasize absurdity.
    3. Banyan trees, putting down air roots, quickly smother other vegetation.

4. An important Hindu religious fair.

5. In the mythic 'golden age' of India even smoke was golden.

6. The word translated as 'white' is the Marathi *shubhra*, which means white, clean, pure, nice, etc.

7. Anything given during an eclipse is inauspicious, but desperate beggars seek to hurry gifts along by shouting before an eclipse is over. The reference here is to the desperate condition of Dalits under the Republic.]

* * * *

It is unlikely that any one organization will ever unify all Dalits. Differences in philosophy and strategy are quite as pronounced in the Dalit population as in the rest of Indian society, and personal conflicts among leaders are quite as common. However, since the 1930s there have been repeated efforts to develop large-scale interstate organizations that could mobilize numbers in defence of rights and still remain distinctively responsive to the felt needs of the Dalit community. Unfortunately such organization has required precisely the resources Untouchables have not had: large numbers of individuals who are fluent in English, the de facto *all-India language; a large pool of middle-class skills and incomes; freedom to participate without suppression; access to the national media.*

The policies of Scheduled Caste educational benefits and public sector job reservations have begun to reduce some of these limitations; there is a slowly growing Dalit middle class, in spite of chronic sabotage within these programmes and continuing limited access to incomes from land or private sector jobs. However, other impediments remain. Civil service regulations restrict overtly political activity by government employees. More importantly, Untouchable employees in both the private and the public sector are seen as tokens whose function is to improve the dominant society's image — social protest activity, however legal, often brings sharp retribution by higher-caste co-workers and supervisors. The ultimate bitter irony is that the same efforts that bring job retribution are routinely ignored by the Indian media, thus blocking Dalit ability to communicate with one another and the dominant society.

There have been no complete solutions to these problems, but there are occasional breakthroughs. Beginning in the 1970s, one association begun by Dalit government employees, BAMCEF, constructed a multistate base, a chain of journals printed in several different languages, and an ideology that emphasized co-operation among Dalits, tribals, religious minorities and low-status Hindu castes. Members come from a variety of these groups, and have jobs that range from peon to skilled technician to administrator. Organization style has emphasized identification with the poor rather than middle-class display. An offshoot, D-S4, was developed to tap the resources of employees' families, as well as the small community of Dalit professionals. The following excerpts from BAMCEF's English-language publication, The Oppressed Indian, *describe a multistate campaign to 'Educate, Organize, Agitate'.*

Kanshi Ram (centre), president of BAMCEF, visiting a branch office in Nagaland, a predominantly *adivasi* (tribal) state in northeastern India. With him are L. Panger Ao, Convenor of BAMCEF's Kohima unit; and Weku G Kenye, a local BAMCEF activist. *(Oppressed Indian)*

Marching to Awaken the Ambedkarite Masses

The Oppressed Indian (April 1983; May 1983)

At this juncture, twenty-five years after the sad demise of Babasaheb, some of the socially conscious followers of Dr Ambedkar launched D-S4 (Dalit Shoshit Samaj Sangharsh Samiti) under the leadership of Mr Kanshi Ram to lead the caravan of Babasaheb Ambedkar to its set destination. Through this newly formed organization a number of programmes are being launched from time to time to awaken, educate and organize the oppressed and exploited people. The 'People's Parliament', 'Poona Pact Denunciation Programme', etc. are some of the prominent programmes which not only aroused the masses but motivated them to a great extent. 'Come back the old days of Ambedkarite era', said some.

The latest venture — 'Message of D-S4: Miracle of Two Feet and Two Wheels', launched by D-S4 on 15 March 1983, in which hundreds of cyclists

Dalit home, destroyed by rural violence in Andhra Pradesh. (Courtesy E.V. Chinnaiah)

under the leadership of Mr Kanshi Ram set out to travel 3000 km distance covering thirty-five important places in seven states of northern India within forty days, is a unique one. After covering 3000 km by cycle, 300 km will be covered on foot around Delhi. It will come back to Delhi on 17 April 1983.

To some it may appear absurd and to some it may even become a thing to joke about. When we are moving in the electronics age with superjet and space vehicles moving at the speed of thousands of miles in a minute, how are these two wheels moved by two feet going to help us? It is really a question that will arise in the minds of the common people. But to such critics, the reply is very simple. Nay, they need no reply; the timely action will suffice.

What is the objective behind this venture which made Mr Kanshi Ram bicycle for 3000 km and lead the team of hundreds of cyclists at the age of fifty years? It was observed at Delhi and elsewhere that 85 per cent of the oppressed and exploited people that Dr Ambedkar nourished for years and built up their movement, have today become the tools in the hands of the ruling castes. Their habits have been so spoiled that they never feel shame when they are used by others. Whenever rallies are organized by political parties to show their strength, these poor SC/ST, OBC and minorities people rush to ride their vehicles and are paid for this. They are happy to go and strengthen the hands of their oppressors and exploiters. They neither feel shame for it nor do they think what harm they are doing to their own existence. They can build up the organization of others but can never think of their own. Most of the so-called Ambedkarites shout the slogans of 'Ambedkar Zindabad' [Long Live Ambedkar] and immediately after that they fall at the feet of Indira Gandhi [Congress (I)] or Atal Behari Vajpayee [Bharatiya Janata Party] and ask for a ticket. Theory of compromise has become a convenient tool for the so-called Ambedkarite leaders! This is happening not only around Delhi but all over India.

Need to Awaken and Educate Our People
To mend their habits and make them aware of how harmful such action is from the organizational point of view, Mr Kanshi Ram, president of D-S4, launched the 3,000 km bicycle march and 300 km walk to educate the oppressed and the exploited people that they need to build up their own organization and independent movement. Nothing can be achieved without struggle, and all struggles need the timely organization of agitations. If some agitations are required for securing rights or rightful demands it requires a show of strength. But our people are habituated to go in the buses and trucks, as they are always doing for other political parties.

Trucks, tractors, buses, cars and rail — all are in the hands of capitalists and those who are holding power. They can use them conveniently as and when they need them for their own benefit. The very same facilities cannot be available to the oppressed and the exploited people. They cannot organize their agitations around these machines. Bicycle is the best weapon for them in their agitations. If their two feet are all right they can reach any place to make their presence felt.

As planned, the cyclists' campaign extended over several weeks, the organization's journals reporting events in rallies in small villages and larger urban centres. Although the campaign was designed to be peaceful, the project was not always uneventful.

Nangal: The Place to Remember
Nangal, which is famous for a big dam erected there to supply water for irrigation to the land of Punjab and thereby become a continuous source of livelihood for the people of Punjab, made its place in the history of D-S4 struggle when D-S4 overpowered the Punjab police and their *goondas* [hoodlums] in the show of strength that took place on 31 March 1983.

The cycle march which started from Kiratpur Sahib reached Nangal at 11.00 a.m. When the procession was moving ahead shouting slogans, a Sikh motorcyclist pushed the leading girls. Both girls fell down and many other D-S4 cyclists too. Immediately the Sikh youth was caught and the people gathered there gave him a good slap. The procession then started again towards Dr Ambedkar Library, Guru Ravidas Mandir and Nangal Township. They were welcomed there by the people.

In the evening when the cyclists were preparing for their night halt, one ASI and two constables with rifles in their hands reached there in a jeep and caught hold of Mr Umrao Singh, driver of the *matador* [supply truck]. When he saw this unexpected development he said 'Why do you catch me? If you want anything, meet the president of D-S4.' They listened to nothing and took Umrao Singh to the police station, using disrespectful language against Kanshi Ramji. In the police station the local Sikh leaders were sitting. [The confrontation pits Sikhs from higher castes who dominate the rural Punjab economy against a mixed group of Dalits, some of whom are Sikhs from low-status castes and some non-Sikhs. Although Sikhism formally rejects casteism, untouchability has remained an important social and economic reality.]

Immediately after this, Mr Kanshi Ram instructed all the cyclists to reach the police station on their bicycles. On reaching the police station they shouted slogans. It continued for one and a half hours. In the meantime, the police brought inside the police station some Sikh *goondas* of the town and handed *lathis* [heavy poles] to them. Comrade Chhotu Ram, in the meantime, tried to get the issue settled but with no result. The police immediately opened the gate and let the *goondas* loose in a *lathi* charge. They also put off their uniforms and helped the *goondas* to beat D-S4 cyclists. It was very shameful on the part of the Punjab police that instead of getting the issue settled they came down to the level of *goondas*. D-S4 cyclists gave a fitting reply. Mr Aman Kumar was forcibly taken inside. Then they made Mr Kanshi Ram the target of attack. During the scuffle two of the activists received injuries. They were given treatment immediately. The news of shameful acts by the Punjab police spread immediately to all parts of the district. Thousands of Dalit-Shoshit people rushed to the Nangal police station. A group of Nihang Sikhs from Anandpur Sahib also rushed there. More than 5,000 people reached within no time. They all demanded justice. The entire situation was in the control of D-S4 by this time. Prominent leaders of different parties and organizations also reached there. They tried to compromise. They tried to save the culprits. They insistently requested Mr Kanshi Ram to come inside and speak to the leaders. The crowd demanded that the Dy. SP/SP [Deputy Superintendent and Superintendent of Police] should come out. The Dy. SP came out and took Kanshi Ram for discussion. After discussion, Mr Kanshi Ram gave the complaint against the police in writing, on the basis that immediate action will be taken against the culprits. At 11.30 p.m. the procession came back to Ravidas Mandir.

Next day on 1 April 1983, at about 1.00 p.m., more than 10,000 people in the form of a procession reached the Nangal police station and were converted into a public meeting.

Addressing the meeting, Mr Kanshi Ram said that yesterday the Dy. SP gave us assurance in front of all that before your departure the action will be taken against the guilty police and *goondas*. But no action has been taken so far. We have therefore come here to demand justice. Now we called the people from the surrounding Nangal area. If by the evening no action is taken the people from the whole Punjab will be called for demand of justice. He further said, we are fighting against injustice. How can we tolerate it if we ourselves do not get justice? We will not tolerate injustice even if we are compelled to overstay in this town for a long time for this purpose.

Among the local leaders, Sant Baba Nand Singh Barmauta said that the present government belongs to the rich. Sant Tirth Singh, in charge of Jivan Singh Gurudwara of Anandpur Sahib, said that wherever there was injustice the Nihangs [a special Sikh sect] have rushed to help. He said, to get justice for yesterday's attack on D-S4 cyclists he would order out the entire army of Nihangs. Sant Kilkhus Singh said that we are prepared to make all sacrifices. Mr Surat Singh demanded justice against injustice. Mr Pritam Singh attributed the cause of this injustice to the social system created by Manu.

Among others who spoke on the occasion were Miss Harvinder Kaur, Baba Singh, Tirsem Lal Sindhu (President, 4th Class Employees Organization), Sarbans Singh (Kakegarm India), Pritam Singh (Village Chief, Mechhpur), Harish Chandra, Comrade Attar Singh (CPI), Dilawara Singh, Singhara Singh (SPI), Sushil Kumar, Jitendra Kumar (Delhi), Mrs Paramit Kaur, Aman Kumar, Kunwar Shyam Singh Tej (Delhi), Dildara Singh (Hydel Project, Central Trade Union).

D-S4 Demand Accepted: Two Police Officials Suspended

On 3 April, SDM, Anandpur Sahib, declared the suspension of one ASI, Mr Ajmer Singh, and Constable Mr Dharan Singh. On this occasion Mr Kanshi Ram and other trade union leaders were present.

Thus three days agitation conducted in front of Nangal police station by Kanshi Ramji was taken back after suspension of the police officials and then the cyclists started for their onward march.

A similar but far more extensive 'awakening campaign' took place from late 1983 through early 1984. The final rally collided with the interests of the governing party and its control of the police in the national capital, but the organization was able to mobilize sufficient opposition support in Parliament partially to counter government efforts to block the rally. The group had less success in dealing with the media, which successfully muffled the impact of the campaign by not reporting it. The campaigners were still able to reach large numbers of their target audience by relying on the flexibility of bicycle technology and by housing campaigners in villages and teeming urban slum hutment areas along their route, but news was available only to those directly contacted and to subscribers of the organization's own publications.

First Phase of 100 Days Social Action Concludes at Delhi

The Oppressed Indian (April 1984)

It is very sad that our government is not only ruling over us but

BAMCEF and D-S4 activists proceeding along one of the national highways leading out of Delhi during the national Bicycle March. *(Oppressed Indian)*

simultaneously exploiting us. Because of this it took fifteen days to get permission for our function. I knew well in advance that for this permission we would have to seek the help of Parliament, and ultimately we had to do this. Today, all you people, both the leaders and workers, see the strength of Dalit-Shoshit people in front of the Parliament. You must know that when the government of the country itself breaks the rules, it is very difficult to work under democratic norms. The entire atmosphere of the country has been disturbed by the present government. We want to tell Indira Gandhi that by delaying our permission for fifteen days she has committed a great blunder. Those of our friends who raised our voice in Parliament, their seats are confirmed.

With these words Mr Kanshi Ram, President of D-S4, alerted the present government of Indira Gandhi while delivering the presidential address at the Boat Club Lawns on 15 March 1984, which was the concluding function organized by D-S4 at the end of the First Phase of 100 Day Social Action for Equality and Self-respect. More than 25,000 Dalit-Shoshit people, including 10,000 cyclists, were present on the Boat Club Lawns.

On 6 December 1983, D-S4 had launched the countrywide Social Action-Struggle for Equality and Self-respect, which commenced from Kanyakumari [the southern-most tip of India] and simultaneously from other places, viz. Kargil (in Kashmir), Kohima (Nagaland) [eastern-most India, where

BAMCEF/D-S4 is predominantly tribal in composition] , Puri (Orissa) and Porbandar (Gujarat), all the five corners of the country.

During these 100 days of the all-India programme thousands of D-S4 activists started for Delhi on their bicycles with blue colour flags flying on the bicycles. In all they covered more than 500,000 km distance by bicycles, addressed more than 7,000 big and small meetings on their way to Delhi in villages, towns and big cities, and awakened more than eight crores of people about the struggle for equality and self-respect. They all came to Delhi along national highways, state highways and link roads.

Delhi and 250 km Range
The cyclists, who started from long distances along the national highways, state highways and link roads, drove the bicycles to the fixed distance and returned. The other activists then started from that very same place. By this means they maintained the link, and this link was maintained till they reached 250 km distances from Delhi. There were thirty such bicycle marches

Dalit women in the city of Pune stage a silent march to protest atrocities against Dalits in the villages of Maharashtra. (E. Zelliot)

all over India. But within the range of 250 km from Delhi, the cyclists from all the villages, towns and cities came directly to Delhi. On their way to Delhi they addressed thousands of public meetings and acquainted Dalit-Shoshit people with the glaring inequalities in all walks of life, and told them how they are being exploited by these 15 per cent Brahmans, Banias [businessmen] and feudal lords.

The cycle marches coming from the five national highways towards Delhi halted on 13 March at Faridabad, Ghaziabad, Shamli and Gannor. During the night all the D-S4 activists in the cycle march were served food and given a hearty welcome by the local D-S4 activists. Big public meetings were also arranged at Faridabad and Gannor, which were addressed by local leaders. Mr Kanshi Ram addressed meetings at Shamli and Ghaziabad.

On the morning of 14 March all the cyclists from the above five places on the national highways started for Delhi. Keeping in view their participation in the Boat Club Rally on 15 March, their arrangements for night stay and food on 14 March were made in JJ [*jhuggi/jhompri*, i.e. shanty] colonies (slum area of Delhi). These JJ colonies are full of millions of Dalit-Shoshit people, most of them coming from the surrounding states to Delhi for their livelihood.

The arrangements for night stay and food for the cyclists coming from Agra and Mathura, Faridabad and Jaipur, and from Gurgaon were made in two parts. For some of them the arrangements were made in Siddhartha JJ Colony, while for others it was made in Ambedkar Nagar. Trilokpuri and Kalyanpuri welcomed the cyclists coming from Aligarh and Ghaziabad, and arranged for their night stay and food. Cyclists from Saharanpur, Mujjafar Nagar and Shamli reached Nand Nagari and Gokulpuri where they were greeted by the local Dalit-Shoshit people and were offered food and shelter for night stay. The cyclists from Chandigarh and Sonepat were welcomed at the Singhu Border by the D-S4 activists from JJ Vazirpur Colony and their arrangements were made at the same colony. Cyclists from Rohtak were accommodated in Mangolpuri JJ Colony and Khyala JJ Colony for night stay. In all, arrangements for all the D-S4 activists coming from the five national highways were made at the *jhuggi/jhompri* colonies on the Delhi border with the help of local D-S4 activists and those volunteers who came in advance from different states to participate in the Boat Club Rally.

All the cyclists crossed the border of Delhi in the afternoon and entered the respective JJ colonies where their arrangements were made. In the evening they moved throughout the colonies chanting slogans like 'D-S4 Zindabad' and 'D-S4 Stands for Struggle for Equality and Self-respect'. All Delhi was stunned to see this unique type of agitation which never took place in the capital earlier.

Public meetings were arranged in all the JJ colonies where the cyclists were halted for night stay. The local D-S4 activists and thousands of other Dalit-Shoshit people participated in the meetings, which were addressed by local leaders.

From Red Fort to Boat Club [both locations of important political symbolism]

Very early in the morning on 15 March all the cyclists resting in different JJ colonies started for Red Fort Parade Ground along the routes already finalized. On their way to Red Fort, they drove in the disciplined way and chanted slogans. By 9.30 a.m. all the cyclists reached Red Fort. From there they started for the Boat Club in a disciplined queue of two each. In addition to the cyclists, thousands of ladies and children reached Red Fort by buses, trucks and trains.

At 11.00 a.m. the rally started from Red Fort to Boat Club. It was led by Kanshi Ramji. At the forefront two D-S4 activists walked slowly with the D-S4 banner in their hands, followed by *matadors*, trucks and buses, etc.

The rally passed through Daryanganj, Delhi Gate, Ambedkar Stadium, Bahadur Shah Zafar Marg, Tilak Brij, India Gate and finally reached the Boat Club where thousands of people were already waiting to welcome the cyclists.

First Time in Delhi

The bicycle rally, wherein more than 10,000 cyclists from all over surrounding area of Delhi within the range of 250 km participated with blue colour D-S4 flags on their bicycles, was unique and organized for the first time. Never before could such a rally be organized by any organization. The Dalit-Shoshit people, including the Scheduled Castes and Scheduled Tribes, had been brought to the Boat Club a number of times loaded into trucks and buses by Indira Gandhi, Atal Behari Vajpayee and many others. But this was the first time they came on their own and that too by their own bicycles, driving the same from more than 250 km distance and also back by the same bicycles. Under the leadership of D-S4, Dalit Shoshit Samaj Sangarsh Samiti, the Dalit-Shoshit people for the first time exhibited their own show of strength. This was too much for the ruling castes and their supporters. It worked as a red signal for these exploiters.

5. Legislatures, Courts, Public Policy

Thus far we have focused on Dalit voices that are part of the informal public opinion process. There are, however, a wide range of articulate Dalit voices that are routinely raised within the formal public policy process, including those of legislators from the reserved Scheduled Caste constituencies. To make this statement is to defy the gods of stereotype, for most Indians are firmly convinced that Scheduled Caste legislators are silent dolts who, at most, raise their voices only to seek narrow privilege. The opinion of many Dalits is, if anything, even harsher: sincere representatives, even though a minority, should be able to produce pro-Dalit and pro-poor policies. The media rarely mentions the speeches and activities of Scheduled Caste legislators; therefore they must be sitting silently in Delhi or state capitals.

There are, in fact, a number of severe limitations on Scheduled Caste influence, but it may be easier to think about these if we first clear away some of the misperceptions. The following speeches to the Indian Parliament (the Lok Sabha) are a sampling of the many given yearly by Scheduled Caste MPs. The first was selected from the period of the Janata Party government and serves to illustrate the continuation of Dalit problems from one party administration to another. The second and third are the product of taking two random volumes of recent Lok Sabha debates from a library shelf. Fellow explorers should be warned that they will need a list of reserved constituencies from election reports or from a biography of parliamentarians. Debate proceedings and reports of parliamentary committees do not specify 'reserved' constituencies, and Scheduled Caste MPs often (as in the second and third examples below) address themselves to issues that are important to Dalits but are by no means exclusive to them.

Ineffective Control of Violence Against Harijans

Shri Kusuma Krishna Murthy (Amalapuram, Andhra Pradesh; Congress-I)

Lok Sabha Debates, 6th Series, vol. XIV, no. 44 (26 April 1978)

Mr Deputy Speaker, Sir, I rise to express some of my views on the working of the Home Ministry. Much has been said about law and order in this country and I would like to add only one thing, that this important subject cannot be dispensed with simply by saying it is a state subject. [At different times, both the Congress and Janata central governments sought to evade responsibility for rising violence against minorities by saying this was entirely a law and order issue and thus under the control of the state governments, not the centre.] Even under the very nose of the central government, in Delhi, the situation of law and order is quite alarming, as we know pretty well. Therefore, the government has to take serious note of it and see that the situation is brought under control because the health and progress of the entire nation depends on law and order.

I would like to stress another equally important situation in India. But before switching on to it, I would like to make a reference to something. Yesterday, on 25 April 1978, in New York, in the United Nations Conference, our External Affairs Minister Shri Atal Bihari Vajpayee, very emphatically stated that India is to step up assistance to the Namibian patriots, both morally and materially, to bring genuine independence to the people of Namibia. He further expressed India's all-out support to the people of Namibia for total eradication of the evil practice of racism and apartheid. Here, I would like to bring to the notice of this ministry that the plight of seventeen crores Harijans in India is drawing the special attention of the entire world and this demonstrates clearly how far we are morally justified in supporting a cause outside our country while forgetting wilfully the equally serious cause in our country. Nowhere in the history of mankind is there any system like a caste system as we possess it in India. This caste system alone has created a section of sub human-beings in this country in the form of Harijans, whose human rights have been trampled systematically for ages. Under this mysterious system, these sub human-beings, namely Harijans, are safe as long as they choose to remain as sub human-beings. Otherwise, they have to face the eternal war of extermination which is silently operating in the form of atrocities.

The nature of atrocities would be clear if we go into certain real instances throughout the country. For instance, in Utta Pradesh let us take up Meerut, the home district of the Home Minister, where in July 1977 virtually the rule of jungle prevailed when one Mr Baleshar, a Harijan, was brutally murdered for growing wheat on land allotted to him by the government, and then the other Harijan women were mercilessly beaten in a bid to intimidate and terrorize them. Here another important thing is that most of the Gram Sabha land was illegally possessed by the high-caste people there, and when we met the Sub-Divisional Magistrate Shri D. S. Bains, he said that the problem was basically social because, somehow, the Harijans were not acceptable as standard human-beings by the rural rich. Apart from this, 92,000 Harijans were deprived of their allotted land and we do not have a precise record as to how many of them have been killed. According to the information supplied by the Minister of Home Affairs, the total number of atrocities on Harijans in Uttar Pradesh in 1977 alone was 4,019. And the other important aspect to be taken into serious consideration here is that when we met the Harijans

119

there, they clearly stated that 'the police do not listen to us and the police do not take down our complaints and we have no place to appeal'.

Coming to Madhya Pradesh, in August, in Kanadia Village of Ratlam District, a grisly incident occurred when four Harijans were brutally murdered and several others seriously crippled. Here the problem was that agricultural land allotted to them by the government was taken back forcibly from the Harijans. An important issue to be taken into consideration is that the Madhya Pradesh Vidhan Sabha [state legislature] was stunned to know that the official machinery moved into action only twenty-four hours after this grisly incident occurred. The Vidhan Sabha was dumbfounded to know that the deceased Harijans were insulted even after they were slain by the assailants who chopped off their noses, their ears and their fingers and tore open their stomachs and terrorized their women folk in a bid to intimidate and molest them. The police station, which was not far away from this place, did not take any action and it appears the officials had prior intimation about this but even then they did not care to take any action in this matter.

The states where the Congress government is functioning are not exceptions in this matter because the Congress has its share of responsibility for the present state of affairs in our country; after all, it has ruled the country for most of the time since 1947. For instance in Andhra Pradesh there were some ghastly incidents of atrocities committed on Harijans. In July 1977, in a place called Chinaogirala in Krishna district, one Harijan was axed to death when the landlords attacked them with knives, spears, axes and other deadly weapons. The landlords and their *goondas* behaved like inhuman brutes when they tore off the sarees and blouses of innocent and helpless Harijan women in a bid to molest them. Similarly in Katapalli Village in Mahboobnagar District in Andhra Pradesh, Harijans were virtually under social boycott imposed by the landlords there for about a month. They were deprived of farm work and put under great stress and strain simply because thirty-five families have been allotted *pattas* [grants of land, part of a programme of small grants to landless villagers] .

If we come to Bihar, this state is a major part of lawlessness in our country. Belchi, Patna, Dharampur, Rohtas, Begusarai, Bihar Sharif and Bishrampur are a few out of many places where countless families of Harijans have been burnt alive. Belchi stands out because of its inhuman brutality. All eight out of the eleven victims who were Harijans were dragged out of their huts where they had sought refuge, and shot dead in cold blood and burnt. Here it was sought to be played down by our Home Minister, Mr Charan Singh, by describing it as a clash between two hardened criminals. But when a nine-member committee from the Parliamentary Forum for Scheduled Castes and Scheduled Tribes, of which I am a member, visited the Belchi village, they came to a clear conclusion that it was a clear case of a massacre of helpless Harijans based on caste hatred.

Again in Madhipur of Monghyr District in Bihar, in July 1977, Harijans were brutally murdered and cut into pieces and thrown into the river Ganga, about which Mr Kapil Deo Singh, Bihar Agriculture Minister, has clearly said that it has created panic and terror among the Harijans of the village.

In Dharampur Harijans were chased and shot dead in their own huts. I went there personally and saw with my own eyes the traces of bullet holes in their mud walls. There, one Mr Shivamuni, aged thirty [who had] studied up to BA, tried to be assertive. He was chased and shot dead in his hut and same was the fate of the other three Harijans who tried to be assertive. Besides three Harijan women were seriously wounded when they tried to save the lives of their husbands. In Rohtas on the Holi day itself thirty-one Harijans were reported to have been burnt alive.

In Bishrampur the brutal killings almost resembled the Belchi incident.

Above all, in Jamatara, mass rape, mass loot and mass arson occurred when the raiders raped six Harijan women and tortured other Harijan women by burning their thighs and breasts inhumanely. The worst part of it is that the police officials who had prior knowledge have not taken any proper action.

These were some of the grisly incidents on which we will be able to come to the clear-cut conclusion that there are three important factors involved in these atrocities. One is the assertiveness by the Harijans and the other is the torturing by the rich and the third one is the splendid silence of the officials. I believe now that I need not lengthen the catalogue of crimes against the Harijans. But the alarming feature is that the atrocities are continuously growing unchecked. This is clear from the Home Ministry's report itself. In 1975 the number of atrocities on Harijans was 7,781, in 1976 it was 5,968 and in 1977 it was 9,225, but according to the report of the Commissioner for Scheduled Castes and Scheduled Tribes there are about 10,000 odd incidents in 1978.

This is the situation in which there is an increase in violence against Harijans, but the way in which the Home Minister is handling the situation is quite disheartening and disappointing. As we know . . . while Rome was burning, Nero was fiddling. Similarly, while the Harijans are burning, Mr Charan Singh is translating them into percentages. Curiously enough he contends that just not more than 1 per cent atrocities on Harijans are committed so far. Probably he means by this that 14 per cent atrocities on Harijans is still permissible in order to complete their quota of 15 per cent reservation.

Thus there is a systematic extermination of assertive Harijans going on in the form of atrocities. It is basically a wrong conception to presume that these atrocities are non-existing in some of the states, but the atrocities are the direct result of some basic factors. They are primarily the assertiveness of the Harijans to protect themselves, and this assertiveness is the direct result of a growing awareness of the basic realities of human-beings. Secondly, the economic inability of the Harijans, but not the physical inability. The economic inability made them completely free from possessing weapons, either secretly or legally, to protect themselves; consequently they are becoming helpless victims. Again this economic inability is the direct result of exploitation of labour. After all the capitalist exploited the labour. Thirdly, the functioning of the caste-infected bureaucrats who are actually in charge of the entire administration continuously. Therefore, whenever and wherever these factors coincide, either intentionally or accidentally the result would be brutal atrocities on Harijans. Evidently the purpose of such dreadful vengeance is to terrorize Harijans to prevent them from becoming assertive. But the multiplicity of atrocities in various dreadful forms cannot suppress them from the growing awareness. I do not know how many of our leaders have realized that this growing determination of the suppressed people to assert themselves is clearly indicative of a new class struggle in India. There is ample evidence from the lessons of history. Without noticing this real phenomenon, some of the Harijan leaders started thinking in terms of demanding more and more guarantees. But I do not insist on such impractical approaches because law is not enough. Constitutional provisions have been proved to be very very ineffective during the last thirty years. There are constitutional provisions in the form of Articles 16, 17, 46, 335 and 338 for the exclusive benefits of Harijans. There is a Commissioner for the Scheduled Castes and the Scheduled Tribes for the exclusive benefits of Harijans. There is a Parliamentary Committee for the Welfare of Scheduled Castes and the Scheduled Tribes. There are a number of practicable solutions in the form of recommendations of Elayperumal Committee and Shilu Ao Committee. Above all the essence of every manifesto of every political party, every time shouts that it was born only for the upliftment of Harijans. Thus, in spite of the existence of so many safeguards the social plight of Harijans today in our country is fast deteriorating — from bad to worse.

The problem is basically social rather than economic in nature. And unless there is a drastic change in the attitude of the people towards our casteism, this problem can never be solved at all and the shameful incidents like washing the statue unveiled by Shri Jagjiwan Ram with Ganga water would go on continuing.

Besides, it is the implementation that matters, not the increase of paper guarantees, and unless the unfaithfulness of the caste-infected bureaucrats towards the principles of the Constitution is penalized, there will be absolutely no use enacting any number of laws for protecting the Harjians. Therefore, there are two practicable solutions. The first and the foremost is, there should be a powerful administrative machinery with state-wide offices under the charge of dedicated Harijans exclusively to strictly penalize the unfaithfulness of any government official towards any measure meant for Harijans.

Before submitting my second solution, I would like to make a few observations.

These Harijans can wait up to any number of decades to secure their just demands constitutionally guaranteed. They can put up with any kind of drudgery and poverty up to any length of time. They can tolerate even if their sheltering huts are burnt down. And they can also suffer the punishment of criminal cases wrongfully inflicted on them. But is it fair on the part of the Government to make us wait helplessly and silently when our very self-respect and modesty is brutally attacked? And is it justifiable on the part of the government to make us wait silently and helplessly when our innocent women are stripped naked in broad daylight and raped before our eyes? 'Nobody can philosophize while his wife is being abducted', emphatically said Harold Laski, the Jew and the 20th Century's greatest political thinker, who knew the inhuman sufferings and tortures in the hands of German Nazis. Therefore, I would like to submit with all my respect to this august House that the government should forcibly take away immediately all the illegal weapons possessed by the rich in the rural areas. If you fail to make the rich surrender their illegal weapons you should kindly give the protective weapons both freely and legally to the helpless Harijans to protect themselves. It is not the question of survival but it is the question of self-respect and modesty

Bicycle marchers entering a village in the northern state of Jammu & Kashmir, with a welcoming band arranged by local Dalits. *(Oppressed Indian)*

of seventeen crores of Harijans who can easily constitute a nation by themselves.

If Gandhiji had not got the communal award modified by risking his life, Dr Ambedkar would have created a safe and respected separate land for Harijans as Mohd. Ali Jinnah did for Muslims. Dr Ambedkar signed the Poona Pact by reluctantly giving up the successfully won separate electorate from Ramsey MacDonald just to save the life of Gandhiji with a fond hope that this nation would be grateful in saving the lives of crores of his people. But India proved time and again that Dr Ambedkar committed a mistake on this issue in believing them and in signing the Poona Pact. I am afraid, that the nation would again have to be partitioned unless the self-respect and modesty of the seventeen crores Harijans in the country is safe and secure. This is not a routine request but a time-bound warning of seventeen crore Harijans in this country.

After all, human life is to live, not just exist.

Employment of Children in Hazardous Jobs

Shri Krishna Chandra Halder (Durgapur, West Bengal; Communist Party — Marxist)
Lok Sabha Debates, 7th series, vol. XXXVIII, nos. 43–44 (3–4 May 1983)

Mr Deputy Speaker, Sir, first I will like to thank Shri Madhavrao Scindia for raising this half-hour discussion in this House. You can well understand how indifferent the honourable Members on the other side [on the governing Congress benches] are towards the children who are the future of our country, as most of them are absent from the House. The earlier speakers have quoted various figures and statistics; I will not repeat them. Mention has already been made about the miserable conditions of child labour in the '*Bidi*' [home-made cigarettes] industry, in mines, in the match factories and in the fireworks units at Sivakasi. A large number of children are employed in the carpet industry also and their conditions of work are equally bad. Sir, what is the purpose of employing children in these places? The purpose is plain and simple exploitation of the children in every possible manner. The wages paid to children are much less than those paid to adult workers. No legislation regarding minimum wages is followed in their case. As a result, those who engage child labour make huge profits for themselves at the cost of these children. The children are paid a meagre two or three rupees; this is the ultimate in exploitation. The employers of child labour are making many times more profit. The honourable Labour Minister, Shri Patil, while replying to the previous speaker a short while ago, practically pleaded his helplessness in this matter. He said that there are already twelve Central legislations on the subject and that he is going to carry out amendments to them. In spite of that, what a large amount of child labour is in existence in our country! Shri Scindia has given some figures about them. But there is a slight difference with my figures. In the *Economic Times* of 10 April last year, 1982, it was stated that there are 20 million child labourers in our country. The International Labour Organization has stated that the total number of child labour in the entire world is nearly 100 million. That means that about one fifth of the entire child labour force of the world exists in my country. This shows what tremendous deterioration in the economic conditions of the people have taken place in the last thirty-five years of the post-Independence era, the low level of poverty to which our masses have fallen. As a result of this staggering poverty, people are forced to send their children, who are the future of our nation, to work in such sub-human conditions. This is not only a socio-economic problem, Sir; we will have to look at it from a humanitarian point of view also. In this context I would like to quote, Sir: 'In 1979 a survey was conducted by the Indian Council of Child Welfare. The Survey Report was that working children form one-sixth of the total labour force of our country and 8 per cent of our child population.' You can understand one sixth of our total labour force are children working in different organized and unorganized sectors, and 8 per cent of our child population. Therefore, the whole thing is a social, economic and humanitarian problem. Everybody has agreed that poverty is the main cause due to which people are compelled to send their children to work. We have to go to the root of the evil. Any piece of legislation, it may be comprehensive, it may be total, but it cannot solve the child labour problem of our country. Therefore, we have to go to the basic question which is, the eradication of poverty. You know, Sir, there is no child labour in Socialist countries!

SHRI M. RAM GOPAL REDDY [Congress (I)] : But there is family planning there which we do not do here.

SHRI KRISHNA CHANDRA HALDER: In spite of family planning, you will not be able to solve this child labour problem.

SHRI A. K. ROY [Independent] : What about the Soviet Union?

SHRI RAM GOPAL REDDY: I have been to Soviet Union. I met our Deputy Speaker there.

SHRI KRISHNA CHANDRA HALDER: The main question is poverty. Man is exploited by man. One class is exploiting another class of people. That is why the children of my country are the most exploited. Whether at Sivakasi or at any other place employing child labour, no register is maintained. Mr Scindia mentioned an accident in which thirty-two children were killed. When they visited the site of the accident, they found that there were no registers at all! That is the problem. They were told that no child was working there! Our approach should be to remove poverty. Such conditions should be created in which children would not be compelled to work as labourers. So long as we are not able to create a social system which is free from exploitation, we will not be able to prevent children from being engaged as labourers.

SHRI MADHAVRAO SCINDIA [Congress (I)] : It is the exploitation of child by man.

SHRI KRISHNA CHANDRA HALDER: So long as the exploitation is there, not only the labourers will be exploited but even the children of our country will be exploited. To stop this evil, we have to change our society. We have to form a classless society. But it will take time. We have to fight. We have to struggle. We have to change our economic, social and political structure also. Unless we can do that, it is not possible to eradicate this evil.

Before that we must have a comprehensive legislation. I want to put one question to our Labour Minister. Whether you are going to convene a meeting of all the Labour Ministers of different states, trade unions, *kisan* [peasant] organizations and social organizations to take their suggestions so that the best form of legislation could be brought forward before Parliament whereby the child labour problem could be minimized to a great extent?

MR DEPUTY SPEAKER: It is a very good question. I am appreciating your question. (Interruptions from the floor)

SHRI KRISHNA CHANDRA HALDER: Don't laugh. Those who employ child labour are anti-national.

MR DEPUTY SPEAKER: They are anti-social.

SHRI KRISHNA CHANDRA HALDER: I agree with you, Sir. They are anti-social.

SHRI MADHAVRAO SCINDIA: This is too serious a question to be made a subject of mirth. The general mood of the House should be serious.

SHRI KRISHNA CHANDRA HALDER: I am handicapped. I am waiting to put my questions. Most of the honourable Members are absent. I am here. I love our children. I love my nation. I want to say that there should not be exploitation even of children.

Therefore my submission is that we should look to the root of this evil and try to solve the basic problems. Sir, India has one fifth of the total child labour in the world, one sixth of the total labour force in our country consists of child labour. This is the magnitude of the problem! To solve it effectively we have to rise above party considerations, and view this as a national problem and to take steps unitedly at the national level with a national outlook. With that end in view, I suggest that a meeting be convened of all the Labour Ministers or Chief Ministers of different states, all trade unions, *kisan* organizations and social organizations, etc. and to consider their suggestions in the matter and a way should be found to combat the evil. If we cannot advance step by step towards a solution of this problem, then these children, the future of the nation, about whom Shri Scindia has rightly said that 'they should also bloom like beautiful flowers', they will wither away untimely. Otherwise they could make the country prosperous, they could make the country strong, and they could carry our country forward. But all these ill-fated children are withering away even before they start blooming. I would like a reply to the suggestions given by me. I would like you all to rise above party considerations and view it as a national problem and to find a solution at the national level. I want to know whether you accept my suggestions in this regard. Unless you do that, the nation will not forgive you. Be it the 20-point programme of Smt. Gandhi or a 120-point programme. To save the children who are the future of our nation, the people of our country will take to the battlefield, if necessary, and they will uproot the very foundations of this exploitation. You will not be able to stem that tidal wave however hard you may try. Still, there is time. To solve this national problem, whether you will come forward or not depends on you. I hope you will follow the right path. With that, Sir, I conclude.

Limitations of Proposed Mines (Amendment) Bill

Dr V. Kulandaivelu (Chidambaram, Tamil Nadu; Dravida Munnetra Kazhagam)
Lok Sabha Debates, 7th series, vol. XXXX, nos. 19-20 (19-20 August 1983)

Mr Chairman, Sir, on behalf of my party, the DMK, I would like to participate in the debate on the Mines (Amendment) Bill and express my views. At the outset I would like to say that the Bill is a laudable one in the sense that it lays stress on removal of certain practical difficulties experienced in enforcement, provision for additional safety regulations, closer association of workers with the safety measures, provision for minimum penalty in cases of gross negligence, etc. thus protecting and safeguarding the interests of the workers of the mines overall.

But, Sir, there are some lacunae in the Bill, although I cannot deny that there is some improvement over the previous Bill. With the passage of time we are now more conversant with the occupational health hazards, which have been on the increase in recent years. So, we should not have a cursory discussion on the Bill in the House. As you are interested in safeguarding the interests of the workers involved in mines, suggestions of the experts in the field of occupational hazards should be called in and taken into consideration. I am happy that at least after three decades the Bill is coming for a review.

Sir, with this preamble I would like to comment on certain aspects of the mines. There are both open and closed mines, and each has its own hazards. As a medical man I would like to enlighten this House on certain medical aspects of how the poor workers are exposed to health hazards. It may be an acute or an instantaneous one because of the collapse of the wall of the mine, fall of debris or it may be due to the machinery involved in mining. Further, the injury may happen at the site or during transit or disposal of the minerals.

Sir, to enumerate a few examples, the people may have carbon monoxide exposure and toxicity, or fire and explosion endangering the life of the individual. It may result in bronchial asthma and excessive breathing difficulty and even chronic disease process in some cases. We cannot detect it by ordinary means. Some may think that it is due to some infection or some other disease. But it is actually not so. It may be due to insult of the lung tissues due to the minerals of the mines as well as coal dust and other dusts. So, their manifestation may be acute, sub-acute or chronic in nature.

In our country one may think, and even doctors may think, that the disease process is primarily due to TB. I wish to point out that health hazard cases have to be followed up with further critical observations. The factory medical officer, who may not be conversant with occupational hazard, may think that it is due to TB prevalent in that area and also in the country. But the fact is, it is not so. TB may be present in an individual where the precipitating cause is the mineral dust, foreign body or silicon, which may lead to fibrosis of the lung and even resist the curability of TB. When an individual with a rheumatoid disease is exposed to coal, he may develop a severe type of pneumonia. To assess such disease processes and manifestations of dust and coal exposure, a competent officer in the field of industrial health hazard is essential.

There are some honourable Members who made references about the association of trade unions. I agree with the honourable Members that trade unions try to protect the interests of the labourers. But I may say that even there, only some influential workers among the trade union can claim adequate compensation, whose cause will be taken up with the administrative people. The poor and innocent people are uncared for. What is the solution in this regard, I would like to know.

The Minister has mentioned in the Bill about the chief inspectors. I wish to point out that the owners and the management agencies are exploiting the labourers. They are bribing the chief inspectors. They have even gone to the extent of bribing the medical officers. I want to ask the Minister what provision is made in this Bill to check this bad practice.

I can suggest at this juncture that there must be a reinforcement machinery which can secretly maintain its activity to check and to avert the malpractice of chief inspectors and exploitation by the owners of the mines. They should check the activities of the people who work in collusion with the private owners. The chief inspectors and the owners responsible for this must be given severe punishment.

In the Bill you refer to compensation. When calculating compensation for the morbidity of the individual exposed to the hazardous agent, we can say definitely whether an injury is a chronic one or an instantaneous one or an acute one. So, in that respect I want to know how far the Minister is going to compensate the worker who develops injury or affliction instantaneously without chronic morbidity. If we are working it on the basis of the work executed by the workman, it will not serve the purpose.

At this stage, while referring to compensation and an alternative job, what I wish to say is this. It is practical family experience that invariably it is the breadwinner of the family who is afflicted with some dangerous disease and ultimately he succumbs to the injuries caused by the agent of the mines. So we have to make adequate provision by way of giving employment to the dependants to save the family from misery. Compensation alone will not serve the purpose. The dependants of the workers should be given adequate employment opportunity. I would therefore suggest to the honourable Minister that mere paper work will not serve the purpose, mere lip service will not serve the purpose. The Act must come into force, but it should be put into real action to protect the interests of the workers. With these words I conclude.

* * * *

Unfortunately, the problems that stand between Dalits and greater influence over public policy are too substantial to be bridged fully by minority representatives, however active some may be. The limitations have been especially jarring to many Dalits because they contrast sharply with the unique international conditions of the years just before Independence, years in which Congress, Muslim League and British colonial divisions allowed a few men like Ambedkar unusual leverage. Since Independence, the power of private wealth as well as caste dominance has solidified at many levels of the Indian polity, intensifying the political problems of a Dalit minority that faces both economic and caste oppression. All of the fluid, fragmented political parties continue to issue election manifestos that promise solutions to Dalit problems, but none has yet produced those solutions, and Dalits themselves are deeply divided over which party represents the best – or least bad – practical alternative.

These problems are compounded by geographic dispersion that leaves Dalits a chronic minority in constituencies above the level of a few city council seats. Ambedkar originally sought to circumvent the effects of this social geography by instituting special legislative seats for which only Untouchables would vote, but the Poona Pact referred to in Murthy's speech created the existing hybrid system – guaranteed proportional representation, but from constituencies in which all local adults vote. Election reports in the 1970s included data on the Scheduled Caste populations in each parliamentary constituency that confirmed Dalit agruments: in only a few of the reserved constituencies do Scheduled Caste citizens constitute as much as a third of the total. In most of the reserved constituencies, Dalits are only 15 to 25 per cent of the possible electorate, and thus remain a minority in what are presumed to be their 'own' constituencies.

Dalits are, of course, an especially vulnerable minority. Political commentators have usually assumed that they can determine the party preference of the majority of Dalit citizens by finding which party has won the greatest number of reserved Scheduled Caste legislative seats, but this is, of course, an unreliable gauge. Not only do many neighbouring non-reserved constituencies have quite as high a proportion of Dalit residents; Dalits in any constituency must also deal with the possibility of economic sanctions or physical violence if results from local ballot boxes do not produce the 'right' results. When local elites are sufficiently divided there is room for uneasy Dalit manoeuvre, but this type of elbow room is not always available. Even where Dalit communities are able to act on independent political calculations, local studies show a wide variety of partisan choices that are shaped by local experiences with activists in India's increasingly kaleidoscopic party system. (Some of these studies are reviewed in Joshi, 1981.) There are a few localities where Dalits have occasionally been able to operate as an effective swing vote, but in most constituencies this remains a hardy myth and a persistent mirage. The most common political reality is frustration.

Dalits are by no means alone in their growing frustration with the electoral system. Increasingly, many Indians have looked to the courts as one alternative way to influence public policy. There have been some important breakthroughs as progressive legal activists have developed a body of public interest and human rights precedents. However, there are also inherent limitations to this strategy, and they are particularly acute for Dalit citizens. Effective use of the judicial system as it exists in India today requires levels of money and information that the average Dalit does not possess. It also requires a judiciary free of caste bias; with some honourable and outstanding exceptions, this too is missing.

The constitutional basis of Indian law is itself a mixed blessing. As we saw in Chapter 2, many of the economic rights of the poor that men like Ambedkar regarded as essential to the development of social democracy (rights Ambedkar incorporated in his own draft constitution, States and Minorities), were either blocked altogether or were consigned to non-juridical 'Directive Principles' of the final Indian Constitution. Juridical sections of the Constitution include many features critically important to Dalit interests, but they also include features that can be interpreted in ways that block socio-economic change. The ebb and flow of judicial interpretation thus becomes a central element in Dalit hopes for progress.

The following article spells out a Dalit argument for progressive judicial activism, and traces the way in which judicial opinions since Independence have approached or departed from the author's goals. The article was written in the wake of one particular Supreme Court decision (in the Minerva Mills case) that used an economically conservative interpretation of the jusdiciable 'Fundamental Rights' section of the Constitution (Part III) to override objectives based on the non-jusdiciable 'Basic Principles' (Part IV). The case involved private industrial property, but had potentially profound implications for a range of other policy issues. The author is a Dalit specialist in constitutional law, head of Siddharth College of Law (a school begun by Ambedkar), and chairman of the board of Legal Studies of Bombay University.

Human Rights and the Primacy of the Constitution's Directive Principles

Professor D. N. Sandanshiv, *Siddharth College of Law Magazine,* **1980–1**

While intervening in the debate on the third reading and adoption of the Constitution, Dr Babasaheb Ambedkar administered these words of admonition:

> The third thing we must do is not to be content with mere political democracy. We must make our political democracy a social democracy as well. Political democracy cannot last unless there lies at the base of it social democracy . . . We must begin by acknowledging the fact there is complete absence of two things in Indian society. One of these is equality. On the social plane, we have in India a society of graded inequality which

means elevation of some and degradation of others. On the economic plane, we have a society in which there are some who have immense wealth as against many who live in abject poverty.

On the 26th January, 1950, we are going to enter into a life of contradictions. In politics we will have equality and in social and economic life we will have inequality . . . We must remove this contradiction at the earliest possible moment or else those who suffer from inequality will blow up the structure of political democracy which this Assembly has so laboriously built up.

The Preamble to the Constitution of India expresses in the most resounding terms the goal placed by the people of India before them. They resolved to constitute India into a sovereign, socialist, secular, democratic republic and proclaimed to all citizens: 'JUSTICE, social economic, and political; LIBERTY of thought, expression, belief, faith and worship; EQUALITY of status and of opportunity; and to promote among them all FRATERNITY, assuring the dignity of the individual and the unity and integrity of the nation.' These objectives declared in the preamble to the Constitution of India have been transformed in details in other parts of the Constitution in general and in Part III and Part IV in particular. Part III of the Constitution comprises the Fundamental Rights and Part IV deals with the Directive Principles of State Policy.

The Indian Constitution embraces within its fold the political and civil rights movement of the USA and the social and economic rights movement of the USSR. The Constitution is conscious of the existing socio-economic-cultural situation and it aims at bringing about radical transformation in that situation. Hence there is a momentous significance in both the Fundamental Rights, which are enforceable in the courts of law, and the Directive Principles, which are non-enforceable in the courts but are nevertheless fundamental in the governance of the country. Both Parts III and IV of the Constitution represent the ideological urges regarding the Individual Fundamental Rights and the Community Fundamental Rights of the people . . .

Rights and freedom can be enjoyed only within a concrete social situation. Freedom is not an abstraction. It does not exist in a social vacuum.

What is the socio-economic-political situation in India? This is a very pertinent question for the purpose of understanding enforcement and enjoyment of the rights by its citizens.

India is confronted not only by the problem of economic inequalities but also by social inequalities. These problems are age-old. India acutely suffers from poverty and caste. Poverty and caste are inter-related. A caste is an enclosed class. There are poor people in every caste. However the percentage of poverty-stricken persons in higher castes is ascendingly low, whereas it is descendingly high in the lower castes . . .

The relevant provisions of socio-economic rights enshrined in the Constitution can be classified under two categories. One category is meant to extend protection against exploitation in any form on the ground of Untouchability and thereby puts a bar against discrimination against these persons. The second category comprises the provisions imposing obligations on the state to take positive action to create better socio-economic conditions for the enjoyment of rights guaranteed under the Constitution . . .

The Directive Principles laid down by the Constitution require the state to strive to promote the welfare of the people by securing and protecting as effectively as it may a social order in which justice — social, economic and political — shall inform all the institutions of national life. They require the following: the state is to direct its policy towards securing an adequate means of livelihood for all, the ownership and control of the material resources of the community are also to be distributed as best to subserve the common good; the operation of the economic system must not result in the concentration of wealth or the means of production to the common detriment; there is to be equal pay for equal work; the wealth and strength of all must not be abused and nobody should be forced to enter a vocation unsuited to their age or strength; children must be given opportunity to develop in a healthy manner and must be protected against exploitation.

Another Directive Principle imposes an obligation on the state to promote with special care the educational and economic interests of the weaker sections of the people, in particular the Scheduled Castes and Scheduled Tribes, and to protect them from the social injustice and all forms of exploitation.

Social justice is an objective of the Indian Constitution . . . Social justice demands preferential treatment to the weaker sections to correct the imbalance existing in the society. When justice is administered, 'equal' treatment may result in injustice. Social justice, therefore, requires special treatment for the backward peoples. In short, social justice helps to bring about a just society by removing imbalances in social, educational, economic and political life of the people. Social justice may be defined as the right of the weak, aged, destitutes, women, children and other underprivileged persons to the protection of the state against ruthless competition in life with those who are socially higher, economically richer, politically in authority and educationally advanced.
. . .

The Supreme Court is the highest court entrusted by the people of India with protecting the citizen against any social, economic or political injustice, and with correcting the errors of all the other courts and tribunals involving miscarriage of justice.

It would be of great interest to an objective observer to know that constitutional jurisprudence, which was expected to be developed by the Supreme Court of India on the guidelines of JUSTICE, social, economic and political; LIBERTY of thought; EQUALITY of opportunity, and FRATERNITY, has not been developed on the proper guidelines. Dwelling on the role of the Supreme Court, Shri R. K. Garg, Supreme Court Advocate, writes that:

> The citizen is often shocked; why did the Supreme Court lean in favour of vested interests? The reason is simple. Laws are enacted to recognize or to

create old and new rights. These rights become vested rights defended by vested interests. The Courts are there to enforce these rights. By habit, training, and equipment, judges get used to paying an awesome respect for vested rights, which are the bedrock of the legal framework given to them for administering justice.

In the last thirty years we have witnessed four distinct periods, with four pronounced attitudes of the Supreme Court towards regulating and controlling the legislature and the executive in the governance of India. The distinct role of the Supreme Court can be analyzed in the light of its attitudes in deciding cases involving relations between the Fundamental Rights and the Directive Principles of State Policy.

From 1950 to 1960 was broadly the period of consolidation of the nascent Indian democracy. Energies during this period of free India were directed to build capitalism, and to eradicate feudalism only to the extent found necessary to release resources for the growth of capitalism. In 1951 the Court in State of Madras v. Champakan Dorairajan, while giving its opinion on a point of reservation to Scheduled Caste students in medical and engineering colleges, held that 'The Directive Principles have to conform to and run subsidiary to the chapter on Fundamental Rights.' [The decision applied the equal individual access rules of the fundamental rights section to high-caste students in a way that blocked affirmative action policies for low-caste students that sought to implement the Directive Principles and break prevailing patterns of high caste dominance in the professions.] . . . This led to the First Amendment Act of 1951, adding Clause (4) to Article 15 with a view to ensure reservations in educational institutions to the Scheduled Caste and Scheduled Tribe students. The First Amendment Act, 1951, can be taken as a necessary step to whittle down the effect of the Court's decision.
. . .

The Supreme Court was thus conservative in its approach to the matters of social justice but it was very 'liberal' in protecting the fundamental right to property. This could be seen in decisions like Chiranjit Lal Chaudhry v. Union of India, and Bella Banerjee. The court in these cases insisted on compensation at market value of property taken by the state for public purpose, and it did not make a distinction between acquisition and requisition for the purpose of awarding payment of compensation to the owners of private property taken by the state. At the same time the court was timid about protecting a personal [civil] freedom in A. K. Gopalan v. Union of India in 1951, and reduced the guaranteed right to liberty to a mere provision in the Code of Criminal Procedure.

Between 1960 and 1967 we saw a mild tilt in favour of the downtrodden people. The decision in Industrial Relations showed a marked shift in favour of the workers. The response of the court to the First Emergency proclaimed in 1962 was one of avoiding embarrassment to the state; but with the passing of time, decisions on preventive detention cases tended to become more humane and reduce the rigours of the decision in Gopalan's case. However, in the matter of right to private property the court still emerged a strong protector, as could be seen in new ground created in Kochunni's case in 1960.

The period from 1967 to 1973 was marked by the court announcing in the Golaknath case that Parliament cannot take away or abridge the Fundamental Rights of Part III [by reducing the absolute right to private property in order to encourage land reform] , and that the earlier decisions on this point were erroneous. During this period the Supreme Court became defiant of the legislature and the executive, and defended vested interests. The individual emerged stronger than the community.

This necessitated the 24th and 25th Constitutional Amendment Bills. The Amendment Bills were held valid in the Keshvanand Bharati case of 1973, . . . though it also laid down the doctrine of 'basic structure' as a limitation on the amendatory powers of Parliament. At the end of this period, the vested interests thus received a powerful blow in the decision on the Keshavanand Bharati case.

Between 1973 and 1980 the right to life, liberty and equality gained new dimensions. In the period of the Emergency the court was called upon to deal with several laws of social and economic reforms in diverse fields. Social and economic justice found new dimensions in terms of the Directive Principles in this period, presumably because of the proclaimed emphasis on the 20-Point Programme. Smt. Gandhi's government enacted social and economic legislation specifically directed towards socio-economic justice. These laws included Abolition of Bonded Labour Act, Debt Relief Act, and so on.

During this period the absolute right to property had become a 'dirty word and a dirty deed'. The absolute right to property was deleted from Part III of the Constitution by the Janata government. However the recent decision in the Minerva Mills case has reversed the wheels of history by once again relegating the Directive Principles to a position subordinate to individual Fundamental Rights. The majority judgement of four to one has declared the amended Article 31 (c) [which permitted elimination of absolute right to private property] to be unconstitutional. This is a great blow to the emergence of a just social order in India.

It is notable that Smt. Indira Gandhi's government has not hesitated to declare its determination to get rid of the 'basic structure' theory and to restore the primacy of the Directive Principles so that social and economic reforms are not rendered impossible.

The dissenting opinion written by Mr Justice Bhagwati in the Minerva Mills case cogently and forcefully supports the view for establishing socio-economic justice in India. His Lordship convincingly proves the primacy of Directive Principles over Fundamental Rights. He observes:

> The Indian Constitution is first and foremost a social document. The majority of the provisions are either directly aimed at furthering the goals of socio-economic revolution or attempt to foster this revolution by establishing the conditions necessary for its achievement . . . The Fundamental Rights are no doubt important and valuable in a democracy, but there can be no real democracy without social and economic justice to

the common man, and to create socio-economic conditions in which there can be social and economic justice to everyone is the theme of the Directive Principles. It is the Directive Principles which nourish the roots of democracy, provide strength and vigour to it, and attempt to make it a real participatory democracy, one which does not remain merely a political democracy but also becomes social and economic democracy, with Fundamental Rights available to all irrespective of their power, position, or wealth . . . It is axiomatic that the real controversies in the present day society are not between power and freedom but between one form of liberty and another. Under the present socio-economic system, it is the liberty of the few which is in conflict with the liberty of the many . . . The dynamic principle of egalitarianism fertilizes the concept of social and economic justice; it is one of its essential elements and there can be no real social and economic justice, where there is a breach of the egalitarian principle.

Unfortunately the majority judgement in the Minerva Mills case is handed down by Chandrachud C. J. This judgement stands out as a contrast to his earlier views [on the relationship of the Fundamental Rights and the Directive Principles] in the Keshavananda Bharati case . . . The majority judgement in the Minerva Mills case has denied primacy to the Directive Principles over the Fundamental Rights. The clock has been put back. Hindrance is created on the road to a just social order.

Thus one may examine the use of Fundamental Rights in India from any angle or any approach and he will have to reach the conclusion that these rights are indeed largely useless and meaningless to those who are victims of the caste system and the established social order. Unless these two monsters are killed, a just social order will be a mirage and the Fundamental Rights merely ornaments in a paper constitution.

Let the 'defenders and protectors' of the Fundamental Rights look at atrocities committed against the Scheduled Castes, let them see the landless labourers working in the bondage of an advanced and powerful class, let them know the pangs and sufferings of millions of unemployed, let them find out the unhygienic conditions in which slum-dwellers are living like dogs, let them look around at homeless people wandering from one place to another in search of a piece of bread, let them find people who are denied clean water to drink — and by seeing the pathetic conditions of the defenceless teeming millions, their 'defenders and protectors' hearts may be touched by the miseries. That may make them less aggressive in defending and protecting the Fundamental Rights against the Directive Principles. They are better advised to visit the dens of poverty, squalor, ignorance and illiteracy before they again protect the Fundamental Rights of a privileged few against the Directive Principles of millions of underprivileged.

* * * *

Recently Dalit voices have also been raised on the international scene, seeking indirectly to press for improved policy performance at home. In 1982 three organizations of Dalit immigrants in North America — VISION, the Ambedkar Mission of Canada and the Shri Guru Ravidas Sabha in California — sponsored testimony by one of their members, Dr Laxmi Berwa, to the United Nations Sub-Commission on Human Rights. Later in 1982 the president of the Delhi-based Dalit action organization, BAMCEF, represented Dalits and other Indian minorities at the International Conference Against Discrimination in Osaka, Japan. In 1983 an expanded international coalition of Dalit associations supported further UN testimony, this time by Shri Bhagwan Das, an Indian Supreme Court advocate and pioneering Dalit publisher and activist. Das subsequently addressed the 1984 World Conference on Religion and Peace in Nairobi, Kenya — very much against the wishes of the official Indian delegation to the conference.

All of this marks a sharp break from the earlier post-Independence period, when Dalits appeared on the international scene only when acceptable to the government or to associations dominated by higher-caste Indians. Most reaction to the change has been a combination of hostility and disbelief from people who find it difficult to accept the reality of Dalit desperation and anger. However there have also been instances of support from other Indian progressives. The following excerpts are from Dr Berwa's speech to the UN in 1982, and a supportive editorial that appeared some weeks later in the Indian Express, *India's largest chain of English-language newspapers.*

Testimony by Dr Laxmi Berwa to the UN Sub-Commission on Human Rights (Geneva, Switzerland, 31 August 1982)

Mr Chairman, Members of the Commission, and Guests:

Today is a big day in the history of millions of Untouchables when their concern is raised in the world body like the United Nations Human Rights Sub-Commission. Many of you who are not familiar with the Indian caste system must be wondering who these Untouchables are. As one of them I would like to tell you what it is like to be an Untouchable in India.

For 2000 years the Untouchables, who make up one-seventh of India's population (approximately 105 million by the government's estimates), have been assigned to the dirtiest, lowest paid jobs and are landless slave labourers, shunned socially by higher castes (Brahmans, Kshatriya, Vaisya) and neglected in social services and education.

They are not allowed to drink water from village wells or it 'pollutes'. They are landless slave labour in villages where 80 per cent of India lives. They are carriers of human excreta on their heads, and of dead animals. They are not allowed to revolt or they are crushed, killed, burnt alive and their women raped. Last year there were 15,000 attacks on Untouchables reported (*Toronto Star*, 11 January 1982). They live in constant fear of attack by other Hindus. Their good clothing or good living cause serious concern and resentment among high-caste Hindus. The press and media are partial and controlled by high-caste Hindus. What we hear is only 5 per cent of what really takes place. Police and the judiciary are controlled by the high-caste Hindus. Before Independence the Hindus were blaming the British for the conditions of the Untouchables. Now after thirty-three years of India's Independence, the slavery and dependence of landless Untouchables has increased and so have the atrocities and killings.

The *Globe and Mail* [Toronto] wrote on 3 December 1981, 'Although the outrage at Deoli was particularly horrifying, it was by no means a rare occurrence. Murderous beatings, and gang rapes of Untouchables are reported several hundred times a year, and less news-worthy humiliations are every day happenings.' The worst attacks have recently taken place at Deoli, near Agra. Twenty-four people including seven women were slaughtered because of refusal to do forced labour and their demand for justice. Two small boys, aged four and eight, were pinned down against the wall and shot to death. Six weeks after this, five armed men at dusk entered the village of Sadhupur near Deoli and started to shoot. In fifteen minutes they killed ten people like rabbits, including five women and two children . . .

[Similar recent events are detailed in subsequent paragraphs.]

VISION sent a letter to the Prime Minister on 14 June 1982 regarding the recent carnage of the Untouchables in Uttar Pradesh, Tamil Nadu, Bihar, Gujarat and many other states, stating its concern and asking to meet her in Washington, D.C. [during a planned official visit]. However, the Prime Minister wrote in a letter dated 22 June 1982 'It does not help for those who are living in affluence abroad to comment on situations about which they have little knowledge.'

The free world owes a duty to the Untouchables, as it does to all suppressed people, to break their shackles and set them free and help restore human rights to them. The Indian Prime Minister should know that when it is a question of slavery, bonded labour, violation of civil and human rights and atrocities on harmless people, it is not an internal problem. It is a problem which will haunt any honest, free person with a conscience, any person with compassion for humanity, any person with a respect for human dignity, whether these people are in India or abroad. Whether they are Indians or non-Indians, Black, White or Oriental. Where are the ideals of the late Mahatma Gandhi or the late Pandit Nehru, if a government cannot protect the weaker sections of its society?

Each year the Commissioner of Scheduled Castes and Scheduled Tribes brings out his annual report with observations and recommendations, but little action is taken because the Indian government has offered step-motherly treatment to its own citizens. The government has to protect its electoral votes. In the *Times of India* (10 July 1982), Mr Sham Lal shed some light on this human tragedy. In 'The National Scene: Showing Them Their Place', he writes:

> The village of Bangalwa in Bihar is only the latest locale. The place is different but it is a replay of the same bloody drama each time. A murderous gang of armed men, all drawn from the landed castes, descends on a village and mows down a whole lot of Harijans with guns. What is the provocation? Perhaps a mere feeling that the Harijans are getting too big for their boots. Or a desire to teach them how to keep their traps shut and

play dumb in courts of law when they are asked to bear witness in cases impugning their betters. The mass killings may be an act of revenge or a mere warning. The insolent message they carry is much the same in either case. The place of the Harijans is at the very bottom of the social ladder in the village, it says, and if they want to save their skin they had better stay where they are.

The political scenario which follows is no less sickening than the drama. Everyone expresses his sense of horror over the spilling of innocent blood. Every party sheds tears for the victims. There is a promise of new security measures. But what does this mean in a society where even the police are infected by the very virus which turns so many members of the so-called higher castes into wild beasts?

This explains the new aggressiveness of the dominant castes everywhere. They have the run of the village scene. They hog most of the gains of development, whether it is easier credit, higher yields from the land or better prices from farm produce. No party wants to stick its neck out in fighting them because this can be highly risky in terms of loss of electoral support . . .

. . .

Such is the plight and the human rights violations against these semi-slaves of India, who are in a constant state of terror and humiliation which is like the condition of Jewish people in Hitler's time. As Dr B. R. Ambedkar, the Father of the Indian Constitution, wrote, 'For the ills which the Untouchables are suffering, if they are not as much advertised as those of the Jews, are not less real. Nor are the means and the methods of suppression used by the Hindus against the Untouchables less effective because they are less bloody than the ways which the Nazis have adopted against the Jews. The anti-Semitism of the Nazis against the Jews is in no way different in ideology and in effect from the Sanatanism [orthodoxy] of the Hindus against the Untouchables.'

Finally, if this state of affairs continues, it is time to listen to what Dr Ambedkar had to say: 'On 26th January, 1950 . . . we will have equality in politics and in social and economic life we will have inequality . . . We must remove this contradiction at the earliest possible moment or else those who suffer from inequality will blow up the structure of political democracy which we have so laboriously built up.'

Members of the Commission, this is the end of my testimony and the rest lies with you as to how best you can help these millions of Untouchables to restore their human dignity.

Not an Internal Matter

Editorial, *The Indian Express*, **(17 October 1982)**

Dr Laxmi Berwa, a representative of three Dalit organizations in North America, might well feel flattered by the government of India's reaction to his recent presentation of the Dalit case before the UN Sub-Commission on

Human Rights in Geneva. While an Indian official in Geneva reminded him that 'it is an Indian matter', elsewhere other officials got busy trying to berate the Minority Rights Group in London, which had helped Dr Berwa to appear before the Sub-Commission. The Indian delegate should have been embarrassed at the support so enthusiastically and gratuitously extended to him by the Rumanian and Russian delegates . . . It makes one sad to recall that it was India which won credit for securing the first intervention in the world organization in a case of violation of human rights. The South African case ranks as a fine precedent. Others followed in due course. So did the International Bill of Rights comprised in the Universal Declaration of Human Rights and the two International Covenants on Human Rights which India ratified, however belatedly, and with reservations. Today, no democracy seriously argues that a violation of human rights is an internal matter. Such a plea is not only wrong, but also counter-productive. It arouses suspicion that there is something to hide and invites even greater international interest.

The above episode is not a solitary one. It fits comfortably into a pattern of illiberal and intolerant Indian responses to international concern for human rights. Recently, Mr T. N. Kaul, the Indian government's representative on UNESCO's Executive Board, opposed the claims of the International Press Institute and the World Press Freedom Committee to attend the forth-coming General Conference of that organization as observers. What was even worse, he dilated on press freedom in terms that would please a Jagannath Mishra or a Gundu Rao. 'Freedom is all right but there is no absolute freedom anywhere', he said and threatened to revive his objections against participation by these two prestigious organizations before the General Conference of UNESCO when it meets on 23 November. He will prepare himself well by then with the help of willing officials in New Delhi. Mr Kaul threw dark hints about their funds and threatened, 'I have only told part of the story of these organizations.' His outburst will add little to India's prestige abroad. Indian attacks on international organizations which keep vigil on the state of press freedom the world over are ill-timed, to say the least. The nationwide protests against the Bihar Press Bill have been widely reported in the foreign press.

Attacks on Mr Berwa and his organization, Volunteers in Service to India's Oppressed and Neglected (VISION), as well as on its allies, will inflict even greater damage to India's prestige, besides being morally reprehensible. VISION did try the 'internal' channels for representation but was rebuffed by two Indian Prime Ministers, Mr Morarji Desai and Mrs Indira Gandhi. The Dalits have come to realize, quite bitterly, that their fellow countrymen do not leave their caste prejudices behind when they cross their national frontiers. The same prejudices linger among Indians abroad. For the Indian government, however, there is only one way to silence foreign criticism. It is earnest, sustained effort for reform at home.

6. Designs for Struggle

Most of the Dalit struggle for liberation still lies ahead. The road that struggle takes will invariably have important consequences that extend far beyond the Untouchable minority, for in spite of 20th Century changes the Untouchables are still concentrated at the bottom of the two hierarchies — caste and class — that define so much of Indian life. The vast bulk of the Untouchable population cannot move without radically restructuring Indian society.

But can they move? And how? There are Dalit proponents of all the prominent strategies for change in India: Gandhian moral reform; orthodox Marxism; Western economic developmentalism, of both the capitalist and socialist varieties. All of these schools of thought are well represented in the Indian and international literature. However there has also been an expansion and diversification of an indigenous Dalit tradition that has spread to Dalit communities throughout India, and these views are much less well known outside Dalit circles. They do not constitute a cohesive and unified perspective — indeed, there is intense internal dispute — but there is a community of communication within which individuals and organizations argue and evolve.

The following pieces illustrate some of the diverse theories and styles within this movement. The first is an English translation of a manifesto originally written in Marathi in 1973 by some of the early leaders of the Dalit Panther movement in Bombay. The Manifesto became one of several points of controversy within the Panther organization, which has since both fragmented and spread across India. The document does not represent the views of all who identify themselves with the Panthers, while at the same time it represents important themes in the thinking of activists in a variety of Dalit organizations. The second and third articles were originally published in The Outcry, the occasional publication of a Dalit-sponsored organization in Canada. The author of the second, L. R. Balley, is the publisher of Bheem Patrika, a Dalit newspaper in the Punjab. The author of the third is one of Balley's colleagues whose work occasionally appears in Bheem Patrika. The exploration closes with a further sampling of Dalit poetry, which so often captures the diversity and ferment of this movement.

Dalit Panthers Manifesto

Dalit Panthers (Bombay, 1973)

Revolutionary Stand of the Panthers
Today we, the 'Dalit Panthers', complete one year of our existence. Because of its clear revolutionary position, the 'Panthers' is growing in strength despite the strong resistance faced by it from many sides. It is bound to grow because it has recognized the revolutionary nature and aspirations of the masses with whose smiles and tears it has been bound up since its inception. During last year, motivated attempts have been made, especially in the far corners of Maharashtra, to create misunderstandings about our members and our activities. Misconceptions about the objectives of the 'Panthers', about its commitment to total revolutionary and democratic struggles, and about its policies, are being spread. It has, therefore, become necessary clearly to put forward our position. Because 'Panthers' no longer represent an emotional outburst of the Dalits. Instead its character has changed into that of a political organization. Dr Babasaheb Ambedkar always taught his followers to base their calculations about their political strategy on deep study of the political situation confronting them. It is necessary and indispensable for us to keep this ideal before us. Otherwise we might mistake the back of the tortoise for a rock, and may be drowned in no time.

The present Congress rule is essentially a continuation of the old Hindu feudalism which kept the Dalits deprived of power, wealth and status for thousands of years. Therefore, this Congress rule cannot bring about social change. Under the pressure of the masses it passed many laws but it cannot implement them. Because the entire state machinery is dominated by the feudal interests, the same hands who, for thousands of years, under religious sanctions, controlled all the wealth and power, today own most of the agricultural land, industry, economic resources and all other instruments of power, therefore, in spite of independence and the democratic set-ups the problems of the Dalit remain unsolved. Untouchability has remained intact. It remains intact because the government did not do anything to eradicate it except passing some laws against it. To eradicate untouchability, all the land will have to be redistributed. Age-old customs and scriptures will have to be destroyed and new ideas inculcated. The village organization, the social organization, peoples' attitudes — all these will have to be restructured to suit true democratic objectives. We must pay attention to the objective process of social development and make an historical analysis of the power that imprisons the Dalit and which has succeeded in making him tie his own hands. The Hindu feudal rule can be a hundred times more ruthless today in oppressing the Dalits than it was in the Muslim period or the British period. Because this Hindu feudal rule has in its hands all the arteries of production, bureaucracy, judiciary, army and police forces, in the shape of feudals, landlords, capitalists and religious leaders who stand behind and enable these instruments to thrive. Hence the problem of untouchability of the Dalits is no more one of mere mental slavery. Untouchability is the most violent form of exploitation on the surface of the earth, which survives the ever-changing forms of the power structure. Today it is necessary to seek its soil, its root causes. If we understand them, we can definitely strike at the heart of this exploitation. The oppression of Dalits still exists despite the lives and work of our two great leaders — Jotiba Phule and Babasaheb Ambedkar. It is not only alive, it is stronger. Hence, unless we understand and give shape to the revolutionary content latent in the downtrodden lives of Untouchables, not a single individual seeking a social revolution would be able to remain alive in India. Truly speaking, the problem of Dalits, or Scheduled Castes and Tribes, has become a broad problem; the Dalit is no longer merely an Untouchable outside the village walls and the scriptures. He is an Untouchable, and he is a Dalit, but he is also a worker, a landless labourer, a proletarian. And unless we strengthen this growing revolutionary unity of the many with all our efforts, our existence has no future. The Dalit must accordingly accept the sections of masses, the other revolutionary forces as part of his own movement. Only then will he be able to fight his enemies effectively. If this does not take place, we shall be condemned to a condition worse than slavery. We must develop and help this consciousness ripen every year, every month, day, hour and every moment. Then alone shall we possess the right to be called human beings at all. It was for this that Doctor Ambedkar made us realize our humanity even in our state of beast-like exploitation. We should, to be successful, accept and understand a thing only after deep study, with a calm mind. We should not fall prey to slogans and outbursts. We must uproot the varna system, caste system that enslaves us in its snares. The soil in which they survive and grow must be made infertile. We must understand that the caste nature of the term Dalit is breaking down.

What has the Government Done for the Dalits?

When India obtained independence in 1947, the face of the administrative class changed. In the place of the king came the President. In the place of the king's prime minister came the 'people's representative'. In the place of the Vedas, Upanishads, Manusmriti and Gita, came the Constitution. On a blank page, independence, equality, brotherhood proliferated. From 1947 to 1974 is a long period of time. In these twenty-seven years the Congress government, turning the electoral process into its own capital, has been ruling with a monopoly. Four five-year plans, five general elections and three wars have gone by in this post-independence 'coming of age'. But the problems and needs of the Dalits, of the entire population, have been kept in a sort of deep freeze by the government. Beyond preserving state power in its hands, the government has done nothing else. On the contrary, by raising slogans of people's rule, of socialism, 'garibi hatao' [eliminate poverty], and green revolution, it has crushed the Dalits, the landless, poor peasants and the working class under its feet. Gambling with their lives, tempting a handful amongst them, the government tried persistently to endanger their very existence. Using divisive tactics that split people along religious, caste and other lines, they endangered the very integrity of democracy. In a democracy where men cannot exercise self-respect, well-being and an importance to their lives, where man cannot develop his individuality and his society, where those who wet with their blood every grain of the country's soil have to starve, where men have to forgo the land under their feet, the roof over their heads, where the upright have to break down and fall, where men have to see their mothers and sisters raped, in such a democracy, independence cannot be called true independence. The struggle for independence was a struggle under the leadership of national capitalists, landlords, feudals, for their own benefit. It was not under the leadership of the people, or of the Dalits. And Dr Ambedkar had always said that it should be of the latter. That man called Gandhi, in whose hands the leadership of the struggle rested, was deceitful, cunning, an orthodox casteist and one who gave shelter to those who wanted to preserve class rule. Merely to preserve the unity of the Independence struggle, he flirted with problems of the Dalits, of untouchability, of the people. And that is why Babasaheb (Ambedkar) called him, time and again, the enemy of the people, the villain of the nation. Babasaheb used to say, Gandhism means preservation of religious authority, Gandhism means traditionalism, Gandhism means casteism, Gandhism means preservation of traditional divisions of labour, Gandhism means incarnationism, Gandhism means the holy cow, Gandhism means worship of images, Gandhism means an unscientific outlook. The British gave up their rule because of the seamen's mutiny, the emergence of the Azad Hind army, because of the struggles of the peasants, workers and Dalits. Because of these they could no longer remain in power. Giving independence to Gandhi and Gandhians meant that the British wanted their own interests in the country to be looked after. This was the sort of borrowed independence we got. True independence is one that is snatched forcibly out of the hands of the enemy. One that is like bits thrown to a helpless beggar is no independence. In every house and every mind the flame of true independence has to be ignited. This did not happen. That is why the Dalit, the worker, the landless and the poor peasant did not become free, the muck at the bottom of the pond remained where it was and, in fact, the government that retained the status quo kept on telling bigger and bigger lies to the Dalits.

What Have Other Parties Done for the Dalits?
The Left parties, having fought five elections, have grown bankrupt. They are now interested in moving from elections to elections. In 1967 the Left parties united against the Congress. There was such opportunism in the united front that parties like the Communists joined hands with communalist parties such as Jan Sangh and Muslim League. In some states, Left united fronts came to power. But the absence of a clear-cut programme made the anti-Congress stand useless. In the task of putting some alternatives before the people, of solving the problems of the Dalits, of establishing the rule of the poor in the country, all the Left parties proved powerless. As a result, revolutionary people's groups lost faith in electoral democracy. Uprisings

like Naxalbari took place and the spark spread around the country. With the 1972 elections, things came back to square one. The Congress sat like a beast on the head of the Dalits, of the people; famine struck, the very livelihoods of crores [millions] of people were uprooted, animals perished. Factories were shut down, workers faced unemployment, everyone was harassed by the mounting price rise. The full eclipse that Congress rule represents for the life of the country has not yet terminated. But our Left parties, playing the politics of parliamentary seats, are still wasting time trying to get recognition from the Congress. Not one dares to turn revolutionary to take up the problems of the people. All those Left parties who do not possess political power have ignored questions of a social revolution. They have not combined the class struggle with the struggle against untouchability, have not raised a voice against cultural and social domination along with economic exploitation. Untouchability is nothing but an extremely poisonous sort of exploitation. This exploitative system was given birth by Hindu feudalism and thrives for its benefit. The framework of untouchability is simply widening with the help of the army, the prisons, the legal system and the bureaucracy. Under the name of high-flown philosophy and liberation of the soul (moksha, nirvana), Dalits have been deprived of earthly happiness, and have been looted of all they possess. With the industrial revolution, machines came into being. Dalits were harnessed to the machines. But in the minds of the upper castes, feudalism survived. Because the owners of the machines could make a profit only by keeping the social structure intact. Only if a social revolution grips the minds of the Dalits, will there be a political revolution. If this takes place, the upper caste, the upper class, will lose the power it possesses. The stand that is taken by the Left parties prevents the spread of revolutionary ideology amongst the people. Because struggles really and truly meaningful to the Dalits were not conducted, Dalits have grown poorer. They have had to face innumerable atrocities.

The Republican Party and Dalit Panthers

The problems of the Dalits today, be they social, political or ethical, cannot be solved within the framework of religion and caste. This is what Doctor Babasaheb realized after his defeat in the 1952 general elections. A scientific outlook, class consciousness and a completely atheistic and fighting humanism alone could add an edge to the struggles of the Dalits. For this purpose, Doctor Ambedkar wanted to transfer the then-existing Scheduled Caste Federation [SCF] into a broad-based party. This could not happen during his lifetime. After his death, his 'followers' simply renamed SCF as the Republican Party and started to pursue casteist politics. They never united all the Dalits and all the oppressed. Above all, they conducted the politics of a revolutionary community like the Dalits in a legalistic manner. The party got enmeshed in the web of votes, demands, select places for a handful of the Dalits and concessions. So the Dalit population scattered over the country, in many villages, remained politically where they were. The leadership of the party went into the hands of the middle class in the community.

Intrigue, selfishness and division became rife. Destroying the revolutionary voice of Doctor Ambedkar, these contemptible leaders made capital out of his name and set up their beggars' bowls. This is Doctor Ambedkar's party, they said. This is Doctor Ambedkar's flag, they said, and filled their coffers. And thus, except the *satyagraha* [civil disobedience campaign] of the landless conducted under Dadasaheb Gaekwad's leadership, the party did not take up any programme worth its name. The atrocities against Dalits grew endemic. In a period of one to one and a half years, 1,117 Dalits were murdered. The land grew barren, not a drop of water was available. Honour was violated, houses gutted, people killed. Along with the very question of living, physical indignities grew sharper. What did the Republican Party do? The party got caught in the net cast by a cunning ruling-class leader like Yashwantrao Chavan. Its life perished. Unity vanished, impotents filled the party. If we put our future in the hands of such impotent leaders, we will forgo our very lives, and that is why today we have to announce with deep pain that we are no blood relatives of the Republican Party.

The Dalits (Oppressed) of the World and Panthers
Due to the hideous plot of American imperialism, the Third Dalit World, that is, oppressed nations, and Dalit people are suffering. Even in America, a handful of reactionary whites are exploiting Negroes. To meet the force of reaction and remove this exploitation, the Black Panther movement grew. From the Black Panthers, Black Power emerged. The fire of the struggles has thrown out sparks into the country. We claim a close relationship with this struggle. We have before our eyes the examples of Vietnam, Cambodia, Africa and the like.

Who is a Dalit?
Members of Scheduled Castes and Tribes, neo-Buddhists, the working people, the landless and poor peasants, women and all those who are being exploited politically, economically and in the name of religion.

Who are our Friends?
1. Revolutionary parties set to break down the caste system and class rule. Left parties that are left in a true sense.
2. All other sections of society that are suffering due to the economic and political oppression.

Who are our Enemies?
1. Power, wealth, price.
2. Landlords, capitalists, money-lenders and their lackeys.
3. Those parties who indulge in religious or casteist politics, and the government which depends on them.

Burning Questions before Dalits Today
1. Food, clothing, shelter.

2. Employment, land, (removal of) untouchability.
3. Social and physical injustice.

   The struggle for the emancipation of the Dalits needs a complete revolution. Partial change is impossible. We do not want it either. We want a complete and total revolutionary change. Even if we want to move out of the present state of social degradation alone, we will have to exercise our power in economic, political, cultural fields as well. We will not be satisfied easily now. We do not want a little place in the Brahman Alley. We want the rule of the whole lane. We are not looking at persons but at a system. Change of heart, liberal education, etc. will not end our state of exploitation. When we gather a revolutionary mass, rouse the people, out of the struggle of this giant mass will come the tidal wave of revolution. Legalistic appeals, requests, demands for concessions, elections, *satyagraha* — out of these, society will never change. Our ideas of social revolution and rebellion will not be borne by such paper-made vehicles. They will sprout in the soil, flower in the mind and then will come into full being with the help of a steel strong vehicle.

Dalit Panther is not a Mere Slogan
The way we look at our questions is the first step to solving them. Panthers will paralyzingly attack untouchability, casteism and economic exploitation. This social system and state have taken many a cruel path to convert us into slaves. Turned us long into '*shudras*'. In the present modern forms of slavery there are mental chains of slavishness. We will try to break them. In our struggle we will become free.

Our Programme
1. More than 80 per cent of India's population lives in the villages. Of these, landless peasants are 35 per cent, and 33 per cent of all landless agricultural labourers belong to Scheduled Castes. (Those Dalit poor peasants who own pieces of land, own a negligible amount.) The question of landlessness of the Dalit peasants must be resolved.
2. Feudal survivals are still to be found in the villages. Due to this, Dalits are cruelly oppressed and exploited. Landlords and rich peasants get social prestige along with wealth. Due to this, the atrocities on the Dalits have grown endemic. This system has clamped itself on the Dalit's chest, affecting every part of his life, from day-to-day living to the deeper economic questions. This system must be destroyed.
3. Landless peasants must immediately get excess land through the application of the land ceiling act. Waste and jungle land must likewise be distributed.
4. The wages of landless labourers must be increased.
5. Dalits must be allowed to draw water from public wells.
6. Dalits must live, not outside the village in a separate settlement, but in the village itself.
7. All means of production must belong to the Dalits.

8. Exploitation by private capital must cease. Foreign capital must be confiscated without compensation.

9. Social, cultural and economic exploitation must be removed and socialism must be built in India. Misleading nationalization must give way to a true introduction of socialism.

10. All Dalits must be assured of daily wages.

11. Unemployed Dalits must be given unemployment benefits.

12. All Dalits must be given free education, medical facilities, housing and good quality cheap grains.

13. When giving employment in educational institutions, the requirement to declare one's caste and religion must be immediately removed.

14. The government must stop giving grants to religious institutions immediately and the wealth of religious places must be used for the benefit of Dalits.

15. Religious and casteist literature must be banned.

16. The division in the army along caste lines must be ended.

17. Black-marketeers, hoarders, money-lenders and all those exploiting the people economically must be destroyed.

18. The prices of essential commodities must be reduced.

We will build the organization of workers, Dalits, landless, poor peasants through all city factories, in all villages. We will hit back against all injustice perpetrated on Dalits. We will well and truly destroy the caste and varna system that thrives on the people's misery, which exploits the people, and liberate the Dalits. The present legal system and state have turned all our dreams to dust. To eradicate all the injustice against Dalits, they must themselves become rulers. This is the people's democracy. Sympathizers and members of Dalit Panthers, be ready for the final struggle of the Dalits.

* * * *

India Needs a Cultural Revolution

L. R. Balley (*The Outcry*, 1984)

India is passing through a very critical stage. All norms and moral codes seem to have collapsed. It has been aptly described that there is working anarchy in the country. But how long will it last? If none else is prepared to ponder over it, let the radicals, at least, think over their role and responsibility for the progressive transformation of Indian society.

Dr B. R. Ambedkar had said: 'History bears out the proposition that political revolutions have always been preceded by social and religious revolutions.' But since for many centuries no effort has been made to usher in a cultural revolution in India, a vast majority of Indians are still deeply engulfed in acute poverty, supernaturalism, superstitions and a quagmire of rites, rituals and astrological predictions. Priests have a sway over the people and they continue, unchecked and unashamedly, to prey upon them parasitically. Gold and jewellery worth crores of rupees remain deposited in numerous temples and shrines without any productive utility and without contributing anything to the welfare of the needy and the poor. All this without the slightest protest from the so-called high castes, who boast of being the only custodians of the spiritual and philosophical treasure, or even from the so-called low-caste Hindus who are the victims of this system.

The Shankaracharya of Puri [head of a major Hindu temple] openly defies law: he publicly preaches untouchability; he denied entry [to the temple] to the Prime Minister of India, Mrs Gandhi. But why? Because, according to Shankaracharya, she married Feroze Gandhi who was a Parsi. It is well known that Feroze was converted to Hinduism before marriage and the marriage between Feroze Gandhi and Indira was performed according to Vedic rites. Not only this, after his death he was cremated according to Hindu rites. Despite this, Shankaracharya regards Mrs Gandhi as a non-Hindu and does not allow her to enter his temple.

Entry in Jagannath Temple at Puri is open to 'orthodox Hindus only'.

This attitude, this behaviour and practice of Shankaracharya, is against the Indian Constitution. Not only this, his act is a criminal offence. But he could not be arrested and prosecuted for fear of Hindu reaction. On the other hand, the followers dragged those who condemned Shankaracharya to the court of law. No Hindu of repute and prominence has criticized the Shankaracharya or demanded action against him.

In this context the following conversation between a Hindu leader and Dr Ambedkar is very significant:

Dattopant Thengdi: The members of RSS (Rashtrya Swayamsevak Sangh) do not believe in untouchability.

Ambedkar: Whether you handful of people believe it or not, is not of much consequence in the context of solving the problem.

Thengdi: You said this because of the smallness of their numbers.

Ambedkar: Not necessarily because of that. There is an additional reason, which is of greater importance. Suppose on some critical social or religious issue your Golwalkar (the RSS chief) lays down a particular line and the Shankaracharyas give a different verdict. Whose decision will carry weight with the ordinary orthodox caste Hindus?

Thengdi: Of course Shankaracharya's.

Referring to the above quoted conversation in the *Weekly Organiser* of 18 March 1984, Mr Dattopant Thengdi comments thus: 'There are many who would be tempted to flaunt the label of social reformer, but "Guruji" (Golwalkar) preferred a secondary role for himself in the wider interests of society.'

When this same question was put directly to Golwalkar he replied, 'It does not matter whether you or I recognize a Shankaracharya. The point is that the "touchables", whom we want to give up "untouchability", accept their authority. They recognize neither you nor me. For them, the Dharmacharyas' (religious preachers) word is a religious commandment.'

What does the conversation indicate, and where does it lead us to? It once again proves beyond any doubt that to a caste Hindu the commandment of

his 'guru', the religious preacher, is supreme. All laws, however revolutionary
and beneficial for human dignity, peace and prosperity, are inferior to it.

How was such an imprint made? When did it happen? None among the
Hindus has ever endeavoured to answer these questions. But did they not
think of answering these questions? This is because the answer to these
questions cannot but lead to the conclusion that it is the Hindu religion which
is responsible for inculcating the idea of untouchability, practices of social
disabilities, hatred and prejudice into their minds.

One may object to this conclusion of mine. Therefore, I want to clear their
doubts, real or unreal.

What is Hinduism? 'Hindu religion, as contained in the VEDAS and
SMRITIS, is nothing but a mass of sacrificial, social, political and sanitary
rules and regulations, all mixed up. What is called religion by the Hindus is
nothing but a multitude of commands and prohibitions.'

'What the Hindus call religion is really law or at least legalized class-ethics.
Frankly, I refuse to call this code of ordinances religion' (Dr Ambedkar,
Annihilation of Caste, section 23).

Of what kind are the commands and prohibitions laid down in Hinduism?
Here are some examples:

1. Property: the Shudra [low castes] can have no property. His master
takes his possessions; a Brahman confidently siezes the goods of his Shudra
(slave). (Manusmriti VIII, 417)

2. Wealth: the wealth of the Shudra (shall be) dogs and donkeys. (Ibid.
X, 52)

3. Dress: the dress of Shudras (of the lower order) shall be the garments of
the dead; (they shall eat) their food from broken dishes; black iron (shall be)
their ornaments; and they must always wander from place to place. (Ibid.
X, 52)

4. Murder: a Shudra can be slain at the pleasure of his master, and the
same is the penance for killing a Shudra as is prescribed for killing a crow,
chameleon, a peacock, a duck, a swan, a vulture, a frog, an ichneumon, a
muskrat or a dog. (Apastamba 1, 9, 25, 13)

5. Education: if a Shudra listens intentively to a recitation of the Veda
his ears shall be filled with molten tin or lac. If he recites Vedic texts, his
tongue shall be cut out. If he remembers them his body shall be split in
twain. (One who tried to educate a Shudra was punishable.) He who tells
law to a Shudra and he who enjoins upon him religious observances, he indeed
together with that Shudra sinks into the darkness of the hell called Asamvritta.
(Dharam Sutra XII 4, 5, 6)

6. A Shudra is denied the right to give evidence.

7. A Shudra is severely punishable for offences of insult of and assault
on the members of the twice born.

8. Some of the important punishments for suppressing and crushing the
Shudras were as below:

(i) For using an ironic expression against a Brahman, a Shudra shall suffer
corporal punishment.

(ii) A once born man (a Shudra) who insults a twice born with gross invective shall have his tongue cut out, for he is of low origin.

(iii) If a Shudra mentions the name and caste of the twice born with contempt, an iron nail ten fingers long and red hot shall be thrust into his mouth.

(iv) If a Shudra arrogantly teaches the Brahman their duty, the king shall cause hot oil to be poured into his mouth and ears.

(v) A Shudra who raises his hand or a stick, shall have his hand cut off: he who in anger, kicks with his foot, shall have his foot cut off.

(vi) A low-caste man (Shudra) who tries to place himself on the same seat with a man of a high caste, shall be branded on his hip and be banished, or the king shall cause his buttocks to be gashed.

(vii) If out of arrogance he spits (on a superior), the king shall cause both his lips to be cut off: if he passes urine (on him), the penis; if he breaks wind (against him) the anus shall be cut off and gashed in.

(viii) If he lays hold of the hair of a superior let the king unhesitatingly cut off his hands, likewise if he takes him by the feet, the beard, the neck or the scrotum, his hands shall be cut off.

Tons of scriptures were written which contained details and directions of punishments, prohibitions and commandments against the Shudras. Following the dicta of these scriptures a society of discarded people was established by the law of the country: (1) by establishing the institution of slavery; (2) by creating the class of Untouchables; (3) by creating a society of unseeables, unapproachables — a society of enemy classes arising out of hatred, false dignity and the idea of supremacy of the ruling classes called Dwijas ['twice-born'] and caste Hindus; (4) by creating classes whose water is impure; (5) by making a class of *Abhojaniyas*, i.e. those whose food cannot be taken; (6) by making these people serve perpetually with or without payment; (7) by putting them to menial work of an unclean nature, like sweeping latrines; (8) by making them live in ghettos outside the villages, with an idea of perpetuating untouchability; (9) *by denying them proper and adequate education*; (10) by denying them access to public institutions and places; (11) by shunning them in private life.

In order to enforce various methods of segregation such heinous institutions as child marriage and *sati* (burning of the wife at the husband's pyre) were introduced, some of which are still prevalent in the country.

The first evil of such a code of ordinances, misrepresented to the people as religion, is that it tends to deprive moral life of freedom and spontaneity and to reduce it (for the conscientious at any rate) to a more or less anxious and servile conformity to externally imposed rules. Under it there is no loyalty to ideals, there is only conformity to commands. But the worst evil of this code of ordinances is that the law it contains must be the same yesterday, today and forever. They are iniquitous in that they are not the same for one class as for another. But this iniquity is made perpetual in that they are prescribed to be the same for all generations. The objectionable part of such a scheme is not that they are made by certain persons called prophets or law-givers. The objectionable part is that this code has been invested with the character of finality and fixity. Happiness notoriously varies with the conditions and circumstances of a person, as well as with the conditions of different people and epochs. That being the case how can humanity endure this code of eternal laws, without being cramped and crippled?

It is the Hindu religion that has cramped and crippled a large number of people in India. Commenting on this peculiarity of Hinduism, Dr Ambedkar remarked on 1 January 1948 . . .

> Besides the Shudras, the Hindu civilization has produced three social classes whose existence has not received the attention it deserves. The three classes are:
>   (i) The Criminal Tribes, who number 20 millions or so;
>   (ii) The Aboriginal Tribes, who number about 15 millions; and
>   (iii) The Untouchables, who number about 50 millions.
>   The existence of these classes is an abomination. The Hindu civilization, gauged in the light of these social products, could hardly be called civilization. It is a diabolical contrivance to suppress and enslave humanity. Its proper name should be infamy. What else can be said of a civilization which has produced a mass of people who are taught to accept crime as an approved means of earning their livelihood, another mass of people who are left to live in full bloom of their primitive barbarism in the midst of civilization and a third mass of people who are treated as an entity beyond human intercourse and whose mere touch is enough to cause pollution? (*The Untouchables*, preface, p. i)

Another tall talk about Hinduism is its toleration. What do the massacres, brutalities, uprootings, segregations, discriminations, disabilities and prejudices against the Untouchables in the whole of the country show? Does all this exhibit kindness and compassion? The reality is:

> Hinduism preaches separation instead of union. To be a Hindu means not to mix; to be separate in everything. The language commonly used, that Hinduism upholds Caste and Untouchability, perhaps disguises and conceals its genius. The real genius of Hinduism and social unity are incompatible. By its very genius Hinduism believes in social separation, which is another name for social disunity and even social separation. Hinduism cannot create that longing to belong which is the basis of all social unity. On the contrary Hinduism creates an eagerness to separate. (*What Congress and Gandhi Have Done to the Untouchables*, p. 187)

It is because of Hinduism that India, even after thirty-seven years of Independence, has not become a nation; it is still a warring multitude of castes and communities. Therefore, in order to make India a united country and to make themselves countrymen, Indians first and Indians last — there must be a cultural revolution.

What should be the object of a revolution, and how to achieve it?

The first and foremost object of this revolution should be to free every man and woman 'from the thraldom of the *Shastras* (Scriptures), cleanse their minds of the pernicious notions founded on the *Shastras*. It is no use telling people that the *Shastras* do not say what they are believed to say, grammatically read or logically interpreted. What matters is how the *Shastras* have been understood by the people.' Not only are the Shastras to be discarded, but also their authority has to be totally denied. In short 'you have got to apply dynamite to the Vedas and Shastras, which deny any part to reason, to Vedas and *Shastras*, which deny any part to morality.'

The cultural revolution must aim at

> a complete change in the fundamental notions of life. It means a complete change in the values of life. It means a complete change in outlook and in attitude towards men and things. It means conversion. It means new life. But a new life cannot enter a body that is dead. New life can enter only a new body. The old body must die before a new body can come into existence and a new life can enter it. To put it simply, *the old must cease to be operative before the new can begin to enliven and to pulsate.*

Therefore, 'such a religion (as Hinduism) must be destroyed . . . there is nothing irreligious in working for the destruction of such a religion. Indeed I hold that it is your bounden duty to tear the mask, to remove the misrepresentation that is caused by misnaming this law as religion. This is an essential step' (*Annihilation of Caste*, Section 23).

How to bring in this cultural revolution? No doubt, the Indian soil is not congenial to complete change. But change has to be made.

Here are some, *only some*, preliminary measures that can lay the foundation of such a cultural revolution:

Priests: In India the priesthood is the only profession where proficiency is not required. The profession of a Hindu priest is the only profession which is not subject to any code. Mentally a priest may be an idiot, physically he may be suffering from a foul disease, such as syphilis or gonorrhoea, morally he may be a wreck. But he is fit to officiate at solemn ceremonies, to enter the *sanctum sanctorum* of a Hindu temple and worship the Hindu God. All this becomes possible among the Hindus because for a priest it is enough to be born in a priestly caste. The whole thing is abominable and is due to the fact that the priestly class among Hindus is subject neither to law nor to morality. It recognizes no duties. It knows only of rights and privileges. It is a pest which seems to have been let loose on the masses for their mental and moral degradation. The priestly class must be brought under control: (1) It would be better if priesthood among Hindus is abolished. But as this seems to be impossible at present, the priesthood must at least cease to be hereditary. (2) Unless he (the priest) has passed an examination prescribed by the state and holds a *sanad* (certificate) from the state permitting him to practise. (3) No ceremony performed by a priest who does not hold a *sanad* shall be deemed to be valid in law and it should be made a penal offence for a person who has no *sanad* to officiate as a priest. (4) A priest should be the servant of the state and should be subject to disciplinary action by the state in the matter of his morals, beliefs and worship, in addition to his being subject along with other citizens to the ordinary law of the land. (5) The number of priests should be limited by law according to the requirements of the state, as is done in other public services.

Such steps will democratize the priesthood by throwing it open to every class and will certainly help to kill Brahmanism; such stops will also help to kill caste, which is nothing but Brahmanism incarnate.

Shrines: All shrines should be brought under some discipline, if not control. The resources and influence of the shrines should be bridled in such a way that these may not be able to continue poisoning, narrowing and communalizing the minds of Indians. In order to combat communalism, its sources of origin and nourishment must be dried up. Most of the shrines have become centres breeding communalism, ill-will, hatred and even social disabilities. Therefore, all shrines should be open to inspection and be made to conform to the country's laws and secular and social needs.

Secular morality: What is secularism? It is a doctrine of basing morality solely on considerations of well-being of mankind in the present life, to the exclusion of all considerations drawn from belief in God or in matters of life after death.

Moral values are placed on a firm foundation when they are referred back to the innate rationality of man. They need no other sanction than the good of humanity.

In the words of Dr Ambedkar, 'Morality does not require the sanction of God. It is for his own good that man has to love man. It is nothing but another name for brotherhood of men.'

Food: Food habits of Indians have become a source of strife, communal disturbance and tension. Indians must stop quarrelling over food. Those who are non-vegetarian must not distinguish and differentiate between beef and pork.

Social integration: Countrywide plans should be drawn up and executed sincerely to break social stagnation and segregation, and to bring social integration in Indian society. For this purpose, inter-state, inter-community and inter-religious meetings, particularly of young boys and girls, should be regularly arranged at the national level through governmental and non-governmental agencies, so that young people come nearer to each other and cross the caste boundaries in matrimonial ties.

If, in the beginning, only these plans are executed, a good beginning can be made, and they say 'well begun is half done'. If we march sincerely the *Cultural Revolutions* will be completed within no time.

* * * *

Cover of *Kondwada* by Daya Pawar (Poona: Magora Press, 1974).

Humanism as a Dalit Perspective

Professor G. Singh (*The Outcry*, 1984)

Although humanism as a creed has roots in Protagoras's philosophy, yet the philosophy of humanism is as old as man as a conscious being himself. The philosophy of humanism has been enriched by eminent philosophers, poets, scientists, social crusaders and scores of other scholars and intellectual giants. Humanism, as it has come down to us through centuries, *is any system of thought or action which assigns a predominant interest to the affairs of men as compared with the supernatural or the abstract.* It is a philosophy of which man is the centre and sanction. Actually, humanism as a philosophy represents a specific and forthright view of the universe, the nature of man and the treatment of human problems (Corliss Lamont, *The Philosophy of Humanism*, p. 10). Humanism is the viewpoint that men have but one life to lead and should make the most of it in terms of creative work and happiness; that human happiness is its own justification and requires no sanction or support from supernatural sources; that in any case the supernatural usually conceived of, in the form of heavenly gods or immortal heaven, does not exist; and that human beings, using their own intelligence and co-operating liberally with one another, can build an enduring citadel of peace and beauty on this earth (Corliss Lamont, *The Philosophy of Humanism*, p. 12).

J udging by this explanation of humanism, Ambedkar generated a humanistic philosophy rich in content and having various dimensions of its own.

Man and Nature

Like all other humanistic philosophers such as Feuerbach, Marx, Russell and others, Ambedkar held a realistic view of man and nature. It is for this reason that Ambedkar accepted the Buddhist view of nature. According to it . . . there is no soul in the highest form that can be said to be governing this universe (Ambedkar, *The Buddha and His Dhamma*, p. 253) . . . Every change stands in some relation to cause, and that cause in relation to an effect and again that effect in relation to another cause . . . That is why Ambedkar, a true humanist, denied any eternal substance inside the cause which is transferred to the effect. The whole world is always in flux and there is nothing that is eternal in the universe. Thus, Ambedkar, by accepting Buddhism, denied any place to supernatural forces such as Paramatma or Atma, etc.

Ambedkar also rejected the idea of an individual soul which is said to be immortal, eternal and permanent. The doctrine of immortality of soul subordinates body and mind to this abstract thing . . . Man's personality, according to him, therefore, is the combination of physical and mental elements. Again, for Ambedkar, man's thinking is affected by objective reality, but not absolutely.

It is this view which leaves room for the freedom of man, to which Ambedkar aspired. It is for this reason that he rejected economic determinism or historical materialism, while accepting other aspects of Marxism such as a materialistic outlook on the universe and the economic reconstruction of abolishing capitalism in favour of socialism and communism — an ideal society. (For details see Ambedkar's lecture on 'Buddhism and Marxism', delivered at Kathmandu, 1954.) W. N. Kuber rightly speaks of Ambedkar's urge for human freedom and writes:

'He stood for human dignity and freedom, for simplicity, integrity, liberality, equality, social and economic justice, material prosperity and spiritual discipline and he was opposed to any social order or institution or any creed or practice, which involved injustice, violence and suppression of human personality' (W. N. Kuber, *Ambedkar — A Critical Study*, p. 292). Like M. N. Roy, Ambedkar had unshakeable faith in the creativeness of man. Both these humanists agree that men, being creative in nature, possess the capacities to change the world over.

Social Ethics and Morality

Like all great humanists, Ambedkar believed in the necessity of morality for just relations in the society. Rather, his contribution is distinctive and conspicuous in this context. Society, says Ambedkar, cannot maintain right relations between man and man or even endure without some standards of sociability. Another name for these standards is morality. And morality, further, is synonymous with Buddhist Dhamma, believes Ambedkar. As he wrote, 'Dhamma is righteousness, which means right relations between man and man in all spheres of life' (*The Buddha and His Dhamma*, p. 316).

These right relations must be established on the basis of social principles of *Liberty, Equality and Fraternity*. These three principles, according to him, must serve as basis of any morality.

What is valuable and everlasting in Ambedkar's concept of society and morality, is his rejection of any divine sanction behind moral imperatives.

'Morality arises from the direct necessity for man to love man. It does not require the sanction of God. It is not to please God that man has to be moral. It is for his own good that man has to love man', argues Ambedkar (*The Buddha and His Dhamma*, p. 316). But morality must be sacred and universal and society must abide by it for the social good. Because, in the absence of any sacred moral code, the best among the citizens cannot be protected; society can't become a harmonious whole and the full growth of the individual cannot be facilitated. Ambedkar as a true democratic humanist — and also like Feuerbach, Russell, M. N. Roy and Sellars — was an ardent believer in atheistic morality, otherwise known as secular morality or rational morality. W. N. Kuber rightly praises Ambedkar's zest for establishing humane relations in society in the following words:

Ambedkar's chief concern in life was to meet the challenge of wrongly idealised social relations which threatened the whole of human existence and shook the foundation of a moral and just social order. The aim of his mission was to arouse in men and women the passion for right relations (Kuber, *Ambedkar — A Critical Study*, p. 297).

One thing which is purely humanistic and unique in Ambedkar's concept of morality is that the purpose of following morality is not the attainment of salvation or Moksha, i.e. liberation from bondage of Karma. It is rather to create social harmony. Ambedkar, like Marx and Russell, believed in and worked for the establishment of classless society. Ambedkar did this by accepting the Buddhist way of life, which for him is no different from the Marxist way of life.

Democracy and World Peace

A humanist is he who not only has ardent faith in democracy but he who also defends it and enriches its philosophy with passion. In this respect, then, Ambedkar was a humanist through and through. Democracy, in the political sphere, stands for belief in 'One man one vote', he said. But for him democracy was not this alone. In order to complete the philosophy of democracy, Ambedkar held, social and economic aspects of it must also be realized. In the social sphere democracy requires right but equal social relations among the members of society. He emphatically elaborated and enriched the concept of social democracy: 'Democracy is a mode of associated living. The roots of democracy are to be found in social relationship in terms of the associated life between the people who form the society' (Dhananjay Keer, *Ambedkar: Life and Mission*, p. 487). What is significant about Ambedkar's view of democracy is that he did not regard democracy as a mere form of government, as was and is the fashion . . . The basis of his democracy is humanistic and is consonant with the idea of human good. Its basis is rational human relations. That is why any sort of curb on the human mind, either in the form of distinctions based on untouchability or caste system or class structure, appear to Ambedkar abominable and inhuman. Therefore, he struggled against these inhuman practices and succeeded in putting 'a good part of mighty Manu upside-down' (H. N. Mukerjee, *Gandhi, Ambedkar and the Extirpation of Untouchability*, p. 23).

Dr Ambedkar was cosmopolitan in thought and practice. Like Marx, M. N. Roy, Russell and others, he stood for world peace. He thought and preached Buddha's gospel of peace in the world and renounced war. In order to establish peace in the world Ambedkar held that redemption of a world communist society is indispensable. Like a humanist he wanted this stage of communist (casteless, and classless) society [to] usher in peacefully, and more so through a rationalistic way of life, in order to be durable. He yearned for the change of the whole world, a new world in which man would feel a free and creative being in a new culture. In fact, Ambedkar held that man can realize his natural self only in such a society.

Abolition of Capitalism

The dehumanizing effects of capitalism debase man, wrote Marx. Marx wrote that capitalism has left intact 'no other bond between man and man but naked self-interest, but callous cash-payment'. 'It has dissolved personal dignity into exchange value, torn off the veil of feeling and affection from family relationship, and reduced them to purely financial connections.' With the same spirit, Ambedkar noted that capitalistic economy debases noble feelings of man. Therefore, Ambedkar pleaded for its destruction . . . Capitalism breeds exploitative values and therefore it must be abolished and replaced by the establishment of genuine socialism.

Ambedkar's concept of constitutional state socialism is unique and more humanistic, because he believes that democratic organization must remain its concomitant partner; for otherwise the abolition of capitalism would necessarily lead to dictatorship wherein democracy might not be possible and dignity of man be underrated. Writes Dr Jatava, 'Indeed, Ambedkar aspires for a society based on a common mode of life, in which human dignity and individual integrity may be connected with principles of social fellowship without any consideration of caste and creed' (Dr Jatava, *The Social Philosophy of B. R. Ambedkar*, p. 154). Thus Ambedkar's humanism aims at a socialized and co-operative economic order and emphasizes a socialistic ideal to be achieved and worked out by democratic means, so that all men and women can enjoy the fruits of economic productivity and prosperity without any distinction.

* * * *

Karl Marx
Narayan Surve, *On the Pavements of Life*, (trans. Krisna Chaudhari and P. S. Nerurkar)

> In my first strike Marx met me thus
> I was holding his banner high on my shoulder.
> In the midst of the procession
> Sister Janaki Akka asks me 'Recognized him?
> he is our Markus, our father.
> born in Germany
> wrote bagful of books and
> returned to dust in England;
> what a Sanyasin, dear friend,
> all lands are equal to him.
> He too had a few kids just like you.'
>
> Afterwards I was addressing a meeting.
> '— then why this depression?
> — poverty . . . where lies its origin?'
> Again there came forth Marx;
> 'I tell you' says he and
> spoke unobstructed to the end.
>
> The other day he stood listening to my speech
> at a gate meeting.
> — 'now we alone are the heroes of history
> of all the biographies too — henceforth — '
> He was the first to applaud then
> laughing boisterously
> he put his hand on my shoulder and said:

'– Are you a poet or what? . . .
nice . . . very nice . . .
I too liked poetry
Goethe was my favourite.'

Buddha

Daya Pawar, *Kondwada*, 1974 (trans. Eleanor Zelliot and Jayant Karve
with A. K. Ramanajun)

I never see you sitting in
Jeta's garden
sitting with eyes closed
in meditation, in the lotus position,
or
in the caves of Ajanta and Ellora
with stone lips sewn shut
sleeping the last sleep of your life.

I see you
walking, talking,
breathing softly, healingly,
on the sorrow of the poor, the weak,
going from hut to hut
in the life-destroying darkness,
torch in hand,
giving the sorrow
that drains the blood
like a contagious disease
a new meaning.

Siddharthangagar

Daya Pawar, *Mogawa*, 1972 (trans. Vidya Disit, Jayant Karve, Eleanor Zelliot)

O Siddhartha! [a name of the Buddha]
The town of your name [a slum area of Bombay]
in this twentieth century
has been struck by the tyrannical plough of power.
Each hut
is uprooted like a worthless stone.
Over the sign board with your name on it
a police van was driven.
Clothing, mats in each hut –
the huge earnings of umpteen generations –
scattered by police clubs.
A bunch of naked little children,
screaming and moaning, came onto the road.

> – Hey, call that woman in Delhi!
> – On, someone phone that minister!

> – Oh, isn't it nice, dear.
> – That hell in front of our apartment is going away –

These were the shouts heard in the air.
Before their eyes the surrounding land was cleared.
In air conditioned glass apartments
power has taken the pose of the three monkeys
If anyone asks, the sahib has left town —
that message has been left with his Personal Assistant.
O Siddhartha,
You made a tyrant like Angulimal [a robber]
tremble.
We are your humble followers.
How should we confront
this ferocious Angulimal?
O Siddhartha,
If we fight tooth and claw,
Try to understand us.
Try to understand us.

It's Reddening On The Horizon

J. V. Powar, *Times Weekly*, 1973 (trans. P. S. Nerurkar)

These twisted fists won't loosen now
The coming revolution won't wait for you.
We've endured enough; no more endurance now
Won't do letting down you blood's call to arms
It won't do:
    the seeds of revolution have been sown since long
    no use awaiting the explosion now;
    even if you take to your heels now
    no use; life's certainty is no more.
How will they snuff the fire within?
How will they stop minds gone ablaze?
No more reasoning now;
    unreason helps a lot
Once the horizon is red
What's wrong with keeping the door open?

Bibliography

The books and articles listed here are representative rather than a definitive bibliography. They include the works cited by the editor in the Introduction and subsequent editorial notes, but there is also a sampling of works designed for both general readers and specialists, whether interested in further information about untouchability or about the broad background of the Untouchables' Indian world.

Abbasayalu, Y. B. *Scheduled Caste Elite* (Hyderabad: Osmania University, 1978).

Aggarwal, Partap C. *Halfway to Equality* (Delhi: Manohar, 1983).

Ambedkar, Bhimrao. *passim.* Relatively easily accessible sources include:

—— , *Dr Babasaheb Ambedkar: Writings and Speeches* (Bombay: Education Department, Government of Maharashtra, 1979 —). Multi-volume series edited by Vasant Moon.

—— , *Thus Spoke Ambedkar*, ed. Bhagwan Das (Jullunder: Bheem Patrika Publications, 1969 —). Multi-volume set.

—— , *The Buddha and His Dhamma* (Bombay: Siddharth College Publication, 2nd edition 1974). Also available in Hindi and Marathi.

—— , *Source Material on Dr Babasaheb Ambedkar and the Movement of the Untouchables*, compiled by B. G. Kunte and B. N. Phatak (Bombay: Education Department, Government of Maharashtra, 1982).

Atyachar Vidrohi Samiti. 'The Marathwada Riots: A Report', *Economic and Political Weekly*, 12 May 1979, pp. 845–52.

Bakhru, Mira. 'Distribution of Welfare: People's Housing Scheme in Karnataka', *Economic and Political Weekly*, 10 March 1984, pp. 427–36 and 17 March 1984, pp. 473–80.

Berreman, Gerald. 'Race, Caste, and Other Invidious Distinctions in Social Stratification', *Race*, 13:4.

—— , *Caste and Other Inequities: Essays on Inequality* (Delhi: Manohar, 1979).

Béteillé, André. *Caste, Class, and Power* (Berkeley: University of California Press, 1965).

—— , *Inequality and Social Change* (Delhi: Oxford University Press, 1972).

Bhatt, Anil. *Caste, Class, and Politics: An Empirical Profile of Social Stratification in India* (Delhi: Manohar, 1975).

Bose, Pradip Kumar. 'Social Mobility and Caste Violence', *Economic and Political Weekly*, 18 April 1981, pp.713–16.

Breman, Jan. *Patronage and Exploitation: Changing Agrarian Relations in South Gujarat* (Berkeley: University of California Press, 1974).

Brown, Judith. *Gandhi's Rise to Power* (Cambridge: Cambridge University Press, 1972).

Chitnis, Suma. *A Long Way to Go* (Delhi: Allied Publishers, 1981).

Das, Arvind (ed.) *Agrarian Movements in India: Studies of 20th Century Bihar* (London: Frank Cass, 1982).

David, A. K. (ed.) *The New Wind: Changing Identities in South Asia* (The Hague: Mouton Press, 1976).

Desai, I. P. 'Anti-Reservation Agitation and Structure of Gujarat Society', *Economic and Political Weekly*, 30 May 1981, pp.819–23.

Dumont, Louis. *Homo Hierarchicus: An Essay on the Caste System*, trans. A. Sainsbury (Chicago: University of Chicago Press, 1970).

Dushkin, Lelah. 'Backward Class Benefits and Social Class in India, 1920–1970', *Economic and Political Weekly*, 7 April 1979, pp. 661–7.

Frankel, Francine. *India's Green Revolution: Economic Gains and Political Costs* (Princeton: Princeton University Press, 1971).

Frykenberg, R. E. (ed.) *Land Control and Social Structure in Indian History* (Madison: University of Wisconsin Press, 1969; and Delhi: Manohar, 1984).

Galanter, Marc. *Competing Equalities: The Indian Experience with Compensatory Discrimination* (Berkeley: University of California Press, 1984).

—— , 'Untouchability and the Law' in A. W. Murphy, *et al.* (eds.) *Law and Poverty* (Bombay: N. M. Tripathy, 1973).

Gandhi, Mohandas, K. *passim*. Complete works have been published by the Publications Division of the Government of India Press as *The Collected Works of Mahatma Gandhi* (Ahmedabad: Navajivan Press).

Gokhale, Jayashree B. 'The Dalit Panthers and Radicalization of the Untouchables', *Journal of Commonwealth and Comparative Studies*, vol. 17, no. 1, pp. 77–93.

—— , 'Bhakti or Vidroha: Continuity and Change in Dalit Sahitya', *Journal of Asian and African Studies*, vol. 10, nos. 1–2, pp. 29–41.

Gough, Kathleen and Hari Sharma (eds.) *Imperialism and Revolution in South Asia* (New York: Monthly Review Press, 1974).

Hazari. *Untouchable: The Autobiography of an Indian Outcast* (reprinted in 1969, New York: Fredrick A. Praeger Co.).

Hiro, Dilip. *Inside India Today* (London: Routledge and Kegan Paul, 1976).

Joshi, Barbara R. ' "Ex-Untouchable": Problems, Progress, and Policies in Indian Social Change', *Pacific Affairs*, vol. 53, no. 2, pp. 193–222.

—— , 'Scheduled Caste Voters: New Data, New Questions', *Economic and Political Weekly*, 14 August 1981, pp. 1357–62.

—— , *Democracy in Search of Equality: Untouchable Politics and Indian Social Change* (Delhi: Hindustan Publishing; and Atlantic Highlands, New Jersey: Humanities Press, 1982).

—— , 'Whose Law, Whose Order: "Untouchables", Social Violence, and the State in India', *Asian Survey*, July 1982.

Juergensmeyer, Mark. *Religion as Social Vision: The Movement Against Untouchability* (Berkeley: University of California Press, 1982).

—— , 'What If the Untouchables Don't Believe in Untouchability?', *Bulletin of Concerned Asian Scholars*, vol. 12, no. 1.

Kamble, N. D. *Poverty Within Poverty* (Bangalore: Institute for Social and Economic Change, 1979).

—— , *Bonded Labour in India* (Delhi: Uppal Publishing, 1982).

—— , *Atrocities on Scheduled Castes and Scheduled Tribes in Post-Independence India* (Delhi: Ashish Publishing, 1982).

Keer, Dhananjay. *Dr Ambedkar: Life and Mission* (Bombay: Popular Prakashan, 1962).

Khan, Mumtaz Ali. *Mass Conversions of Meenakshipuram* (Madras: Christian Literature Society, 1983).

Khare, R. S. *The Changing Brahamans* (Chicago: University of Chicago Press, 1970).

Khosla, Dinesh. *Myth and Reality of the Protection of Civil Rights Law in India* (Delhi: Hindustan Publishing; and Atlantic Highlands, New Jersey: Humanities Press, forthcoming).

Kishwwar, Madhu and Ruth Vanita. *In Search of Answers: Indian Women's Voices from MANUSHI* (London: Zed Press, 1984).

Klass, Morton. *Caste: The Emergence of the South Asian Social System* (Philadelphia: Institute for Study of Human Issues, 1980).

Kosambi, D. D. *Culture and Civilization of Ancient India* (London: Routledge and Kegan Paul, 1965; and Delhi: Vikas Publishing, 1981).

Kothari, Rajni (ed.) *Caste in Indian Politics* (Delhi: Orient Longmans, 1970).

—— , *Democratic Polity and Social Change in India* (Bombay: Allied Press, 1977).

Kumar, Krishna. 'Educational Experience of Scheduled Castes and Scheduled Tribes', *Economic and Political Weekly*, 3 and 10 September 1983, pp. 1566–72.

Lynch, Owen. *The Politics of Untouchability: Social Change in a City of India* (New York: Columbia University Press, 1969).

—— , 'Political Mobilization and Ethnicity Among Adi-Dravidas in a Bombay Slum', *Economic and Political Weekly*, vol. 9, no. 39, pp. 1657–68.

Mahar, J. Michael (ed.) *The Untouchables in Contemporary India* (Tuscon: University of Arizona Press, 1972).

Marla, Sarma (For the Gandhi Peace Foundation). *Bonded Labour in India* (Delhi: Biblia Impex, 1981).

Marriott, McKim and Inden, Ronald. 'Toward an Ethnosociology of South Asian Caste Systems', in K. David (ed.) *The New Wind* (The Hague: Mouton, 1977).

Mencher, Joan. 'The Caste System Upside Down: Or, The Not-So-Mysterious East', *Current Anthropology*, vol. 15, no. 4, pp. 469–93.

—— , *Agriculture and Social Structure in South India* (Delhi: Oxford University Press, 1974).

Miller, Robert. 'They Will Not Die Hindus: The Buddhist Conversion of Mahar Ex-Untouchables', *Asian Survey*, vol. 7, no. 9, pp. 637–44.

Minority Rights Group. *The Untouchables of India*, revised edition of the report by Dilip Hiro (London: MRG, 1982; and Bangalore: Dalit Sahitya Akademy, 1984).

Moffat, Michael. *An Untouchable Community in South India* (Princeton: Princeton University Press, 1979).

Omvedt, Gail (ed.) *Land, Caste, and Politics in Indian States* (Delhi: Authors Guild Publications, 1982).

—— , and Eleanor Zelliot, 'Introduction to Dalit Poems', *Bulletin of Concerned Asian Scholars*, vol. 10, no. 3, pp. 2–10.

Pandey, S. M. *Development of Marginal Farmers and Agricultural Labourers*

(Delhi: Sri Ram Centre for Industrial Relations, 1974).

Parvathamma, C. *Scheduled Castes and Tribes: A Socio-Economic Survey* (New Delhi: Ashish Publishers, 8/81 Punjabi Bagh; 1984).

Patankar, Bharat and Gail Omvedt. 'The Dalit Liberation Movement in Colonial India', *Economic and Political Weekly*, February (Annual Number) 1979.

Radakrishnan, P. 'Land Reforms and Social Change: Study of a Kerala Village', *Economic and Political Weekly*, 24 and 31 December 1983, pp. A143–A150.

Ram, Nandu. 'The Limited Education', *Seminar*, December 1981.

Ram, M. S. A. (ed.) *Social Movements in India*, 2 vols. (Delhi: Manohar, 1978 and 1979).

Sachidananda. *Social Dimensions of Agricultural Development* (Delhi: National Publishing House, 1972).

Sandanshiv, D. N. (ed.) *Law and Social Justice* (Bombay: Siddharth Publications, 1978).

—— , *Reflections on the Counter-Revolution in Marathwada* (Aurangabad: Anand Publications, 1978). Also available in Japanese translation.

Shah, Vimal P. (for Indian Council of Social Science Research). *The Educational Problems of Scheduled Caste and Scheduled Tribe College Students: A Statistical Profile* (Delhi: Allied Publishers, 1982).

Sheth, N. R. *The Social Framework of an Indian Factory*, revised 2nd edition (Delhi: Hindustan Publishing, 1981).

Shivakumar, S. C. and Chitra. 'Class and Jati of Asthapuram and Kanthapuram', *Economic and Political Weekly*, vol. 14, pp. 263–86.

Srinivas, M. N. 'The Future of Indian Caste', *Economic and Political Weekly*, Annual Number, February 1979.

—— , *Social Change in Modern India* (Berkeley: University of California Press, 1966).

Thorner, Daniel and Alice. *Land and Labour in India* (Delhi: Asia Publishing House, 1962).

Verba, Sidney, B. Ahmad and Anil Bhatt. *Caste, Race, and Politics* (Berkeley: Sage Publications, 1971).

Yagnik, Achyut and Anil Bhatt. 'The Anti-Dalit Agitation in Gujarat', *South Asia Bulletin*, vol. 4, no. 1 (1984), pp. 45–60.

Zelliot, Eleanor. 'Dalit: New Cultural Context of an Old Marathi Word', in Clarence Maloney (ed.), *Language and Civilization Change in South Asia* (Leiden: E. J. Brill, 1978).

—— , with Joanna Macy. 'Tradition and Innovation in the Contemporary Buddhist Movement in India', in A. K. Naraian (ed.), *Studies in the History of Buddhism* (Delhi: B. R. Publications, 1980).

—— , 'Dr B. R. Ambedkar', in Ainslee Embree and Stephen Hay (ed.), *Sources of the Indian Tradition*, revised edition (New York: Columbia University Press, forthcoming).

Public Documents

Government of India. *Census of India*. 1961, 1971, 1981.

Government of India, Department of Social Welfare. *Report of the Committee on Untouchability, Economic and Educational Development of the*

Scheduled Castes (The Elayaperumal Report). 1969.

Government of India, Lok Sabha Secretariat. Periodic reports of the Parliamentary Committee on Welfare of Scheduled Castes and Tribes. (Detailed studies on topics ranging from job discrimination in particular industries to violence.)

Government of India, Ministry of Agriculture. *Report on the Committee on Panchayati Raj Institutions.* 1978.

Government of India, Office of the Commissioner for Scheduled Castes and Tribes. *Report of the Commissioner for Scheduled Castes and Tribes.* (Issued annually.)

Current Information Sources

The following are some of those agencies and publications likely to be sources of current English language information. Rates are for individual subscriptions in 1984.

Dalit Voice. Fortnightly newspaper; includes notices and advertisements from other publishers and agencies of interest. Domestic — Rs.20; international (air) — $20. c/o Dalit Sahitya Akademy, 109/7th Cross, Palace Lower Orchards, Bangalore, India — 560 003. See also the occasional publications of the Akademy.

Economic and Political Weekly. Leading Indian news and research publication. 284 Shahid Bhagatsingh Road, Bombay, India — 400 038. International subscriptions at $40 (sea mail) and $75 (air mail).

India Now. Monthly publication including both independent reports and reprints from publications in India. Subscriptions: US and Canada — $10; overseas (air) — $16. Correspondence: US — *India Now*, POB 2456, Pullman, Washington 99163; Canada and overseas — *India Now*, POB 37, Westmount, Quebec, Canada H3Z 2T1.

Indian Social Institute. Occasional research publications. Lodi Road, New Delhi-110 003.

Jantak Lehar English Monthly. Ambedkarite Dalit publication, companion publication to a Punjabi weekly. Domestic — Rs.12; Britain (air) — £5; US/Canada (air) — $12. c/o Jantak Lehar, Opposite 4 Marla, Model House, Jullunder, India-144 003.

Manushi. Monthly, published alternately in Hindi and English, exploring the Indian scene through the eyes of women in all walks of life. Domestic — Rs.30; US/Canada (air) — $19; Britain (air) — £11.50. c/o Manushi Trust, CI/202 Lajpat Nagar I, New Delhi, India-110 024. (Subscriptions are for six issues; subscribers please specify English or Hindi edition.)

People's Education Society (PES). Annual publications, including writings by staff and students as well as business reports, of affiliated institutions. PES was founded by Dr Ambedkar; staff and student body are mixed, but the institutions' primary focus is on Dalit and other low income students. c/o PES, Anand Bhavan, Dr Dadabhai Naoroji Road, Fort, Bombay, India-400 023.

People's Union for Civil Liberties. Civil and human rights organization publishing occasional reports as well as newsletters to members. c/o Dr Rajni Kothari, President, 1 Court Road, Delhi, India-110 054.

People's Union for Democratic Rights. Civil and human rights organization with special interest in economic rights. Occasional reports. c/o Dr Vaid, Secretary; D-11, Staff Quarters, Delhi-110 054.

Prajabandhu. Dalit fortnightly published in English and Telegu. International rates on request. c/o E. V. Chinnaiah, Bheem Bhavan, Nellore-4, Andhra Pradesh.

Audio-Visual Materials (English language)

Minorities: Who Do They Think They Are? Slide/tape or video cassette teaching package for secondary schools. World seen through the eyes of three different minorities: the Native Americans (North American tribal peoples), the Untouchables of India, and the Travellers ('Gypsies') of Britain. Available for purchase (£16.00 plus £2 p&p), c/o Minority Rights Group, 29 Craven Street, London WC2.

An Indian Story: Enquiry Into Suppression of Civil Rights. Award-winning documentary by Tapan Bose and Suhasini Mulay. Explores socio-economic roots of police violence in north Indian state of Bihar, including interviews with local Untouchables, tribals and other low status Hindu castes. 58 minutes, colour, 16 mm, English subtitles. Enquiries: in India — Suhasini Mulay, B-42 Friends Colony West, New Delhi-110 065; in Canada — IPANA, POB 37, Westmount, Quebec H3Z 2P1; in US — Deepak Kapur, 49 Pinewood Avenue, Albany, New York 12208.

Tragada Bhavai. Documentary of performances and social milieu of a rural theatre troup based in the Koli community of Gujarat. Though not emphasized in the film, this is an Untouchable community, and the film makes it possible for viewers to compare traditional Dalit cultural life with the radical changes we have described above. 42 minutes, colour, 16 mm, English narration, filmed by Rodger Sandall and Jayasinhji Jhala. c/o Documentary Educational Resources, 5 Bridge Street, Watertown, Massachusetts 02172.

Bombay: Our City. Documentary by award-winning producer Anand Patwardhan; first released in early 1985. Daily life of Bombay slum-dwellers, including conflicts with political authorities. In their own words, slum-dwellers describe the clash between 'urban beautification' and the low income citizens' search for a place to live and work. 82-minute and 57-minute versions available, both colour, 16mm, English subtitles. Rental in the US: Icarus Films, 200 Park Avenue South, New York, New York. Rental and other enquiries in Canada: IPANA, Box 37, Westmount, Quebec, Canada.